Why Not Kill Them All?

Why Not Kill Them All?

The Logic and Prevention of Mass Political Murder

WITH A NEW PREFACE BY THE AUTHORS

DANIEL CHIROT
AND
CLARK MCCAULEY

Princeton University Press
Princeton and Oxford

Second printing, and first paperback printing, with a new preface, 2010
Paperback ISBN: 978-0-691-14594-5

The Library of Congress has cataloged the cloth edition of this book as follows

Chirot, Daniel.
Why not kill them all? : the logic and prevention of mass
political murder / Daniel Chirot and Clark McCauley.
p.   cm.
Includes bibliographical references and index.
ISBN-13: 978–0–691–09296–6 (hardcover : alk. paper)
ISBN-10: 0–691–09296–6 (hardcover : alk. paper)
ISBN-13: 978–0–691–09296–6 (hardcover : alk. paper)
ISBN-10: 0–691–09296–6 (hardcover : alk. paper)
1. Genocide. 2. Social conflict. 3. Conflict management.
4. Genocide—Prevention. I. McCauley, Clark R. II. Title.
HV6322.7.C47 2006
304.6′63—dc22   2005037887

British Library Cataloging-in-Publication Data is available

This book has been composed in Electra

Printed on acid-free paper. ∞

Printed in the United States of America

3   5   7   9   10   8   6   4   2

TO OUR CHILDREN,

Claire and Laura Chirot

AND

Thomas, Richard, and William McCauley

Contents

Preface to the Paperback Edition

Since the hardcover of our book went to press in 2005, much has changed in the world. Unfortunately, most of the contemporary conflict situations we discussed, especially in chapter 4, have not improved, and the potential for more catastrophes remains high. This leads us to believe that what we wrote five years ago remains useful and timely.

A rare example of improvement is the situation in Northern Ireland, but the peacemaking process was already substantially completed as early as 1998. The integration of both Ireland and the United Kingdom into the European Union, as well as the modernization of Ireland, removed most of the reasons for the Republican-Loyalist divide, though historical legacies of mistrust persist. Fatigue on both sides, and the efforts of both the British and American governments, made important contributions to the settlement.

In Darfur, however, the disaster continues, albeit in a more confused, somewhat less violent, and less clearly focused form. Meanwhile, the threat of a renewed war between northern and southern Sudan has increased, and violence between various southern groups has greatly escalated. If there is no new threat of war between Croatia and Serbia, in neither Bosnia nor Kosovo has there been any significant ethnic reconciliation. The Israeli-Palestinian conflict is no closer to being settled. The murderous Russian-Chechen War is over for the time being, but the issues that caused it are far from settled, and Chechnya continues to be brutally repressed by Moscow's local warlord ally. Ethnic wars and general repression continue in Burma, and Pakistan is in the midst of a new ethno-religious civil war that promises to produce massive civilian deaths. The civil war in Ivory Coast, to which we devoted some space, ended with a 2007 agreement between the north and south, but a briefing by the International Crisis Group on July 2, 2009, explains that none of the important problems between the contending parties has been resolved. The opposing armies and various militias remain armed and in control of much of the country, and even if there is no killing going on now, the potential for a resumption of the events of 2002–2003 remains high. We could go on and list all of the old problems that persist and produce large-scale massacres, as in the eastern Congo or Afghanistan. We could list new ones that have come up or returned after periods of quiet and have the potential to cause large numbers of noncombatant deaths, as in parts of India or in Nepal; but it was never our intention to produce a catalogue of such situations, only to use some to illustrate important points.

This does not change our opinion, stated frequently throughout the book, that most potential ethnic, religious, economic, ideological, regional, or international tensions are managed in far less extreme ways. Genocidal episodes of mass murder and all-out war remain quite rare compared to all the possible conflicts that exist. This has always been so. The persistence of some bitter conflicts that do produce the killing of large numbers of noncombatants on the basis of their membership in particular communities at war with each other does, however, point to the fact that once conflicts reach such a level, solving them becomes very difficult. The best way to prevent such situations from arising is to be aware of the potential for deadly conflict before a critical stage is reached. Some excellent international organizations devote themselves to discussing dangerous conflicts and bringing them to the world's attention, particularly the International Crisis Group (http://www.crisisgroup.org) and the Before Project (http://beforeproject.org). There is also an increasing amount of useful knowledge coming from countries that have experienced serious internal conflicts—for example, Kumar Rupesinghe's edited work *Responding to Civil War: An Examination of a Third Generation Early Warning and Early Response System* (published in Colombo, Sri Lanka, in 2009 by the Foundation for Co-Existence).

It is not really all that difficult to see early warning signs for those who understand the political dynamics in specific parts of the world, and are armed with the psychological insights to understand the situations that exacerbate emotional tensions. What our book does is to spell out those dynamics and explain the thinking of those who engage in extreme violence in order to help observers of particular situations evaluate the potential for catastrophic conflict.

Since the hardcover of the book was published, many new studies of genocidal mass political murder have appeared. While any effort to provide a full list would entail a long bibliographic essay, a few new books stand out. Ben Kiernan's *Blood and Soil: A World History of Genocide and Extermination from Sparta to Darfur* (Yale University Press, 2007) is an unusually comprehensive and wide-ranging discussion of many different kinds of cases, with each one examined in great detail. Two books on the Armenian case show how much more balanced recent scholarship has been in this area. One had already appeared in 2005 but escaped our attention; the other is more recent. These are Donald Bloxham's *The Great Game of Genocide: Imperialism, Nationalism, and the Destruction of the Ottoman Armenians* (Oxford University Press, 2005) and Taner Akçam's *A Shameful Act: The Armenian Genocide and the Question of Turkish Responsibility* (Metropolitan Books, 2006). More recently, two excellent books on Central Africa have appeared: Gérard Prunier's *Africa's World War: Congo, the Rwandan Genocide, and the Making of a Continental Catastrophe* (Oxford University Press, 2009) and René Lemarchand's *The Dynamics of Violence in Central Africa* (University of Pennsylvania Press, 2009). These are all specific and historically grounded "case studies" that show how conflictual situations can degenerate into genocidal mass killings; in many ways they offer more insight than the often overly simplistic quantitative databases currently favored by traditional political scientists.

In 2009 Daniel Goldhagen published *Worse than War: Genocide, Eliminationism, and the Ongoing Assault on Humanity* (Public Affairs). Goldhagen is a controversial scholar adept at gaining wide public attention by drawing clear moral lines where others see greater complexity. Whatever one may think of his work, however, its indictment of governments, including the present administration in the United States, for not doing enough to prevent mass political murder is certain to bring this topic to the fore once more.

Work on how to prevent politically motivated mass murder has proliferated in recent years, but it is not certain that we really know more about how to prevent it than we did earlier. There is a strong temptation to dichotomize actors into "blameless victims" and "evil perpetrators." This leads to calls for more international justice, as if somehow the imposition of an international criminal court could prevent and even stop the "killing by category" that includes noncombatants defined by ethnic, religious, or political identity. We discussed the limitations of such an approach in the book, particularly in chapter 4, but perhaps we did not go far enough. There remains the possibility of direct military intervention, but if we have learned anything from the American wars in Iraq and Afghanistan, or the involvement of United Nations troops in the Congo, it is that in practice "humanitarian" interventions are costly, often ineffective, and morally very problematic because the reasons for such actions are generally motivated by less-than-pure benevolence.

The very definition of "genocide" comes from the Nazi genocide against the Jews. This is in some ways unfortunate because the Holocaust was such an extreme case. Only the most racist of anti-Semites could have believed that Jews were an existential menace to Germany. There were no Jewish revolts, or demands for German territory, and the illusion of Jewish power had to ignore the fact that Jews were less than 1 percent of Germany's population in 1933. On the other hand, in most other twentieth-century and even contemporary cases of genocidal violence, the conflicts between various communities were and are quite real and threatening. High stakes cannot excuse genocide or any kind of mass murder, as the victims are always disproportionately helpless noncombatants who play little or no political role; but simply criminalizing perpetrators misses the point that they may feel desperate themselves. Indeed, hard as it may be for most of us to understand this, Hitler's motivation was neither cynical nor opportunistic. He genuinely believed that Jews were a deadly menace, a disease that had to be wiped out, even if there was no real evidence that any of this was true. Our point is that it is as important to understand the motivations, fears, and hopes of the killers as it is to expose their viciousness.

Certainly, as Kiernan's new book points out, and as we discussed in our first chapter, in the past there were mass killings and ethnic cleansings based almost entirely on greed and convenience—it was easy to grab territory by liquidating the resident population. European colonizers were frequently guilty of such acts. But in recent decades, such cynical violence by perpetrators who are merely greedy and callous, but have little reason to feel threatened, has become less likely. That is one of the great contributions of the movement to enlarge human rights, itself motivated largely by the extension of Western conceptions of harm, rights, and justice to all of humanity, not just to citizens of Western countries. On the other hand, desperate competitions for scarce resources, for control of states, and for ideological and religious purity have not gone away.

There is a tendency for groups ranging from international NGOs to large government organizations, including the United Nations, working to prevent intergroup violence, particularly genocide, to promote solutions that do not adequately address the fears and sense of threat felt by the contending parties. Of course, the need to do so vastly complicates any potential remedial action, which is why it is so important to start well before the mass killings get underway.

In this respect, we believe that the classic anthropological studies we cited in chapter 3, explaining how premodern societies worked out ways of limiting the destructive potential of conflict, can still be of use. Similarly, in chapter 4, our translation of these studies into suggestions for conflict management in modern cases remains relevant.

In the United States the arrival of a new administration led by President Obama has placed the prevention and control of mass political murder higher on the national and international agenda than ever before. Samantha Power, whose book on genocide we cite, has moved to a policy position as director for multilateral affairs in the National Security Council. America's new ambassador to the United Nations, Susan Rice, has made it a priority to address these kinds of issues, though it remains to be seen how effective this will be. A commission headed by Madeline Albright and William Cohen has produced a short book called *Preventing Genocide: A Blueprint for U.S. Policymakers* (published at the end of 2008 by the U.S. Holocaust Museum, the American Academy of Diplomacy, and the U.S. Institute of Peace). This book shows how much interest there is in doing something, and how difficult that will be. Only by looking at all of the many causes of such violence, and the multiple ways in which these causes need to be addressed, can real progress be made. Ultimately, we believe that continuing progress will have to come in part from spreading the idea that our enemies are like us, and we need to understand their fears and hopes as much as we need to set up structures that make greater exchanges and rules mitigating conflict possible. We remain optimistic in thinking that this will happen because in so many instances in the past, ways were worked out to limit the damages from conflict. We know the circumstances under which such efforts and rules stopped working, so we know much better than we did even two and three generations ago what needs to be done to prevent such failures. Conflicts and violence will never stop entirely, but they can be contained.

Acknowledgments

We would like to thank Martin Seligman for introducing us and helping us to get started on this project. Subsequently, the Andrew W. Mellon Foundation supported our work by funding some of the activities of the Solomon Asch Center for the Study of Ethnopolitical Conflict at the University of Pennsylvania and a Sawyer Seminar Series of lectures and seminars at the University of Washington. The United States Institute of Peace helped support Daniel Chirot during the final stages of the preparation of this book, and a sabbatical leave from Bryn Mawr College supported Clark McCauley during the same period. David Kauck played a key role, not only by providing ideas, but also in making Chirot's field work in Africa possible. Paul Rozin and Marc Ross introduced McCauley to issues of ethnopolitical conflict, and Carol Rittner first encouraged him to write about genocide. Ed Royzman's ideas about how to conceptualize hate are represented in chapter 2. CARE's Guillaume Aguettant and Brian Cavanagh offered both direct assistance and practical ideas that shaped much of our fourth chapter. Reşat Kasaba, Peter Blossey, and Cindy Chirot read large parts of the manuscript and made important suggestions. Jan Gross's support was a great help as well. We thank all of them. We also wish to express our appreciation of our wonderful editor, Peter Dougherty. Finally, we want to remember Pamphile Koné, a wonderful friend without whom Chirot could not have worked in Ivory Coast's rebel zone, and who died young, as too many Africans do, in 2005.

Why Not Kill Them All?

Are We Killers or Peacemakers?

> You have heard that it was said, "An eye for an eye and
> a tooth for a tooth." But I say to you, Do not resist one who is
> evil. But if anyone strikes you on the right cheek, turn to him
> the other also. . . . I say to you, Love your enemies, and pray
> for those who persecute you, so that you may be sons of your
> Father who is in heaven; for he makes his sun rise on the evil
> and the good, and sends rain on the just and on the unjust.
> —*Matthew 5:38–45*

Our world today is dangerous. It has always been dangerous, but modern technology, a globalized economy, easy communications, and massive migration now spread the effects of crisis in one part of the world to other parts very quickly. We do indeed live in a "global village." But like ancient village societies, we still have our clans and tribes, each with their territories, whose competitive disputes can degenerate into violence and occasional genocidal massacres. Like the agrarian states and civilizations that emerged from stateless societies thousands of years ago, we still have competing religions that usually coexist but set boundaries that can lead to very violent wars and genocidal purges. Like the modern technological societies that came into being in the nineteenth and twentieth centuries, we still have competing nationalisms, and we still struggle to cope with all the changes brought about by modernity. We still generate new ideologies and adapt old ones to support one side or another in the disputes that are produced by the conflicting demands of the modern world. These have produced massive genocidal violence in the twentieth century and may do so again.

Despite this stark prospect, in this book we plan to show that there is no reason to despair. Pre-state societies, agrarian states, different religions, and modern states and societies have also devised ways of mitigating conflicts, so that not all of them have been excessively violent, and relatively few have been genocidal. Without such mechanisms, human history would be far more tragic, and today our species would have little prospect of surviving much longer. We can learn from past attempts to control violence, and we can devise new ways of dealing with crises that may lead to political massacres.

Conflict can become genocidal when powerful groups think that the most efficient means to get what they want is to eliminate those in the way. It can become equally or more murderous when the motive is revenge, and descend to the worst levels of slaughter when there is great fear that the survival of the enemy group might endanger the survival of one's own group. The most intractable cause of genocidal killings emerges when competing groups—ethnic, religious, class, or ideological—feel that the very presence of the other, of the enemy, so sullies the environment that normal life is not possible as long as they exist.

As we proceed through the book, however, we will see that it is possible in many ways to combat the tendency for conflicts to degenerate to such a point. Developing exchanges with other groups lessens the chances that any conflict will reach genocidal proportions. Codes of honor, moral teachings, and formal rules to govern conflict have the same effect. We will explore ideologies that are so absolutely sure of themselves that they demand extreme final solutions that wipe out their enemies, yet we will also find ideologies that are far more tolerant and accepting of compromise. These are not necessarily pacifist ways of thinking, but ones that are based on skepticism about any absolute judgment of others or situations. Enlightenment ideas that originated in the seventeenth and eighteenth centuries can moderate extremism. By exposing the myths that can lead to genocidal wars for the unhistorical fabrications that they really are, objective examinations of the past can make it more difficult to stoke genocidal passions. Emphasizing the worth of individuals, their distinctive attributes, and their rights over those of impersonal communities greatly diminishes the likelihood that intolerant, closed groups will be able to recruit enough members to become dangerous. Enlightenment thinking these days may be an increasingly insecure basis for trying to prevent the kinds of conflicts that could lead to genocide, but it is surely one, despite its Western origins, that is worth trying to preserve, particularly because it faces challenges even within the West.

At a much more modest level, there are many ways of lessening tensions between different communities. We will look at truth and reconciliation commissions. These do not provide universal solutions, but in some circumstances they can help. In some places decentralization and local autonomy can greatly decrease internal tensions. Building up civil society institutions, particularly ones that bring members of different ethnic and religious groups together, can, in the long run remove some of the flammable tinder that many leaders have used to move their people into massacring others. Those who want to set forest fires will always be around, but if they have less material to work with, they are more likely to fail.

We will show that it is possible to devise strategies to help lessen the chances that competition will turn to extreme violence. In addition to the well-known international mechanisms for supporting peace and reducing conflict, there are also many local, small-scale programs such as the ones we will discuss in chapter 4. These are well worth pursuing, not only in troubled areas, but everywhere, because conflicts can always arise. Although their cost is modest, they require patience and humility because they cannot be imposed by force or succeed quickly.

The study of those cases in which the impulse to "kill them all" prevailed can clarify some of the darkest aspects of human history yet also offer hope. We have always known how to do better. Understanding why excesses occur is an important step toward understanding some of the dire conflicts that exist in today's world, and it can provide a foundation for policies aimed at reducing and limiting violent conflict. That can greatly reduce the potential for genocide and lesser kinds of mass political murder.

Ours is a controversial subject. Talk of genocide or of mass political murder arouses deep emotions. Scholars, policymakers, and general publics disagree bitterly about definitions, about what actually happened in historical cases, about who was responsible, about how many died, and about whether or not anything could have been done to prevent these deaths. Disagreement is not just about obvious distortions, such as those few who still deny that the Nazis or the Ottoman Empire committed genocides. There are many cases that are not as clear. Was the patent neglect of famine conditions in Ireland by the British government in the midnineteenth century genocidal? More than a million died in the potato famine, but there were no death camps, no roving squads of killers, only what many would consider criminal disregard by a government that could have done much to help. Was the American bombing of Hiroshima genocidal? Tens of thousands of women, children, and noncombatant men died, but this was part of a war, and some argue that by shortening the war it actually saved more lives than it took. Others consider this one of the great crimes of the twentieth century. How about the U.S. ethnic cleansing of Native Americans such as the Cherokee, when forced expulsions resulted in thousands of deaths? Were these examples of mass murder, even though most of the victims died as a result of hardship, famine, and disease rather than outright execution? We discuss such cases, and not every reader will agree with our conclusions.

Some may think that it is a mistake to look at less clear or less deadly cases of mass killing. It can be argued that the moral force of denouncing and acting against genocide is undermined by any suggestion that more limited forms of violence, such as deadly ethnic riots or localized massacres, are part of the same phenomenon. For example, those who claim that the killing of the Jews by the Nazis was so total and gruesome that there are no comparable cases have already introduced that argument into the debate about definitions of genocide. For those who believe this, comparison with lesser-scale atrocities is itself a form of Holocaust denial. Going back to age-old cases and examining ethnographic studies about pre-state societies may seem to those who want to concentrate on modern crimes to be a trivialization of the subject. Obviously, we think differently, though we can sympathize with such concerns.

It is part of our central contention that all such cases, whether large or small, have a logic and rationale behind them. The perpetrators, and certainly their leaders, always have some reason in mind to justify their action, and we need to take that reasoning seriously, even if we entirely disagree with it. Thus, to say that the Ottoman authorities who initiated the genocide of Armenians really thought that the Armenians threatened the survival of the empire and even the survival of an independent Turkish state infuriates some Armenian nationalists who maintain that there was no such threat, only blind Turkish prejudice. We can debate whether or not there was a real threat, but it seems undeniable to us that the Ottoman leaders thought it was real, and that this is why they acted as they did. Rationality is a very slippery concept, but in general we believe that most political massacres are quite deliberate, are directed by or at least approved by the authorities, and that they have a goal, even if the actual murderers can take advantage of momentary passions and a lust for killing that appears in such events. The rationale behind such actions may be based on false information, on essentializing prejudice, or on reasoning that is more self-interested than logical, but this does not lessen the fact that the perpetrators believe that mass killing is the right thing to do.

Similar controversies arise in any discussion about ways of preventing mass killing. There is a large and rapidly growing literature on conflict resolution and prevention, but little consensus about what works and what does not. Pursuing leaders responsible for mass murder and bringing them to justice? Education campaigns? Strengthening international institutions? Alleviating poverty? Building civil society? Promoting truth and reconciliation commissions? These and others have all been proposed and will be examined. We treat these various approaches with caution, because no single method seems to us to offer a comprehensive solution.

We would never claim that ours is the final word on this important subject. New studies of mass political murder continue to be published, and new cases keep arising. The future holds more genocidal episodes, and some will be on a very large scale. Nothing in our research suggests that the reasons for such mass killings have disappeared or are likely to disappear any time soon. On the contrary, today's world seems poised for a whole new set of massacres, perhaps religiously based, that will combine the horrors of twentieth-century, state-sponsored killing with the faith-based ideological intolerance of the great wars of religion that bloodied many parts of the world in earlier eras. Yet, at the same time, there are ever more international organizations striving to prevent bloodshed, to create conditions that will lead to better conflict resolution, and to promote mediating institutions able to dampen violence and make mass killing less likely. We want to contribute to this effort while remaining realistic about the dangers that face us.

In order to arrive at our policy proposals in chapter 4, we begin by laying out the causes of mass murder for political ends in chapter 1, where we spell out the main reasons for such events. In both modern and ancient times, it has occasionally simply seemed convenient to rid oneself of obstructive enemies by either exterminating or forcibly removing them. Such removals on a large scale invariably resulted in massive death rates, and they still do, as has been shown in such cases as the ethnic cleansings in Yugoslavia in the 1990s and in Darfur in the early 2000s. The desire for revenge has also produced mass murder, as has the fear that if an enemy is not totally destroyed it will strike back. The worst kind of fear is that somehow an enemy group's very survival on earth is so polluting and dangerous that it needs to be entirely wiped out. Hitler believed this about Jews, the Khmer Rouge about Vietnamese and those Cambodians infected by Vietnamese thinking, the Hutu governing elite in Rwanda about Tutsis, and some Protestants and Catholics about each other during Europe's religious wars. The Bible itself mentions many such examples.

This brings up another major controversy that we examine in our first chapter. Are genocides such as those perpetrated by Hitler, or by Stalin's purges and mass killings of millions, events that could only take place in modern societies? No one denies that there has always been a lot of slaughter, but could it be that both the scale and thoroughness of more recent mass murders is of a different order than past events? We will show that even though exceptionally brutal genocidal episodes have always occurred, modern nations have in one aspect raised the stakes of conflicts by turning us all into jealous tribes. This was the norm when humans lived in small-scale societies, but then our numbers were small. It became less common as states turned wars into competitions more between elites than between masses, but in a sense, we have been retribalized on a very large scale.

To better understand why mass murder occurs, we will turn in chapter 2 to the psychology of genocidal killing. Steven Pinker, a psychologist widely known as a defender of the idea that much human behavior is innate and biologically determined, has written that any simplistic view of our species as either naturally violent or peaceful misses the main point.

> The prevalence of violence . . . does not mean that our species has a death wish, an innate thirst for blood, or a territorial imperative. There are good evolutionary reasons for the members of an intelligent species to try to live in peace. . . . Thus while conflict is a human universal, so is conflict resolution. Together with all their nasty and brutish motives, all peoples display a host of kinder, gentler ones. . . . Whether a group of people will engage in violence or work for peace depends on which set of motives is engaged. (Pinker 2002, 58)

No one doubts that different individuals have varying psychological predispositions that lead them to be more or less violent as well as more or less conciliatory, and the same goes for different ethnic, religious, or class-based groups and societies. Different states and nations also have different propensities to be more or less aggressive. It is equally true that changing circumstances can make violence-prone individuals, groups, and societies more peaceful, or vice versa. This was true in the past and remains so today.

We take the position that mass killing is neither irrational nor in any sense "crazy." Humans are predisposed to think of competing groups other than their own in essentializing, that is to say, stereotypical ways, and this obviously leads easily to demonization of entire communities of perceived enemies. Our emotions—anger, shame, fear, resentment— predispose us to violence when we feel threatened, and to mass murder against those who most stand in our way or endanger us. But our psychological predispositions lead us in the opposite direction as well, toward love and an aversion to killing. It is only by accepting this paradox and studying the reasoning that lies behind both violence and peacemaking that we can make some progress in controlling our darker impulses.

This book therefore explores why and under what circumstances competition and conflict between groups, both within single societies and between them, become more or less deadly. How do such conflicts sometimes reach the genocidal level? What mechanisms exist to miti-gate conflicts so as to reduce the chances of such drastic outcomes? By looking at the specific conflict mitigation mechanisms developed by both pre-state and state societies, our third chapter explains why most conflicts, even wars, did not become genocidal. Some very ancient ways of limiting violence have persisted into modern times. In a num-ber of cases, however, both in the past and today, such arrangements have failed. This has led to, and continues to produce, atrocious car-nage.

The huge genocides of the past century—the slaughter of Armenians in 1915, the Stalinist purges of the 1930s, the Nazi Holocaust from 1941 to 1945, the Cambodian destruction of a quarter of its population from 1975 to 1979, the Rwandan genocide of 1994, the mass murders in the Yugoslav wars of the 1990s, and the more recent ethnic cleansing and murders in Darfur, taking place as we were finishing this book—have captured the world's attention and have killed vast numbers of people. But there have been many more less-publicized episodes in other coun-tries, some killing tens of thousands, some a few thousand, some only a few hundred. It is our contention that many of the same impulses that lead to massive genocide are present in these episodes that kill far fewer individuals, but nevertheless encompass the massacre of men, women, and children who are members of groups targeted for elimination by their enemies. Large-scale genocides need the organizational power of government; lesser instances may not need as much organization, though local authorities are almost invariably complicit.

In recent years there have been many excellent studies on this sub-ject, particularly of the major genocides in the twentieth century, but also some examinations of earlier incidents of mass killing. Many such studies are cited in the pages that follow. Our book's aims, however, are broader in three ways. First, we suggest that representing ancient as well as modern examples of mass killing is important in demonstrating the normality of such violence. No continent, no century, no civiliza-tion is exempt from this behavior. Second, we suggest that mass murder is rare in relation to the kind of power imbalance that makes such killing possible. The victors in intergroup violence do not usually try to wipe out the vanquished and all their relatives. Why not? This perspective leads us to look at psychological, cultural, and institutional barriers to mass killing, and to look for these across a range of political forms from pre-state societies to the modern nation-state. Third, and perhaps most important, we suggest that there is a continuum in mass killing that offers a better understanding of the worst examples from examination of smaller and less horrific examples.

Understanding how to control lesser episodes of mass political murder, we believe, is a necessary step toward the control of large-scale genocide, and just as important. By the time Hitler had control of Germany, had conquered most of Europe, and had decided to exterminate Jews, it was too late to do much about it other than to defeat him and destroy his military power. The time to take preventive action would have been years before Hitler came to power, perhaps even decades earlier. The same holds true for other major tragedies of this sort. The final, most terrible steps may develop quickly and in unforeseeable ways, but the conditions that make them possible do not develop overnight. Knowing how they happen can lead to awareness of the coming danger.

The same perspective informs our understanding of pre-state episodes of genocidal behavior. Obviously, when societies were organized as small bands of self-governing kinfolk, conflicts that led to the elimination of one group or another killed very few people, though the consequences for a particular family, village, or clan could be just as genocidal as when large groups have been killed in more modern times. We believe that focusing only on more modern and large-scale genocidal events narrows our understanding of how such events take place and of what can be done to prevent them. In trying to explain the phenomenon of mass political murder, we therefore move back and forth in time and examine cases that include both relatively small numbers of people and very large numbers.

Conflict within and between societies is inevitable, and humans will sometimes resort to violence in such conflicts. But our societies have developed many ways of mitigating conflict, and given the number of potential and actual conflicts that exist, most are either not deadly or not very deadly. Large-scale genocide is quite rare, and even genocidal episodes on a lesser scale are usually avoided. It is when the mechanisms for conflict mitigation break down, or new situations occur in which such mechanisms have not yet been developed, that the worst situations occur. By examining conflict-limiting mechanisms both in pre-state and state societies, we believe we can better understand the general phenomenon of mass killing. Human beings are not by nature either bloody monsters or peaceful angels; rather it is situations, institutions, and socially agreed-upon interpretations of these that move human action toward peace or violence.

Studying what has caused terrible wars and genocidal slaughters in the past and how human societies have sought to control such violence opens a window into our contradictory, frightening, but also redeeming nature. That is one reason to study this subject. There is, however, a more important reason for studying mass, politically motivated murder through the ages. In our retribalized, dangerous world, with its vastly improved communications and advanced technology, we need to develop policies that lessen the probability of genocidal conflicts. This we will do in our fourth chapter, which concentrates on policy recommendations. Again, we will move from large-scale to much more modest proposals, and we will be once more asking our readers to remember that there are no single explanations, no easy answers, and often no clear-cut moral solutions to the problems that lead to terrible conflicts.

At the start of the twenty-first century the admonition from Jesus Christ's Sermon on the Mount quoted at the start of our introduction seems no closer to realization than it did two thousand years ago. Although mass political murder for convenience, for safety, for vengeance, and for supposed purity have afflicted every century, the twentieth century was in many ways the worst ever, and the twenty-first has started off promising to be as bad or worse.

There is evil, and there is good, but ours will not be a book that merely condemns those who commit evil. Rather, we are going to try understanding why evil occurs, and why almost any group of humans is capable of both good and evil. We believe that this is the only way to propose effective methods of countering mass killing, and that it is also the only way to understand our own contradictory impulses.

CHAPTER ONE

Why Genocides?
Are They Different Now Than in the Past?

Qui tacet, consentire videtur.
(He who keeps silent seems to consent.)
—*From a letter written by General von Trotha, commander of
the German army in Southwest Africa, to German
Chancellor Bülow in 1905 (Dedering 1999)*

T he term *genocide* was coined only in 1944 (Lemkin 1944) and
was designated as an international crime by the United Nations
in 1948 (L. Kuper 1981, 210–14). *Ethnic cleansing* is an even newer
term. It came into use during the Yugoslav wars of the early 1990s and
was declared a crime against humanity by the United Nations in 1993
(Teitel 1996, 81). Though the two terms are distinct, there is considerable overlap in their meaning. In practice, modern episodes of ethnic
cleansing have caused large numbers of deaths and often conform to
the United Nations' definition of genocide, which is the attempt to
destroy "in whole or in part, a national, ethnical, racial, or religious
group" (Fein 1990, 1; Freeman 1995, 209). Norman Naimark's historical account of such catastrophes in Europe in the twentieth century
(including the genocide of Armenians in Anatolia in 1915) shows that
what may have begun in some cases as state-sponsored ethnic cleansing
quickly turned into mass killing by deliberate murder, abuse, famine,
and disease. Such, for example, was the case with the Germans expelled
from large parts of eastern Europe after World War II. About 11.5 million civilian Germans were "cleansed" from this area, of whom up to
2.5 million died. Most of these deportations and deaths took place in
the last year of World War II, but more than half a million deaths oc-

curred after the war, particularly in deportations from Poland and Czechoslovakia (Naimark 2001, 14, 110–38, 187).

Neither genocide nor ethnic cleansing is unique to the twentieth century. When the Cherokees were expelled from the southeastern United States in 1838, the resulting death rates certainly mark the episode as genocidal even though it was not the specific intent of the U.S. government at that time to exterminate them. Those who made it to what would later become Oklahoma and survived the hardships and disease remained there, more or less unmolested. Nevertheless, a recent demographic estimate suggests that as many as 20 percent of the sixteen thousand Cherokees deported on the "Trail of Tears" died on the way, and if deaths from disease immediately after resettlement are counted, the death toll may be closer to 50 percent. The damage done to the Cherokees would certainly have been considered genocidal by our own era's standards (Farb 1968, 250; Thornton 1990, 47–80).

The terms *genocide* and *ethnic cleansing* have come to be interpreted in somewhat similar ways, as extreme examples of attempts by a politically dominant group, typically claiming to represent a majority of the people in a given political entity, to get rid of specific ethnic or racial groups viewed as enemies. In fact, the definition of *ethnic* is very fuzzy. The Nazis treated Jews as an ethnic group defined by a common heredity, or what is sometimes called a race, not as a religiously defined one. Bosnian Muslims, Orthodox Serbs, and Catholic Croats also treated each other as ethnic or racial entities, not as religious ones. Nor were the Armenians in 1915 singled out because of their religion, but because the Ottoman authorities perceived them as an ethnic nation, a people sharing a common culture and hereditary kinship bent on carving out a new, hostile state in the heart of Anatolia. Neither conversion nor how any of these people prayed was the issue (Browning 1992a; Glenny 1993; Suny 1993). The biggest case of genocide in the late twentieth century, the slaughter of Tutsis by the Hutus then in power in Rwanda in 1994, had no religious component at all; in fact, on close inspection, it is questionable whether these two groups were really distinct ethnicities at all, as they had intermarried for four centuries, spoke the same language, and practiced the same religions. Gérard Prunier considers them to have been "status groups," in Max Weber's sense, rather than "ethnic groups" (1997). Nevertheless, the rest of the world interpreted Hutus and Tutsis as different ethnicities, and so did many Hutu and Tutsi themselves. This has reinforced the notion that genocides are the most extreme example of ethnic cleansing. Because of the salience of modern examples of genocide and ethnic cleansing, and perhaps because of United Nations focus on such examples, these are now widely considered to be the most common forms of political mass murder.

Despite this currently popular interpretation, it would be shortsighted to think that mass murder and expulsion are limited to ethnic enemies. Genocide is part of a larger phenomenon of mass killing that has, at various times, targeted groups defined in terms of their religion, ideology, economic class, or merely because of the region in which they lived. If religion seems to have been secondary to ethnic and national concerns in twentieth-century examples, or in many of the cases associated with European expansion into the Americas and Australia, that was not always the case in the past; and in the twentieth century itself, ethnicity or nationality were not the only reasons for which certain groups were subjected to mass deportation and murder.

Jews were expelled from Spain in 1492 on religious grounds and could escape this fate by converting, unlike the Jews who faced Hitler's genocide. In the Spanish case, the "cleansing" was religious, not specifically ethnic, at least in the minds of King Ferdinand and Queen Isabella, who ordered the expulsion under pressure from the Catholic Church's Holy Office of the Inquisition. About half of the eighty thousand Jews living in Spain in 1492 fled, and most of the rest converted. About two thousand converted Jews were executed in the period encompassing the decades immediately before the expulsion through about 1530, but the vast majority of *conversos* gradually blended into Christian Spain. As in all cases, the motives for this episode are complex, and the continuing persecution of converted Jews suggests that some of the Inquisitors were specifically anti-Semitic and had "ethnic" rather than purely religious motives. But the king and queen of Spain insisted that this was not their objective, and they tried to protect converted Jews (Kamen 1998, 16–27, 56–60).

A much more recent, and far bloodier example of genocidal persecution that was not specifically ethnic comes from the late 1920s to the early 1930s, when Joseph Stalin, the ruler of the Soviet Union, caused some eight million supposedly prosperous peasants and their families (kulaks) to be killed and deported to deadly work camps in terribly harsh conditions because of their membership in what was defined as an antisocialist economic class. Millions of other people were subsequently killed and deported, often to die of overwork and deprivation in the late 1930s because they were labeled as anticommunists, or as the wrong kind of communist—Trotskyites, Bukharinites, and so on (Courtois et al. 1999, 146–202). This is why in the negotiations after World War II that led to the United Nations convention outlawing genocide, the Soviets made sure that mass persecution on the basis of ideology or class position would not be included as a genocidal act, even though the Western powers wanted such a provision (L. Kuper 1981, 138–50).

Stepping back nine centuries, we encounter yet a different kind of example based not on ethnicity, religion, or ideology, but simply on regional politics. In 1069, William the Conqueror, who had installed himself as the king of England three years earlier, commanded that Yorkshire be cleared of its population in order to break the ability of the Anglo-Saxon lords of that region to continue their resistance to the Norman conquest. No one is sure how many died, but the systematic destruction of villages and crops, the widespread murder and flights into the surrounding mountains, where enslavement by Scottish tribes or starvation awaited the refugees, greatly reduced the population. Two decades later, after the area had been partly resettled by immigrants from elsewhere in England and brought under control by Norman lords seeking peasants to cultivate their lands, the population density of Yorkshire was still only one-fifth that of neighboring territories (Kapelle 1979, 118–90). This was mass expulsion and slaughter purely on the basis of political geography, as Anglo-Saxon peasants in more submissive regions were not treated this way, and Anglo-Saxon lords who collaborated with the new Norman hierarchy were gradually absorbed into the ruling class.

We can label all these cases as examples of mass political murder and expulsion, because whatever categories were used to target victims, the aim was political. That is, a certain group was deemed to pose a

threat of some sort to those in control, and therefore it had to be eliminated. The specific motives and explanations given for these acts varied,
but they were all united by this single theme.

After World War II, the Soviet Union and its political allies in eastern
Europe viewed the German population in the areas they controlled as
a long-range threat that might provoke a resurgent Germany allied with
the United States to claim territories to the east, as it had in 1938 and
1939–and furthermore, both the Soviets and the Slavic peoples of eastern Europe felt that the crimes committed by the Nazis amply justified
revenge against all Germans (Naimark 2001, 108–10). In Bosnia, during the Yugoslav wars of the 1990s, as in the case of William's atrocities
in Yorkshire nine centuries earlier, it was largely a matter of territorial
control that was at issue, though killing was often justified on the basis
of historical claims and retribution (Glenny 2000, 626–49). Jews were
identified by the Spanish Inquisition and monarchy as an encourage-
ment to the backsliding of *conversos* and therefore as a threat to the
project of turning Spain into a thoroughly Catholic society (Kamen
1998, 20). Supposed Trotskyites in the Soviet Union, along with kulaks,
"wreckers" (former Party allies whom Stalin disliked), and vast numbers
of other kinds of undesirables posed an ideological threat to Stalin's
rule and goals. Their presence was used as the excuse for the failings
in Stalin's economic policy, and they had to be eliminated in order
to construct Stalin's version of socialism (Lih 1995). Cherokees were
expelled from Georgia and adjoining U.S. states because white settlers
wanted their land. They were not a direct political threat, but the land
they owned was coveted, and allowing them to stay in place would have
made it difficult to seize (R. Davis 1979, 129–47). Tutsis were perceived
to threaten the political control of the Hutu elite (Prunier 1997, 192–
212). Armenians were thought to threaten the very survival of a Turkish
and Muslim Ottoman Empire (Adanır 2001, 71–81). Finally, Hitler
perceived Jews as a racially polluting, dangerous disease that threatened
the strength of the German Aryan race and as members of a world
conspiracy to overthrow his regime and ruin Germany. That Hitler was
obsessed with the importance of racial purity is shown by his programs
to kill homosexuals, the mentally deficient, and Gypsies, though none
with the single-minded determination with which he pursued those

whom he considered his "race's" most dangerous enemy (Burleigh and Wippermann 1991). It hardly matters how correct Hitler's perception was, or Stalin's, or that of any of the other perpetrators of such acts. The designated victims were viewed as politically dangerous, or at the very least a major impediment to the goals of those in power. Getting rid of them in one way or another was necessary in order to carry out those goals.

This raises the first of two important questions that we need to answer. *What conditions lead to mass political murder or mass expulsions?* What are the causes of such genocidal policies? Clearly, there must be more than one. Even in the short list of examples given above, the ideological and social circumstances of the genocidal episodes varied greatly. William the Conqueror, Governor Lumpkin of Georgia (a fervent advocate of Cherokee removal), and Hitler had quite different motives, aside from all wanting to remove a threat to their interests. William had no racial or strong ethnic prejudices but just wanted to rule. Anglo-Saxon lords who cooperated could be incorporated into his ruling elite, and peasants were there to be taxed and used, not exterminated unless they somehow threatened his control. Their ethnicity was irrelevant. Governor Lumpkin, on the other hand, had contempt for the Cherokees and considered all Native Americans as (in his words) "a savage race of heathens." But he viewed them as more of an annoyance than a major threat and was content to see them expelled to a distant land where, or so he believed, white U.S. citizens had no interests. He even claimed that this was for the Cherokees' own good, to save them from competition with a "superior" race (Lumpkin 1969, 1:57, 2:150). For Hitler, Jews were not just an annoyance, but a deadly disease. At a dinner with Heinrich Himmler, the head of the SS, on February 22, 1942, Hitler said: "The discovery of the Jewish virus is one of the greatest revolutions that have taken place in the world. The battle in which we are engaged today is of the same sort as the battle waged during the last century by Pasteur and Koch. How many diseases have their origin in the Jewish virus!" (Hitler [1941–43] 1973, 332). Stalin had yet another set of reasons for his mass murders. His were based on a particular reading of Marxist-Leninist ideology that saw the elimination of class enemies as a necessary part of the construction of socialism, and he interpreted any obstacle to his project as proof of class-based resistance (Tucker 1990).

These illustrative examples are useful but do not yet create the kind of systematic typology that would help us understand such acts. In order to do this, the term *genocidal* has to be defined simply enough to clear away many of the ideological and historical disputes about what was intentional or in some sense accidental, and what can be justified by some sort of complex rationalization or must be viewed as criminal. A convenient way of doing this is to say that a genocidal mass murder is politically motivated violence that directly or indirectly kills a substantial proportion of a targeted population, combatants and noncombatants alike, regardless of their age or gender. Both mass murders that were planned ahead of time, as in the case of the Jewish Holocaust, and those that were a by-product of an expulsion, as in the case of the Cherokees, are included in this definition. Intent and the ideology behind such killings do matter as we establish our typology, but these may vary considerably from one type to the other, and it is almost impossible to try to adjudicate among competing claims about the intentionality, justice, or injustice of many of these catastrophes. One need only look at the vast literature about, for example, the Armenian genocide to see how contentious an issue it remains to this day, even though no serious historian doubts that something terrible did indeed happen. This does not mean that we ought to avoid all moral judgment when considering genocidal killings; but it does mean that without a general typology we are too prone to see each example as a unique product of a few depraved individuals. Yet, as should become obvious, genocidal events have been common enough to suggest that they cannot be explained as some kind of deviant behavior. On the contrary, given the right circumstances, normal human beings are all too ready to kill by category.

Only a few hundred may be killed if the targeted population is small and localized, or millions if it is large and widespread. Typically, the larger the mass murder, the more likely it is to be studied, and the really huge cases are those that most preoccupy the bulk of the literature on genocidal behavior. As it is our contention that we should not limit ourselves to just these well-known cases to understand why such actions occur, it is self-defeating to try to define *genocide* or *mass murder* in a precise numerical way. If more than a hundred Muslims in a town in India are killed by extremist Hindus, as happened in some of the cases described in Ashutosh Varshney's book (2002, to be discussed below in chapter 4), that is a genocidal act, even if it is very far from being a general genocide directed against the more than 150 million Indian Muslims. If everyone in a small village is killed in a war in Highland New Guinea, as has happened, that is genocidal as well, even if such an event seems almost trivial compared with the major genocides. Most studies of mass political murder focus on the largest events, those that can unquestionably be called genocides, so our typology will be based on what is known about these major events. Only later in the book will we turn to many smaller-scale events to bolster our understanding of the phenomenon, and then we will explain why it is so important to study the whole range of such deadly episodes, not just the major ones that now tend to define the field of genocide studies.

Once established, a typology that sets out the kinds of situations likely to produce genocidal slaughters can then be used to answer the second important question raised by the study of such events. *Are modern genocides and ethnic cleansings different from earlier ones?* No one with any historical knowledge doubts that mass murder of noncombatants and deadly expulsions of whole groups of people are very old, but many sophisticated theorists believe that the thoroughness and scope of such events in the twentieth century far surpassed anything in the past and have been a product of modernity itself. Zygmunt Bauman has written (perhaps hyperbolically): "It is the adventurers and dilettantes like Genghis Khan and Peter the Hermit [who inspired the slaughter of Jews during the First Crusade in the late eleventh century] that our modern, rational society has discredited. . . . It is the practitioners of cool, thorough and systematic genocide like Stalin and Hitler for whom modern, rational society paved the way" (Bauman 1989, 90).

Hannah Arendt, still the most cited of the theoreticians of totalitarianism's crimes, believed that the alienation of modern life was fundamentally responsible for the crimes of both Stalin and Hitlerism (Arendt 1951). This "modernist" view is also the theme of *Eichmann in Jerusalem*—modern bureaucratic conformity was the instrument through which such things can happen (Arendt 1963). She was well aware of how bloody the past was, but nevertheless believed that what had happened under totalitarian regimes in the twentieth century was a different phenomenon. The recent book on ethnic cleansing by Norman Naimark supports this view based on the totality of ethnic cleansing that was planned in the twentieth-century European episodes he studied. These he believed to be more thorough than mass political murders and expulsions in the past (Naimark 2001, 190–91).

Simply enumerating lists of premodern genocidal acts, some of which, like those of Genghis Khan in central Asia and Persia, were on a very large scale, does not entirely refute Bauman's and Arendt's assertions that there is something different about modern genocides. Nor is this a mere academic question, as it is related to the critical issue of what, if anything, we can do to control and prevent such behavior. If modernity itself is to blame, this casts doubt on some of the fundamental moral aspects of social change over the past several centuries. Indeed, both Bauman and Arendt came out of intellectual traditions highly skeptical of the value of modernity, and Bauman has become a leading proponent of postmodernist values. Whether or not his argument holds up to close scrutiny, however, is still open to debate.

The Four Main Motives Leading to Mass Political Murder

Of course the most basic condition for mass political murder is that one group has an overwhelming superiority in power. That superiority can be simply numerical, or it can be the result of technological and organizational superiority that gives one group irresistible force. In modern times it has usually been state power that has made genocide and ethnic cleansing possible. What is puzzling is that when groups are in conflict, one side often gains tremendous power over the other, yet instances of such an imbalance are far more common in history than are cases of genocide and ethnic cleansing. We therefore need to explain what sometimes turns vast power over enemies into mass murder.

Instead of concentrating on the moral implications of genocidal acts, whether direct murder of large numbers of people, or their expulsion under conditions of duress that result in many deaths, we should examine such events from the point of view of the perpetrators. Then it becomes clear that many such events appear to have been a matter of rational choice; on other occasions, however, there was much more involved than a cold-blooded calculus of costs and benefits. We begin with some clear examples of purely instrumental mass killings and mass expulsions and go from there to more complex motives. The typology we use is an adaptation of the one proposed by Frank Chalk and Kurt Jonassohn (1990, 29–32).

CONVENIENCE

Resistance may thwart the material or political ambitions of a group of people who have a preponderance of force to back their goals. There are many ways of handling such resisters. They may be bribed or bought out, and they may be persuaded or forced to compromise their claims to partially satisfy the stronger group. But the leaders of those resisting may believe the costs of giving in are higher than the costs of resistance. Continuing resistance, of course, raises the costs for those trying to impose their will, and eventually, the stronger party may consider mass expulsion or mass murder as the cheapest solution. That was William the Conqueror's reasoning when he "cleansed" Yorkshire. For historical and geographic reasons, this was the most resistant shire of his newly conquered English realm, and after trying to incorporate its nobility, he simply decided that their continuing resistance threatened his rule throughout England too much to let it go on, so he took extreme measures.

The example of the expulsion of the Cherokees is somewhat different, because they were unable and unwilling to put up any serious military resistance. They did, however, claim to have a legal right to their land and so were deemed to be in the way of the white settlers who dispossessed them. The material and military costs for the government were low, as the Cherokees were weak, and in the end, did not resist. But in this case, another element was present, one that did not affect William's actions in Yorkshire: a sense among many U.S. citizens that what they were doing was ethically and legally wrong, so that one of the chief costs was moral. In fact, those responsible for the policy went out of their way to diminish the obvious immorality of what they were doing by claiming to have justice on their side and also by insisting that the Cherokees were inferior human beings who needed to be removed for their own protection. This hypocrisy was a clear attempt to defray the moral cost of what they were doing.

Cherokee removal took place in 1838 but had been prepared by a long series of decisions and laws passed during President Andrew Jackson's administration (1829–37), then executed during that of his successor, Martin Van Buren (1837–41). The Cherokees had made a particularly valiant attempt to adapt to the white man's ways. They had turned a set of loose chieftainships into a constitutional state, developed a system of writing for their language, and gained a considerable level of literacy. They had also become private landowners, and some of them, imitating their white neighbors, had even become owners of black slaves. But these changes did not save them, because the growth of the white American population and the increasing demand for cotton lands created pressures for the removal of Indians. The discovery of gold in Cherokee territory greatly increased that pressure (R. Davis 1979; Hoig 1998, 101–32; McLoughlin 1986, 428–47; Perdue 1979; Persico 1979).

Those pressing for removal of the Cherokees and other Indians often phrased their goals in pious, charitable terms and concocted legalistic justifications for what was mostly a matter of greed and a deeply held prejudice that Native Americans could not really be "civilized" and could not, therefore, contribute to the development of the land as workers, even though they had been market participants in the days of the fur trade. Agricultural expansion, of course, had ended the fur trade. In a long speech to the United States Congress, then Representative Wilson Lumpkin, who subsequently became governor of Georgia, stated the rationale for Cherokee removal as follows: "Reject this bill [to eject the Cherokees from the Southeast to what is now Oklahoma], and you thereby encourage delusory hopes in the Indians which their professed friends and allies well know will never be realized. The rejection of this bill will encourage and invite the Indians to actions of indiscretion and assumptions which will necessarily bring upon them chastisement and injury, which will be deplored by every friend of virtue and humanity" (Lumpkin 1969, 1:57).

This was also Andrew Jackson's rationale. Native Americans were incapable of surviving the competition presented by whites, so before they were exterminated, they should be shipped off to the West where there would be no white settlers for a long time. There has been much debate among historians about whether Jackson was merely an Indian-hating hypocrite, or actually believed that the only way to save what were being called "remnant" populations was to force them to resettle (Remini 1977, 257–79; Satz 1991, 29–54; and more generally on Jackson, Remini 2001). Whatever his sentiments, Jackson deliberately disregarded a Supreme Court decision that prohibited the removal of the Cherokee because of their treaty rights, and encouraged Congress to pass laws defying the court to remove these most "civilized" (that is to say, Americanized) of Indians (McLoughlin 1986, 444–46).

The Cherokee removal was no isolated case. Well over one hundred thousand Native Americans were forcibly removed during the Jackson and Van Buren administrations. In 1831, Alexis de Tocqueville had observed another tribe, the Choctaws, being expelled across the Mississippi from their homeland, and later wrote: "It is impossible to conceive the frightful suffering that attend these forced migrations. They are undertaken by a people already exhausted and reduced; and the countries to which the newcomers betake themselves are inhabited by other tribes, which receive them with jealous hostility. Hunger is in the rear, war awaits them, and misery besets them on all sides. . . . [I] was the witness of sufferings that I have not the power to portray" (Tocqueville [1835–40] 1954, 1:352). Tocqueville discussed the coming fate of the Cherokees, which he correctly foresaw, and concluded this section of *Democracy in America* with what may be the most bitter remarks in his classic work. "The Spaniards were unable to exterminate the Indian race by those unparalleled atrocities which brand them with indelible shame . . . but the Americans of the United States have accomplished this . . . with singular felicity, tranquilly, legally, philanthropically. . . . It is impossible to destroy men with more respect for the laws of humanity" (369).

Another example occurred in Russia in 1860. After almost a century of inconclusive warfare against the Muslim Circassians in the north-western Caucasus, the Russian Empire decided they could not be sub-dued. They were considered "savages" and "bandits," which means that the usual tactic of co-opting their chiefs, turning them into Russian nobles, and transforming the other locals into dependent peasants was not working. The Circassians inhabited a poor and difficult mountain-ous region with few riches, but the area was strategically important, as it controlled a part of the Black Sea coast and access to the Ottoman Empire. The tsar's army launched a four-year campaign to starve, burn, kill, and expel the remaining Circassians. Of about two million, half died, about 120,000 to 150,000 resettled elsewhere in Russia, some 700,000 fled to the Ottoman Empire, and fewer than 200,000 survived in their original homeland. Ukrainian and Russian Orthodox Christian settlers were moved in to replace the local population and guarantee Russian possession of the territory. Some observers drew an explicit analogy with the way in which contemporary Americans were treating their native populations (Shenfield 1999). This example, however, is actually more similar to the eleventh-century Yorkshire case, as the Rus-sians were usually quite willing to incorporate non-Slavic elites and resorted to what amounted to a costly military operation because all else had failed.

In instances such as these a simple calculus takes place. The indige-nous population is troublesome and cannot be controlled or dispos-sessed. To leave it in place diminishes the value of the territory, either as a strategic holding or for economic exploitation. The local population is vulnerable because it is militarily weak, so it is killed or expelled. This was the rationale in the elimination of the Aboriginal population of Tas-mania and some other parts of Australia by its British settlers. The Aborig-ines were fighting back as their land was taken over by whites whose sheep were transforming the island. Though militarily insignificant, the Tasmanians were considered dangerous pests who could not be civi-lized—that is, made to do useful work for the whites. They were rounded up and put in camps where they all died (Hughes 1988, 414–24).

Many episodes of this kind can be found throughout history. Julius Caesar carried out such cleansings, bordering on genocide, during his conquest of Gaul. For example a Germanic tribe on the west bank of the Rhine, the Eburon, were virtually annihilated in 53 B.C. Caesar typically would try to bring conquered Gallic and Germanic tribes under control by promising them safety in return for obedience, but the Eburons, who had submitted, then reneged and massacred some Roman troops. Caesar felt obliged to eliminate their king, Ambiorix, and in order to do that, he targeted the entire tribe (Harmand 1984, 92–93). This action is explained in the *Commentaries* on Caesar's Gallic Wars:

> Caesar himself set out to plunder and lay waste the territory of Ambiorix. This chief was on the run, in terror. Caesar had given up hope of being able to force him into submission, and had decided that in order to protect his own prestige, the next best thing was to strip the country of inhabitants, buildings, and cattle so completely that if any of Ambiorix's people were lucky enough to survive, they would hate their chief. . . . Troops were sent out all over Ambiorix's territory, killing, burning, and pillaging; everything was destroyed and great numbers of people were either killed or taken prisoner. (Caesar and Hirtius [51–50 B.C.] 1980, 189)

In this case, a utilitarian calculation appears to have combined with a second impetus to genocidal behavior—revenge, which goes beyond but may still include a utilitarian aspect.

Many of the massacres conducted by Genghis Khan combined both calculated instrumentality and revenge, as have some forms of modern warfare that deliberately target civilian populations. When the Mongol armies of Genghis Khan swept through what is now Afghanistan in 1219 and 1220, the city of Herat surrendered and was spared damage. But later, it revolted against the Mongols, and Genghis Khan furiously ordered that every man, woman, and child in it be slaughtered and its walls torn down. This was done. The Persian sources claim some two million were killed. This is almost certainly an exaggeration, but still, there were probably three hundred thousand to half a million people packed within the city walls at the time, including many refugees. Afterward, the sources tell us there were about forty survivors. Yet the Mongols did not treat all cities in this fashion. Genocidal massacres like those in Herat were carried out for revenge, but also for sound strategic reasons—to convince other potential enemies that it was better to surrender than to face total destruction, and that reneging after surrendering was fatal. This is what the historian David Morgan has called the "Harry Truman" strategy in 1945–surrender or face complete annihilation of all your cities and people. To those who surrendered, the Mongols, like the Americans, could be quite tolerant (Morgan 1986, 73–83, 91–93).

The controversy about the use of atomic bombs in Japan will never be entirely resolved, but there is at least some justification for saying that the motivation in the bombing of civilian targets in both Japan and Germany by the Americans and British—especially in the last year of World War II, when both Germany and Japan were essentially defenseless against air attack and the allied air fleets were massive—was a sense that "they had it coming." Still, the utility of such bombing seemed, at the time, to be self-evident: "terror bombing" was expected to win the war by breaking the enemy's will to resist (Pape 1995). The importance of the utilitarian consideration is indicated by the fact that, once the war was over, neither the Americans nor the British engaged in continuing massacres (Frank 1999; Garrett 1993; Neillands 2001). It would be misleading to equate the killing of large numbers of civilians for utilitarian and limited ends, whether in modern or premodern warfare, with the deliberate extermination of whole peoples such as that carried out by the Nazis, but of course, for those killed, there is no difference. In either case, the numbers could reach genocidal proportions within the particularly targeted area, whether it was Dresden and Hiroshima in 1945, Herat in 1221, or Yorkshire in 1069.

REVENGE

When Genghis Khan and Caesar committed genocidal acts during their wars of conquest, this was part of a strategy to control populations, with extermination used as a last resort to teach a lesson to those who would not submit, to get them out of the way, and to serve as an example to others who might be tempted to resist. But in these cases, as in some of the bombing of cities during World War II, there was also an element of revenge. Caesar killed "prodigious numbers" in the kingdom of Ambiorix partly because he could find no other way to subdue this region but also because he was infuriated by the "treachery" of this tribe. The historian Jacques Harmand comments that "this was a campaign of extermination that was exceptionally brutal in the history of the conquest [of Gaul] about which it is impossible to deny that it was the only possible answer to the massacre of the [Roman] cohorts the previous autumn" (1984, 93). Ambiorix had promised to submit but had turned on the Roman soldiers left behind as guards, and this required vengeance.

Insisting on "prestige" and "honor" is a rational strategy to impress all potential enemies that attacking "us" is fraught with peril because "we" will avenge our hurt pride. Tying this to a just cause as "we" interpret that term gives "us" the moral excuse to engage in extreme brutality. A recent interpretation of imperial Rome's foreign policy claims that it was primarily based on exactly such a mind-set, insuring dominance by nursing slights to its prestige and honor until an avenging army could be collected, sent to the frontier, and launched into punitive warfare. Reminding all of Rome's potential enemies that punishment was sure to come eventually, even if it often took years to play out, was a far more important part of Roman planning than any immediate strategic or economic goal. If the offender was deemed too hard to control, or Roman honor had been deeply wounded, complete extermination of an enemy people was sometimes planned. This is entirely rational, but was not based on winning any immediate material advantage; rather, the long-term survival of the empire was deemed to depend on its reputation for defending its honor and always extracting revenge. "The goals of such expeditions were not normally 'defensive.' They were not undertaken, for example, to drive the barbarians out of Roman territory; in many cases the enemy will have left by the time the army arrived. The aim was to punish, to avenge, and to terrify—that is to reassert a certain state of mind in the enemy, or even a certain moral equilibrium" (Mattern 1999, 116–17). That is not to deny the economic and strategic importance of maintaining boundaries safely under control, but to emphasize that the Romans interpreted such measures to themselves as matters of justice and honor, and continued to do so as long as they were powerful enough to enforce their sense of international "morality."

Revenge can, however, go well beyond any simple calculation of costs and benefits. For those who have internalized a code of honor that demands revenge, settling the demand becomes a leading goal. That is why so many violent conflicts, both between individuals and between groups, including some significant wars, seem to violate material self-interest. Anger at the thought of injured honor becomes a primary motive in itself.

One of the most terrible twentieth-century examples of a vengeful genocide that had no obvious material rationale was the extermination of the Herero by the Germans in 1904–5 in their colony of Southwest Africa (today's Namibia). This colony had so little strategic or economic value that before the revolt the Germans were considering selling it to the British. In 1904, the Herero people rebelled against their cruel and abusive German masters, and at first succeeded in defeating the small German military force in the colony. When the news reached Berlin, Kaiser Wilhelm II decided weakness and an overly conciliatory governor had produced this uprising and defeat, and he handed control of the territory to the army so that he could bypass parliamentary control. General Lothar von Trotha was sent out with an army of almost ten thousand with the Kaiser's orders to crush the revolt by "fair means or foul." The poorly armed Herero were duly defeated by what was the world's most capable army and driven into the desert. Then von Trotha set up pickets along the entire border with orders to prevent them from returning to their lands. His proclamation is worth reading:

> I, the Great General of the German soldiers, address this letter to the Herero people. The Herero are no longer considered German subjects. They have murdered, stolen, cut off ears and other parts from wounded soldiers, and now refuse to fight on, out of cowardice. I have this to say to them. . . . The Herero people will have to leave the country. Otherwise I shall force them to do so by means of guns. Within the German boundaries, every Herero, whether found armed or unarmed, with or without cattle, will be shot. I shall not accept any more women or children. I shall drive them

back to their people—otherwise I shall order shots fired at them. Signed, the Great General of the mighty Kaiser, von Trotha. (Dedering 1999, 211)

Although some German pamphlets of the time suggested an ill-defined "final solution" (*definitive Regelung*) for the Herero, this was not yet Nazi Germany (Dedering 1999, 215). Eventually, when news of the full extent of what was happening reached Germany, there was outrage among parliamentary Social Democrats. The government was shamed into issuing an order to be more lenient, though with a delay long enough to let von Trotha's work be done. At the next census taken in the colony, in 1911, there were fifteen thousand Herero out of the original population of about eighty thousand. Another five thousand had managed to break out and make it to the British colonies of the Cape and Bechuanaland (now, respectively, South Africa and Botswana). So, at least 75 percent of the Herero were killed or deliberately starved to death in 1904 and 1905. When von Trotha returned to Germany, he was personally decorated by the Kaiser (Drechsler 1980).

This genocide and ethnic cleansing was partly a matter of convenience, to allow the Germans to rule Southwest Africa more easily, but it was much more a matter of "honor" to avenge an uprising deemed to be treacherous and humiliating because of the momentary successes of the Herero. It was also meant to warn imperial Germany's enemies what could happen to them if they violated German "prestige." That, after all, is the reason why "prestige" is so often important. Those who feel that their prestige has been diminished then feel they are vulnerable because they are seen as weak. This might embolden their enemies. The German army felt it had to prove itself ruthlessly determined to crush opponents, and this combined with the element of sheer revenge to make the Germans press on with the destruction of the Herero far beyond the point of this unfortunate people's complete submission.

During World War II, of course, the Germans routinely engaged in such actions in parts of eastern Europe and the Soviet Union, and at times elsewhere. In June 1944, they herded the villagers of Oradour, France, into a church and burned them to death, shooting those who tried to escape. The motive was primarily a deep-seated anger against the local population that obviously hated the intruders. Resistance had been active in that part of France, and there is good evidence that the massacre was planned, not the result of spontaneous anger. Given the timing of the slaughter, there was no prospect that it would materially affect the outcome of the war. It was just for revenge (Farmer 1999).

When individuals feel that a wrong has been committed against them, they seek justice. Despite many efforts to separate justice from revenge, the distinction frequently gets lost. Justice easily becomes a matter of honor. And revenge pursued for reasons of honor and justice against a collective entity, be it a family, a village, a clan, a tribe, or a whole nation removes whatever moral scruples the avenger may have against massacring the supposed offenders. These offenders may have been simply defending themselves against greedy interlopers, or they may have been aggressors themselves. It no longer matters once the stronger party claims that justice is on its side.

The compulsion to extract revenge for past wrongs is hardly limited to retribution for immediate acts. We humans have historical memories and have a habit of explaining our present situation in terms of the distant past, and this includes demands for historical retribution for deeds that happened long ago, and may, indeed, not really have happened at all. Thus, the Bible's Old Testament cites a vengeful God requiring the Israelites to slaughter all of the Midianites except for the virgin young women. The Lord says to Moses:

> "Avenge the people of Israel on the Midianites. . . ." And Moses said to the people, "Arm men from among you for the war, that they may go against Midian, to execute the Lord's vengeance. . . ." They warred against Midian, as the Lord commanded Moses, and slew every male. . . . And the people of Israel took captive the women of Midian and their little ones; and they took as booty all their cattle, their flocks, and all their goods. All their cities . . . they burned with fire. . . . And Moses was angry with the officers of the army. . . . [He] said to them, "Have you let all the women live? Behold, these caused the people of Israel, by the counsel of Balaam, to act treacherously against the Lord in the matter of Pe'or, and so the plague came to the congregations of the Lord. Now,

therefore, kill every male among the little ones, and kill every woman who has known man by lying with him. But all the young girls who have not known man by lying with him, keep alive for yourselves." (Num. 31 [Revised Standard Version])

The latest assessment by archeologists and biblical scholars is that this text was probably written in the seventh century B.C., at least six centuries after the supposed event, but whether or not it actually happened is not the point (Finkelstein and Silberman 2001, 94–122, 281–95). What is clear in this biblical passage is that justice as vengeance prescribes genocide. There are far too many examples of genocidal acts committed for the sake of revenge to dismiss this as something rare. After defeating his rival in a bloody civil war for the imperial Ming dynasty throne, the Prince of Yen, in 1402, tried to win over leading Confucian officials to his side. They refused, and so the new emperor killed thousands of them and hunted down their families until tens of thousands had been slaughtered (Chan 1988, 196–202). Up to a point, this was entirely utilitarian, as it broke the power of the Confucian officials for a very long time, something the new Yung-lo emperor clearly had in mind. This case was based neither on ethnicity nor on religion but was a premodern example of class-based genocide directed against an elite stratum. Nevertheless, if the element of revenge had not been present, it would have sufficed to simply kill the leaders and strip the class of its powers; the persistence of the Yung-lo emperor in tracking down even those who had fled, and their families, suggests that more than just practical considerations were at work (Dardess 1983, 288).

The logic of revenge killing is evident even when the numbers killed are relatively small. In societies with weak or nonexistent states, such as in medieval Iceland (Samson 1991), or until not so long ago in Corsica (Gould 1999) and the American South (Reed 1993; Reed and Reed 1996, 272–73), individual murders were common, and violent feuds between families could last for long periods of time. Families that do not protect their honor in situations where there is no effective state or police to protect their property are likely to suffer. "Cultures of violence" turn out to have an extremely high concern with "honor" for precisely that reason (Nisbett and Cohen 1996). Failure of a family or clan to defend insults to its honor suggests that the group is unable to mobilize for collective action and is therefore vulnerable to predation. Taken to the level of large categories of people, based on ethnicity, religion, class, or region, the same rules may apply and call into play murderous episodes of genocidal vengeance. To fail to take revenge may invite catastrophe later on, and if that is the perception, there is all the more reason to sanction extreme brutality.

Revenge lay behind the rape of Nanjing in 1937–38 by the Japanese army that had just conquered the city. The Chinese had had the temerity to fight bitterly against the invading Japanese earlier in Shanghai, and few modern armies were as obsessed with notions of honor as was the Japanese Imperial Army. Even though the Samurai code of honor forbad the killing of noncombatant civilians, for six weeks tens of thousands of women were raped and up to three hundred thousand Chinese were systematically tortured, beheaded, mutilated, and otherwise murdered. There is no doubt that the whole operation was ordered by top Japanese commanders. It lasted far too long and was too systematic to be ascribed to "battlefield frenzy" or fear of resistance once the city had surrendered (Brook 1999; I. Chang 1998; Fogel 2000). The wanton cruelty of the operation shows how far beyond merely efficient retribution the emotional aspect of vengefulness and injured pride can take perpetrators. Again, if the intent had been only to teach them a lesson about the futility of resistance, quickly executing some number of men of military age would have served the purpose, but extending the outrage over such a long period of time and with such cruelty suggests an emotional reaction far exceeding any utilitarian calculation.

SIMPLE FEAR

An obsession with revenge to save one's honor is partly precautionary, to teach potential enemies a lesson, and partly a reaction to a perceived sense of injustice, but it is also fed by fear that the failure to enforce vengeance will ultimately allow the enemy to regain strength and inflict further punishments. At more extreme limits, nothing stimulates the genocidal impulse as quickly as fear of extermination. A social group of any size that feels its very existence is at stake unless an aggressor or potential aggressor is eliminated will not hesitate to commit massacres in order to save itself. There are countless stories of combatants killing innocent civilians because they identify them all as potentially murderous enemies. The case of a possible massacre of Korean civilians by American soldiers at No Gun Ri in the midst of a panicky retreat in 1950 could be an example of this kind of reaction (Moss 2000). Fear, mixed with a desire for revenge, produced the massacre of Vietnamese civilians by American soldiers at My Lai, even though many commentators have tried to impute deeper meanings to this event (D. Anderson 1998; Lester 1996).

Fear, however, can be much more complex than that experienced in a confused battle. It can be a gnawing, long-term apprehension that an enemy group will, if it ever gets the power to do so, eliminate "us." This explains the extreme examples of cruel murder that soil the histories of virtually every ruling royal or imperial family in premodern history. As members of families fought for power, even surviving babies or small children who might lay claim to the throne were considered dangerous because they could serve as rallying points for opponents to the monarch. Thus royal killing of close kin — brothers, half-brothers, parents, sons, in-laws — and of more distant kin was routine wherever the succession was questioned or unclear.

An extreme example is the systematic fratricide that occurred regularly in the Ottoman Empire's ruling family from the fifteenth to the seventeenth centuries. The son who succeeded to power had his brothers and half-brothers strangled, and their wives and pregnant concubines sown into weighted sacks that were tossed into the Bosphorus. Any survivor posed a mortal danger (Nicolson 1962, 250). When such killings did not eliminate rivals, there were civil wars between surviving contenders (Fine 1994, 500); so of course, murdering family members directly was far safer for the new sultan, and perhaps necessary to avoid having the same fate meted out to him, his children, and his women.

The Ottoman Empire, before the advent of modern nationalism in the nineteenth century, generally behaved tolerantly toward religious and ethnic minorities, but not if it felt threatened. After a particularly serious set of wars between imperial brothers over the succession that led to the enthronement of Selim the Grim in 1513, that sultan turned his attention to the threat presented by the Shiite Muslim Persian Empire of the Safawids. To make sure that the heretical (at least in the eyes of the Orthodox Sunni Muslims) Shiite within the Ottoman realm did not rise up to support the Persians, he had forty thousand of them slain or imprisoned (Parry 1975, 410–11; Zarinebaf-Sahr 1997). When whole groups of enemies were seen as potential rivals who posed a mortal danger, whether relatives who might claim the throne or religious heretics who could help an enemy power, this threat could set off a series of defensive massacres or expulsions.

After the final military victory of the Christians over the Muslims in Spain in 1492, raiding for slaves, looting, and murder continued for more than a century, with Muslim corsairs descending on Spain, and Christians doing the same in North Africa. This continual raiding was punctuated by periodic uprisings of Muslims who remained in Spain, and they were often joined or helped by Moriscos—Muslims converted to Christianity but still treated as a separate community. By the late sixteenth century this situation was aggravated by the perceived threat of the Protestant heresy coming from France. Finally, after a series of revolts and killings, three hundred thousand Moriscos, over 90 percent of those in Spain, were expelled to North Africa in 1609 in one of the most thorough premodern ethnoreligious cleansings on record (Taylor 1997, 78–99).

Deadly ethnic riots, which Donald Horowitz has called "protogenocides," as well as many episodes of deadly ethnic cleansing, are often provoked by fear. The perpetrators are afraid that the targeted group is becoming so powerful that it will dominate, humiliate, impoverish, or perhaps even eliminate them; the offending group must be eliminated or at least put in its place by violence to reduce this threat (2001, 180–82, 431–35).

The story of Serbian-Croat relations, from the increasing tensions between these groups during the first two decades of Yugoslavia's existence after World War I, through the ethnic massacres conducted during World War II, and the rapid return of tensions in the late 1980s and early 1990s, is not so different from the story of the hostility between Christians and Muslims or Morisco new Christians in Spain in the sixteenth century. Without going into details about Yugoslavia, it is easy to see that there was competition over resources and rising fear that if the members of the opposing group were not eliminated through murder and expulsion, then they would commit murders and expulsions. There had been massacres during World War II; and in the early 1990s, ethnic murder began again, giving rise to reasonable fears that new massacres were about to be committed, so that preemptive violence was justified (Oberschall 2001). Here, as in Spain in the sixteenth and early seventeenth centuries, there were voices calling for moderation and understanding, as well as extremists demanding revenge and drastic solutions to eliminate the danger once and for all. The extremists won in both cases, in large part because there had been enough violent conflict in recent history to make such fears entirely plausible. The continual appeal in Yugoslavia to ancient medieval battles and the call for justified historical vengeance were biblical in their fabrication of ancient histories to justify ethnic separation and cleansing, but underneath it all, there was the present fear that to fail at this task might mean the elimination of one's own ethnic nation, or at least, its relegation to poverty and marginality. It hardly matters whether such fears were justified or not, as leaders on all sides convinced their followers that they were (Banac 1984; Djilas 1991; Judah 1997).

Stalin's killing, forced starvation, and deportation of kulaks, and later of potential saboteurs, Trotskyites, and others had much to do with his own fear of betrayal, as well as with his ideological conviction that if such people were not eliminated, their class origins and misconceived ideological positions would destroy socialism. To add to the examples given above, there is his destruction of much of his army's officer corps in 1938. About 40,000 officers were killed, including 3 of 5 marshals, 15 of 16 army commanders, 60 of 67 corps commanders, and 136 of 199 divisional commanders. In many cases their families were slain as well. The primary reason was Stalin's fear that in a coming war with Germany his forces would be defeated, and then an angry army would turn on him, as it had turned on the tsar because of losses in World War I (Laqueur 1990, 91; Tucker 1990, 514–15).

Later, Stalin's persecutions extended to various targeted ethnic groups as well. Ethnic cleansing of Chechens and Ingush from the Caucasus took place on a massive scale in 1944, supposedly to punish them, to take vengeance for their having worked with German invaders, but also because they were difficult to assimilate and posed a potential threat to Soviet rule in strategically important areas—much as some Caucasian peoples had threatened the Russian Empire in the nineteenth century. Some half million Chechens and Ingush were deported, of whom about 20 percent died of hardship. About two hundred thousand Crimean Tatars were also removed from their homeland and sent to central Asia near the same time, and up to 45 percent died. Many Black Sea Greeks, Armenians, and Bulgarians were deported to central Asia during this period for the same reason (Naimark 2001, 92–107). Convenience and vengeance were the primary causes, as these were small groups, but Stalin's fears of betrayal by ethnically hostile people had been exacerbated by the many examples of ethnic groups' collaborating with the Germans during World War II.

Stalin's final ethnic target, the Jews, was pursued for more complex reasons. From the time of the Revolution of 1917 through the 1920s and 1930s, Jews had played a disproportionately large role in the Communist Party, largely because they could provide skilled white-collar workers, professionals, and intellectuals untainted by any association with the old tsarist regime, which was itself anti-Semitic. After the great Party purges of 1937 and 1938, many new Russians holding traditional anti-Semitic views came into the organization, and Stalin eliminated most of the Jews among the old Party leaders. His greatest rivals, Trotsky, Zinoviev, and Kamenev, were Jews. During World War II, Jews continued to play a prominent role in Soviet affairs and could hardly be accused of collaborating with the Nazis, but after the war, prominent Jews began to be attacked, and there is good evidence that Stalin intended eventually to deport all Jews to Siberia. It was clear that he held a deep grudge against them. The Soviet media became increasingly anti-Semitic, and the campaign against them was already well under way when it was stopped by Stalin's death in 1953 (Slezkine 2004, 218–49; Vaksberg 1994; Weiner 2001, 138–62, 191–235).

Simple political fear, or a desire for vengeance, cannot alone explain the massiveness of Stalin's persecutions of various categories of people. In order to understand the murderous paranoia driving his acts, as well as similar genocidal campaigns by a number of other communist leaders in the twentieth century, but particularly those of the Khmer Rouge from 1975 to 1979, we have to turn to the final, and most extreme reason for such policies. We will see that there is a common thread running through the most excessive examples of communist killing, the Nazi genocides, and many other episodes of mass extermination, both modern and premodern.

FEAR OF POLLUTION

Mass murders or deportations that are ethnically, religiously, ideologically, or class based can be caused by a fear of pollution. This is at once the most intense, but also the psychologically most difficult cause to understand for those who do not share the sentiment that a particular group is so polluting that its very presence creates a mortal danger. When the targeted group objectively seems weak or powerless, the reasoning of the genocidal persecutors may appear particularly senseless but nevertheless needs to be understood.

In 1857, a series of large-scale massacres of British colonials occurred in India during the Great Mutiny. The fear and loathing engendered by British rule, and the sense that they had to be eliminated once and for all, both for the sake of vengeance and to prevent their return, resulted in the killing of hundreds of British, including women and children. The most notorious massacre took place in Kanpur and was conducted in public as thousands of Indian inhabitants watched. The killing was religiously sanctioned and was part of a great celebration to mark the elimination of British rule. But later, as a British army unit was approaching the town and exacting terrible revenge on neighboring villages, another batch of more recently captured women and children was secretly executed, probably to eliminate witnesses who might denounce the leaders of the uprising. The first massacre was a great cleansing operation to rid the land of the white Christians; the second was the fearful reaction of the rebellion's leaders, who were then trying to find a way to escape retribution (Mukherjee 1990).

Rudrangshu Mukherjee notes that a British commission of inquiry after the event was certain that the rebels must have raped many Englishwomen, but instead found that there had been no such incidents.

The explanation was that for both Muslim and Hindu insurgents, the revolt and massacres were part of an effort to religiously cleanse an India polluted by "Kafirs," infidel foreigners who had been contaminating the purity of caste and violating the laws of both religions. Not only rapes, but also even "naming the Kafirs" were viewed as impurities. The massacres were therefore as much a reaction to dreaded pollution as to any sense of vengefulness against the British, which is why the first massacre was a public ritual, unlike the second, panicky set of killings that were motivated entirely by ordinary fear of retribution (Mukherjee 1990, 115–16).

Trying to understand the ferocity of the wars of religion between Protestants and Catholics in France in the sixteenth century, in which some 750,000 people were killed, also requires an appreciation of the fear of religious pollution. It happens that the term *massacre* comes from these wars. Until the 1540s, the French word had merely designated the butcher's chopping block, but in 1545 it was used to describe killings of whole populations and the burning of villages in Provence in an effort to cleanse the land of Protestant heresy (Greengrass 1999, 70; Holt 1995). The wars of religion were complex and had several causes, some economic, some related to what amounted to disputes between aristocratic clans, some having to do with struggles for control of the French monarchy. But there was a genuinely theological component to these wars, which included a number of massacres culminating in the St. Bartholomew's Day massacre of 1572. Of all the motives for mass killing, the urge to purify Catholicism of the stain of heresy was at the heart of the worst episodes (Crouzet 1990; N. Davis 1975). Mark Greengrass (1999) has summarized much of the literature on these wars: "Hence the particularly gruesome cruelty meted out towards Protestants, the perverted mutilation of their bodies after their death. This was not sadism as we might understand it. Rather, the heretics were nonhumans, diabolic agents, and their pursuants were God's secret, avenging angels." As in many such extreme cases, during the massacres Catholic mobs repeatedly felt it necessary not only to kill Protestants, but also to burn their possessions and mutilate their bodies in order, somehow, to purify the land by butchering the heretical enemy as animals. Genital mutilation of men and cutting open pregnant Protestant women were part of this ritual of purification, and places where Protestants had celebrated services had to be burned in order to cleanse the ground of pollution (Holt 1995, 2, 86–93).

One is reminded of the horrible brutality that marked the killings in Indonesia in 1965 and early 1966 during one of the worst massacres of civilians in the second half of the twentieth century. A long period of rising tension and open conflict between the Left and the Right, and a rising tide of violence in many rural areas over control of land, culminated in an attempted left-wing coup. This was quickly defeated, and conservative army officers took advantage of their victory to launch a purge of the Communist Party of Indonesia. At least a half million people and perhaps up to one million were killed, mostly by civilians backed by the army (Crouch 1978, esp. 97–157). In East Java, where some of the worst excesses took place, the massacre frequently took on a ritualistic aspect far removed from the ostensibly modern political struggle occurring between communists and anticommunists. Not only were whole families destroyed, but torture and mutilation were common. "Heads, sexual organs, and limbs were displayed along the side of the main road outside Pasuruan. Canals were choked with bodies." Muslim youth groups were the most active and brutal killers as they slaughtered those accused of being communists and anti-Muslims (Hefner 1990, 210). In many cases suspected communists were tied up with their dogs, animals considered highly impure by the Muslims, thus indicating that their owners were not considered to be good Muslims. The "communists" had their throats slit so that they would bleed but not die quickly, and they were then thrown together into rivers and canals to drown or bleed to death attached to their dogs. (This story was told to Chirot and to Robert and Nancy Hefner in 1986 near Malang, East Java, by a former Muslim youth activist who had participated in these events.) This frenzied, ritualized killing was so similar to the atrocities committed in the French wars of religion because it mirrored the same wish to cleanse the land of infidel pollution and danger.

That combination of historical vengeance and the desire to rid the land of religiously polluting people is evident in the Old Testament passage cited earlier, about genocide against the Midianites. Through the Midianites "the plague came to the congregations of the Lord." In the later case of the Amalekites, the Lord, through Samuel, ordered that all of them, and all of their animals, should be utterly destroyed as well, and the Lord is furious because King Saul does not actually kill all of them. This episode of "fanatical fury," as Michael Grant calls the killing of the Amalekites (1984, 72), probably reflects the thoughts of scribes from the Kingdom of Israel, destroyed in 722 B.C. by Assyria, after they took refuge in Jerusalem and wrote a text to warn the surviving southern Jewish kingdom that the Lord is unforgiving of those who violate his commands (Lane Fox 1992, 66–67). Or it might have occurred in response to a seventh-century B.C. text seeking to create religious unity and adherence to the one true God of the Jews. (This is the interpretation of the Pentateuch proposed by Finkelstein and Silberman 2001.) Similarly, the obsession with pollution in the harsh laws set out in Deuteronomy also dates from that time, and these sanctions were refined during the Babylonian captivity to hold the exiled Jewish community together when the greatest danger facing it was assimilation (Douglas 1984, 42–43, 54–58, 107; Finkelstein and Silberman 2001, 296; Lane Fox 1992, 181–82).

The fear of pollution is most acute when there is a sense that failure to ritually cleanse the social and natural order will result in catastrophe or when terrible events have occurred and societies search for explanations, which they then find in their past failure to observe ritual purity. That is when "fanatical fury," a mixture of panic, rage, and a wish for vengeance combine into a frenzied desire to rid the land of the filth causing all these problems, whether in Indonesia in 1965, in France during the sixteenth-century religious wars, or in biblical tales.

The horror of Jews that pervades much of medieval Christian history is also a fear of pollution. Whatever other motives may have contributed to this repugnance—greed, looking for scapegoats in times of trouble, or dislike of merchants and usury—it was fed by something deeper. Georges Duby stresses that the early Carolingian conceptions of the monarch's duty included ". . . presiding over the destiny of all Christianity and . . . leading it to salvation. . . . His other duty was to reduce, or at least halt, the expansion of the Jewish community, a hard core of spiritual opposition which, though rejected, was still full of vitality" (1977, 7).

When Christian Crusaders set out on the First Crusade, their initial acts of violence were directed against French, then German, then eastern European Jews, and finally those they found in the Holy Land. As usual, motives were mixed, but a combination of a desire for revenge and for religious purification, to remove the dishonorable stain of the Jews' treachery against Christ, were more important than any simple economic motive. Jews were generally offered the choice of conversion to Christianity or death. Though forcible conversion was actually prohibited by canon law, and the high churchmen opposed these acts, "Once the crusade had been preached as an expression of love for God and brothers it was impossible for churchmen to control the emotions their appeal had aroused and throughout the twelfth century every major call to crusade gave rise to pogroms against Jews" (Riley-Smith 1987, 16–17).

In times of trouble, notions of Jewish impurity could produce massacres even in the absence of a call to crusades, as in 1320 and 1321 in France and some of the northern Iberian kingdoms. The association with pollution in this case is particularly marked, as both lepers and Jews were targeted. A twelfth-century Anglo-Norman poet, Walter of Wimborne, had earlier written poetry combining images of putrefaction, defecation, leprosy, avarice, Jews, betrayal, and corruption (Nirenberg 1996, 62–63). Jews had been expelled from France in 1306 (and from England in 1290) and then readmitted to France in 1315, so the famines and general discontent that unsettled France in 1320 were blamed on them, and indirectly, on the king who had allowed them to return. In the end, the French monarch had to step in to protect the Jews and put down what was an incipient popular revolt (Jordan 1996, 113, 170).

Anti-Semitism is such a multifaceted phenomenon that it is impossible to cover its many aspects as a unified whole. It is obvious that it consisted of many parts. In early-twentieth-century Vienna, Jews and converted Jews played a major role in the professional and intellectual life of the officially tolerant but actually increasingly anti-Semitic Habsburg Empire (Beller 1989). A relatively liberal era was ending, partly because of rapid social change, partly because seeming outsiders were gaining too much ground, but also because of a growing Germanic nationalist faith that demanded greater purity. Social change, new demands for ethnic and national loyalty, and rising resentment coincided with the spread of popular pseudoscientific theories about race and eugenics, and these fit in well with conservative, religious antimodernism. It was in the Vienna of that period that the young Adolf Hitler absorbed the popular theories about race and history that were to shape his worldview (Schorske 1981, 120–46). Not coincidentally, central Europe in the late nineteenth and early twentieth centuries (like late-fifteenth-century Spain, when Jews were expelled) was also the scene of revived stories about the ritual murders of Christian children by Jews (Kieval 1997).

Trying to explain away fear of pollution on purely material grounds, as a form of class warfare, or as the manipulation of the credulous masses by cynical elites, completely misses the tenacious ferocity of those whose fears lead them to commit dreadful acts that might seem to defy any material calculation. Perhaps it is the incredulity of basically decent people faced with the fanaticism of those who are terrified by pollution that leads them to look for other, more "rational" explanations. Thus, for example, Deborah Lipstadt's book on American reactions to the Jewish Holocaust ascribes some of the unwillingness to face up to what was going on, even in the face of growing evidence after 1942, to well-founded skepticism. The press remembered the exaggerated stories about German cruelty in World War I, and the new stories coming from central and eastern Europe were simply hard to believe (Lipstadt 1986). Reasonable, liberal people could not fathom the depth of hatred and fear that really determined official German policy.

In a way, this disbelief is similar to the rationalizing of some German historians who claim that Nazi racial genocide was a defensive reaction to Soviet class genocide. Such a claim is only plausible if one neglects Hitler's very deep aversion to, and fear of, Jews (Kershaw and Lewin 1997, 7). It was the merit of the psychologist Walter Langer's classified wartime study of Adolf Hitler's mentality (later published in 1972) to point out the many mentions in Hitler's writings of the fear of disease, of pollution, of corruption, and of degeneracy—all of them ascribed to racial mixing and particularly to the Jewish disease. Hitler himself was perfectly clear on this. He wrote in *Mein Kampf*: "Blood mixture and the resultant drop in racial level is the sole cause of the dying out of old cultures; for men do not perish as a result of lost wars, but by the loss of that force of resistance which is contained only in pure blood" (Hitler [1925–26] 1971, 296). And, in one of his most famous passages: "With satanic joy in his face, the black-haired Jewish youth lurks in waiting for the unsuspecting girl whom he defiles with his blood, thus stealing her from her people. With every means he tries to destroy the racial foundations of the people he has set out to subjugate" (325). There may have been a lot of pseudoscientific eugenics in Hitler's ideology, yet these and many other passages in his writing and speeches indicate that his horror of Jews was not merely misunderstood Darwinism but was linked to an obsessive search for purity.

The modern search for a perfect, utopian society, whether racially or ideologically pure is very similar to the much older striving for a religiously pure society free of all polluting elements, and these are, in turn, similar to that other modern utopian notion—class purity. Dread of political and economic pollution by the survival of antagonistic classes has been for the most extreme communist leaders what fear of racial pollution was for Hitler. There, also, material explanations fail to address the extent of the killings, gruesome tortures, fantastic trials, and attempts to wipe out whole categories of people that occurred in Stalin's Soviet Union, Mao's China, and Pol Pot's Cambodia.

The revolutionary thinkers who formed and led communist regimes were not just ordinary intellectuals. They had to be fanatics in the true sense of that word. They were so certain of their ideas that no evidence to the contrary could change their minds. Those who came to doubt the rightness of their ways were eliminated, or never achieved power. The element of religious certitude found in prophetic movements was as important as their Marxist science in sustaining the notion that their vision of socialism could be made to work. This justified the ruthless dehumanization of their enemies, who could be suppressed because they were "objectively" and "historically" wrong. Furthermore, if events did not work out as they were supposed to, then that was because class enemies, foreign spies and saboteurs, or worst of all, internal traitors were wrecking the plan. Under no circumstances could it be admitted that the vision itself might be unworkable, because that meant capitulation to the forces of reaction. The logic of the situation in times of crisis then demanded that these "bad elements" (as they were called in Maoist China) be killed, deported, or relegated to a permanently inferior status. That is very close to saying that the community of God, or the racially pure *volksgemeinschaft* could only be guaranteed if the corrupting elements within it were eliminated (Courtois et al. 1999).

The destruction of one-quarter of the Cambodian population by the Khmer Rouge from 1975 to 1979, some two million people, is a gruesome example. In this case the compulsion to purify Cambodia took many forms: there was the goal of achieving racial purity by eliminating all traces of contaminating Vietnamese blood in the Khmer people, of obtaining class purity by destroying class enemies and their families, of wiping clean the corrupting stain of Western modernity by emptying the cities of people, and of purging the Communist Party of all treachery and opposition. All this was based on a clear utopian vision, based on a fantasy created by French historians and absorbed by Pol Pot and his entourage, that the ancient Khmer Empire had been a perfect agrarian utopia that could be recreated. This time, however, it would be done on an even larger scale, guided by Maoist ideals (Heuveline 2001; Kiernan 1996, 7–8; Kiernan 2001). Particularly telling was the fact that many of the Khmer who were massacred were considered to have become tainted by Vietnamese influence and thus to have become "Khmer bodies with Vietnamese minds" (Kiernan 1996, 424–25).

Bad elements, wreckers and Trotskyites, Khmer bodies with Vietnamese minds, the Jewish disease, Protestant heretics—all of these polluters presented, in the eyes of their killers, deadly menaces. We can turn again to the Old Testament for a dramatic example of how this works. After conquering Canaan, committing a whole series of bloody genocidal massacres, often murdering, as in Jericho, "both men and women, young and old, oxen, sheep, and asses, with the edge of the sword," and supposedly ridding the land of Israel of its enemies (Josh. 3–22), Joshua speaks to his people: "For the Lord has driven out before you great and strong nations. . . . Take good heed to yourselves, therefore to love the Lord your God. For if you turn back, and join the remnant of these nations left here among you, and make marriages with them, so that you marry their women and they yours, know assuredly that the Lord your God will not continue to drive out these nations before you; but they shall be a snare and a trap on you, a scourge on your sides, and thorns in your eyes, till you perish from off this good land which the Lord your God has given you" (Josh. 23:9–13).

Despite this warning, the Israelites did not obey. In the early part of Judges, there is a list of the Canaanite cities in which the Israelites committed neither genocide nor ethnic cleansing (Judg. 1). This angered the Lord, but worse was to follow. The Israelites "went after other gods from among the gods of the people who were round about them, and bowed down to them." The Lord punished Israel by setting its enemies against it and then repeatedly relented, giving them a chance to slaughter their enemies, but they kept on falling back into the same sin (Judg. 2–11). It is quite clear that the reason they kept on worshipping false gods was because they were intermarrying with non-Israelites, and the story of Samson (Judg. 16) is meant to be a sharp reminder of how dangerous it is to love a forbidden outsider.

When these stories were written down, the perceived threat to Jewish survival was that through intermarriage and cultural assimilation they would cease to exist as a distinct religion, a chosen people. To prevent this, their close kin, the heretical or unconverted Canaanites, had to be demonized. But more than this, in a time of extreme stress, when the Jews faced political defeat, it was necessary to explain how things could have gone so badly wrong by blaming it all on their failure to purify themselves—that is, their failure to heed their demanding God. This was an error that the great ideological killers of the twentieth century tried to avoid.

How Distinct Are the Four Motives?

Our four motives are not mutually exclusive. Governor Lumpkin of Georgia, after all, was a racist who saw the Cherokee as inferiors in a society that considered racial mixing a contamination. So even this most instrumental of ethnic cleansings was not entirely free of other motives. Yet, if Cherokee land had not been coveted, they would not have been ethnically cleansed, and once they were removed, there was no push to have them exterminated. The primary motive was greed—

not revenge, fear, or any sense that Cherokees were so polluting that they had to be wiped out.

As noted, motives of revenge and fear often overlap because of the danger of not responding to violence with violence. The enemy might gain strength, and other potential foes may be tempted to attack. Fear makes revenge rational even in the absence of any sense of outrage. We will return to this theme in the next chapter. But again, our cases show the primacy of one or the other on many occasions. It is hard to imagine what the Germans might have feared from a thoroughly defeated Herero population, or why they decreed a genocide, except for revenge.

If many cases have mixed motives, however, the specific reasoning behind each one needs to be analytically disentangled in order to understand why they took place. To take some of our most obvious examples, trying to explain Hitler's obsession with cleansing the earth of Jews by claiming that the main motive was to seize their property, or to gain revenge for their past behavior, is to misunderstand how deep his hatred really was. Similarly, we cannot understand the horror of Europe's wars of religion, or of Stalin's destruction of millions, without understanding the fear of pollution. Distinguishing between motives opens the way to a better psychological understanding of what drives some to mass murder. This is something we will examine more closely in our second chapter.

Are Modern Genocides and Ethnic Cleansings Different? Retribalization and the Modern State

Having some sense of the main causes of genocidal acts, we can address the question of whether or not there is something different about modern versions of mass political murder. Hitler, Stalin, and Mao certainly embodied modern theories about the state and about the role of science (racial in one case, class-based in the other two), and it would be an error to call them mere throwbacks to Genghis Khan. But in their obsessive drive to purify their societies of racial or class pollution, these tyrants were also less than fully modern. Theirs was a search for utopian purity, a "fanatical fury," and a terrible fear of what would happen to them and their cause if they did not cleanse their societies. Such sentiments are very ancient and have been responsible for massacres many times in the past, even if never on the scale made possible by modern bureaucratic states.

Other examples of twentieth-century mass killings and murderous ethnic cleansings—of Armenians, of Herero, of Bosnian Muslims, of Tutsis, of Germans from eastern Europe, and of many cases of deadly, massive, forced population movements and murderous communal violence in southeast Asia, south Asia, the Middle East, the Balkans, and Africa—fit into one or several of the categories described above. Practical power considerations, desires for revenge or to maintain honor, fear of the enemy, and a perception that a bloody cleansing was required all explain such events in the recent as well as in the more distant past.

Despite this, there is something to the argument that the modern world is worse. The scholars who support this argument are not historically naive, and many major analysts persuasively claim that the nationalism underlying twentieth-century genocides and ethnic cleansings is indeed a modern phenomenon constructed to suit the needs of modernizing states—or, alternatively, as a reaction against such states whose dominant elites try to impose their form of nationalism on resistant ethnolinguistic or ethnoreligious groups. Though they each stress somewhat different points, Eric Hobsbawm (1992), Benedict Anderson (1991), Liah Greenfeld (1992), and Ernest Gellner (1983) all share this perspective. Greenfeld goes the furthest in directly implicating German and Russian nationalism for the horrors of Nazism and Stalinism, but similar condemnation is implicit in the arguments of the others, too. Even Anthony Smith (1986), who is accused of being a "primordialist" about nationalism (one who believes that nationalisms are based on very old ethnic identities rather than recently constructed ones), accepts the idea that modern nationalism since the nineteenth century has something different about it.

This is not the place to review once more the vast literature on the rise of nationalism, some of which was cited above. Suffice it to say that virtually all contemporary specialists of this subject believe that modern nationalism has made demands on its people for greater cultural homogeneity, either through conversion to a common language and set of values (as in the United States), or more often, through acceptance of ethnic or religious homogeneity (or both). The notion that a cultural group or "nation" has some right to rule itself became standard in western Europe as a consequence of the French Revolution and the spread of English and French Enlightenment principles (Gellner 1983; Kedourie 1960). That the western Europeans violated these principles in their own imperial ventures contributed greatly to the spread of the same principles and to anti-imperialist nationalisms, as well as to the general moral rejection of colonialism in the second half of the twentieth century (B. Anderson 1991). The complementary notion that a state should represent a nation continues to create problems for those trying to bring peace to many troubled, culturally heterogeneous states from the Balkans to Russia, from Africa to central Asia, south Asia, and southeast Asia.

The identification of state with nation has meant that the modern nation has become the village, the clan, the tribe, or the small city-state with which most people identified in the past. Liah Greenfeld (1992) has claimed forcefully that becoming modern means becoming a member of a larger nation, no longer just a member of a village, region, or religion. The nation for most people today is the chief focus of political identity, and those who, for one reason or another, do not believe that the state they live in legitimately represents their group strive to leave or to create their own nation-state. In a real sense, the modern world has become retribalized, but the new tribe, the nation, includes far more people than tribes did in the past.

It is not just the unlimited, vast scope and unexpected shock of the few great genocides in the twentieth century that have made social scientists and philosophers such as Arendt and Bauman suspect that these events have a uniquely modern component. In modern times, ethnic cleansings have been much more numerous than outright exterminations, and since the midnineteenth century and all through the twentieth, populations have split apart that previously had lived together in relative harmony for long periods of time. The "unmixing" (Rogers Brubaker's term) of ethnolinguistic and ethnoreligious groups that has accompanied the unraveling of great multiethnic states—such as the

Habsburg, Ottoman, British Indian, and more recently colonial African and communist empires—appears as something new because successful agrarian states in the past normally tried to do the exact opposite.

Empires and kingdoms agglomerated diverse groups together by conquest, thus maximizing the rulers' revenues, and usually resorted to mass killings or deportations only when they met intense resistance. In contrast, a growing number of modern states that have emerged from empires have sought to rid themselves of potentially productive populations that have come to be viewed as threats to the nation rather than as sources of revenue. Groups are targeted simply because they speak a different language or practice a different religion (Barkey and von Hagen 1997; Brubaker 1996). Indeed, the Ottoman genocide of Armenians, the Nazi genocide of Jews (Melson 1992), and the Rwandan genocide of Tutsis (Prunier 1997), were all part of efforts to engage in total ethnic cleansing—complete "unmixing" of populations that had lived together, mostly on peaceful terms, for many centuries. Such horrors might have occurred in the past when one people conquered another and found it impossible to otherwise subdue the enemy or use conquered land to their advantage, but there were very few efforts to root out minorities from areas they had long inhabited if they could be controlled without resorting to this extreme.

The many systematic unmixings of populations in the twentieth century in Europe have some parallels in the past, but not many. One precedent is the expulsion of Jews from certain medieval European countries even though they posed no obvious military or political threat. The expulsion of Jews from Spain in 1492, combined with a preoccupation for creating a society of "pure blood," appears particularly "modern," though close examination shows that the "cleansing" was much less thorough than historians once thought (Kamen 1998, 32–34).

Does this mean that large-scale ethnic cleansing of the sort that produced modern ethnic genocides as well as the Yugoslav catastrophes and the dozens of similar events in the twentieth century is part of an alarming contemporary trend? That is what Ted Gurr suggests when he lists 233 "minorities at risk"—close to a billion people in today's world (Gurr 1993, 11, 326–38). Of course, as in the past, not all potential conflicts have or will ever become so extreme, but Gurr's work points out that some have, and perhaps more will. If such catastrophes are indeed more modern, perhaps they will continue to increase, as they seem to have done in the twentieth century.

Any group within the state's borders that does not accept its legitimacy on cultural grounds threatens its very integrity, the life of the state, and of the nation represented by that state. Even if a non-state cultural group wants to be loyal to the state it inhabits, suspicion that it is untrustworthy threatens the state and opens that group up to persecution. Once violent conflict is engaged, the motives of revenge and justice, as well as fear of defeat come into play. These may be ritualized and rationalized as fears of pollution and turn into long-lasting hatreds and potentially murderous feuds.

The rise, once more, of religious fervor in combination with nationalism as a unifying force has already caused significant bloodshed and shows every sign of growing even stronger (Juergensmeyer 1993). This is most evident in Islam (Tibi 1998), but exists elsewhere, too (Juergensmeyer 2000). The execrable behavior of Saddam Hussein and Slobodan Milošević; ethnic and religious extremism in Sri Lanka and Afghanistan; endless rounds of massacres in Rwanda, Burundi, Congo, and Sudan; new wars and outrages in the Caucasus; intercommunal massacres in Indonesia; the inflexibility of many religious Jews and Muslims over contentious issues in Israel and Palestine—these and many other cases are not just exceptions to a beneficent rule. There are too many such "exceptions" (Jowitt 1992). There are contrary cases, of course, as in South Africa, where compassion and forgiveness now have the upper hand over the desire for revenge and ethnic fears, but it would be foolhardy to see any clear trend in that direction.

It might be seen as a sign of hope that, of all the reasons for massacring people, the first, simple convenience, is somewhat less acceptable today than in the past. Even the worst tyrants who engage in such actions claim to be following what they deem to be some higher ethical principle—socialism, democracy, racial purity, national survival, or some other noble goal. Today a Julius Caesar exterminating a troublesome tribe in Gaul would have public relations agents saying that this was done so that the people of Gaul might better enjoy the benefits of the Pax Romana. Even the first century knew something of spin control, as Tacitus ironically observed when he wrote about the subjugation of Britain: "To robbery, slaughter, plunder, they give the lying name of empire: they make a solitude and call it peace" (Tacitus [A.D. 98] 1964, sec. 30).

Today when presumed vital interests, national survival, national honor, religious and ideological purity, or a deep desire for revenge are in play, political massacres of one kind or another are possible and even likely. The possibility of genocide has never been absent, but in modern times control of the state, particularly in economically impoverished and politically unstable areas, has developed new importance: first because state-controlled resources can be crucial for economic advancement and even for physical survival, and second, and more important, because if everyone is supposed to be a member of the nation that supports and legitimizes the state, then any cultural group without control of a state is likely to feel threatened with extinction. Higher stakes intensify the struggle between competing groups for hegemonic control. This means that the kinds of mass political murder and expulsions that characterized the twentieth century are likely to continue to occur in the twenty-first.

CHAPTER TWO

The Psychological Foundations
of Genocidal Killing

> Most of you know what it means to see a hundred
> corpses lying together, five hundred, or a thousand. To have
> gone through this and yet—apart from a few exceptions,
> examples of human weakness—to have remained decent,
> this has made us hard.
>
> —*Heinrich Himmler in a speech to SS leaders in*
> *charge of massacring Jews, 1943 (Fest 1970)*

The four reasons for genocidal killings discussed in chapter 1 are (1) practical, material ends that require the elimination of opponents who are in the way; (2) desire for what is perceived to be justified revenge; (3) fear of the enemy; and (4) a need to rid the environment of dangerously polluting others. But there is more to it than that, because we know that most human beings, all but those most habituated to extreme brutality or a small number who seem to lack normal emotional reactions to bloody violence, have to overcome a sense of horror when they engage in or witness slaughter firsthand. Carl von Clausewitz, the greatest European theoretician of war, and himself a veteran soldier who had been in many deadly battles, told his wife that the sight of Russian Cossacks butchering Napoleon's soldiers as they retreated from Moscow in 1812 was "ghastly," and he added: "If my feelings had not been hardened it would have sent me mad. Even so it will take many years before I can recall what I have seen without a shuddering horror" (quoted in Keegan 1994, 8). How do feelings get hardened? How is it that so many can be found to commit mass murder? What are the psychological mechanisms that overcome the horror most people feel when confronted by such spectacles?

Our examination of the psychological studies on this subject will find that there are actually many ways to get people to massacre others, and in the end, given the right circumstances, we will discover that it is not so difficult to explain why this happens. The disgust most of us feel at the thought of butchering others can be overcome by turning killing into a routine that desensitizes the killers, by training, and by good organization. Able leaders can get their followers to commit terrible acts by appealing to their emotions and sense of duty. Any combination of intense fear, anger, and hate of potential victims can suffice to justify genocidal behavior. Being humiliated by an enemy creates the desire for justice and revenge that easily fuels these emotions and turns them into enduring sentiments that produce yet more conflict and cycles of violence. Eventually, many normal individuals can quite easily be turned into brutal killers, even if that is not true of everyone.

How to Get Ordinary People to Become Butchers

During the slaughter of Jews by the Nazis, SS chief Himmler, who himself supposedly vomited, or at least was shocked and paled the first time he witnessed Jews being massacred (Padfield 1990, 342–43), recognized the revulsion this produced. And for this reason the killings that had begun as mass shootings at close range, with brains and blood spattering the executioners, were turned over to death camps, where the murder was impersonal, chemical, less bloody, and largely out of sight of regular soldiers (Browning 1992b, 24–25, 49–50). Killing large numbers of people is hard and unpleasant work, and few of us would relish the thought of working in a human slaughterhouse.

This shift in the Nazis' methods is supported by the findings of Paul Rozin and his colleagues, who have found that we tend to be repelled by anything that reminds us of our animality, and so we surround sex, eating, hygiene, body products, birth, and of course, death with all kinds of rituals (Rozin et al. 2000). Seeing people being slaughtered reminds us of our own vulnerabilities and eventual fate. To massacre we need some way of ritualizing and distancing ourselves from what we are doing to avoid identification with the victims.

There is good evidence that those who carry out genocidal massacres have to be motivated and trained to overcome any scruples that would otherwise hinder their activities. Genghis Khan sometimes carried out abominable massacres—in Herat, for example, as described in chapter 1—but his men were evidently not eager for this work. To make sure that they dispatched the appropriate number of unarmed civilians, the men were obliged to cut off ears and bring them to their superiors to show that they had fulfilled their quotas (Chalk and Jonassohn 1990, 109). When Mongol warriors were not at war, they engaged in gigantic hunts in which an entire area would be surrounded, and the large animals in this zone would be forced into an ever-shrinking circle, until they were bunched together, at which time they would be slaughtered *en masse*. This was good training in Mongol cavalry tactics, but also got men used to butchering on a large scale in a socially approved way (Morgan 1986, 84–85).

Christopher Browning's great work on Nazi Jew killers reports that they drank heavily to prepare themselves and often used native (usually Ukrainian, Latvian, or Lithuanian) auxiliaries to do the work, and these, also, were given ample amounts of liquor as well as being subject to threats and inducements to get them to perform their task (Browning 1992b, 52, 80, 163). After the deed has been done a few times, it becomes easier to do it again, as the killers become desensitized. Once the first hurdle has been passed, and men have killed a few helpless victims, it is not so difficult to turn them into mass butchers.

But it is more than the disgust that many feel when observing mass slaughters that must be overcome. There is also the issue of legitimacy. Most humans have a sense of fairness that governs relations with others (Homans 1974), and the most primitive sense of fairness is the reciprocity principle (Cialdini 2001). If someone helps, befriends, or supports you, or gives you a present, then you owe that person help, friendship, support, or a gift in return. Similarly, if someone insults or hurts you, or takes something from you, you owe them insult, punishment, and recovery of your property. What counts as help or harm can vary from one culture to another, but the general principle of reciprocity is found in every culture. Reciprocity means that killing those who seem directly threatening appears fair, but killing those who cannot harm us is more questionable.

The inclination against killing unless threatened oneself is well understood by those who train and lead soldiers. Much military pomp is an elaborate way of ritualizing and rendering killing acceptable. In battle it is relatively easy to get soldiers to fight against other soldiers who are clearly intent on killing them, but much harder to get them to kill civilians who, on the face of it, are not threatening. The psychologist Ervin Staub, for example, reports that American soldiers told to shoot at what appeared to them to be civilians were unwilling to do so, but under orders, and with experience, their scruples were overcome, and killing became more routine (Staub 1989, 26, 126).

The psychology of rationalization that underlies the way in which reluctance to kill is overcome goes by the name of "dissonance theory." Dissonance is an unpleasant arousal that comes from seeing ourselves as having chosen to do something wrong, stupid, or sleazy—that is, something at odds with our positive self-image (Sabini 1995). The less outside pressure is imposed on us, the less we can excuse our acts, and the greater the dissonance; but even when we can say, "It was an order," killing usually involves some feeling of responsibility. Therefore, to get rid of dissonance, we change our beliefs about what is right and wrong to bring our beliefs into line with our acts. Americans reduced the dissonance between their professed ideals and the reality of the immense suffering they imposed on ethnically cleansed Native Americans by claiming that it was "for their own good," and it was this rationalization that so outraged Tocqueville and led to his bitter commentary on what was being done to the Indians (Tocqueville [1835–40] 1954, 1:369).

A striking example of this kind of psychology at work is the set of famous "obedience" experiments carried out by Stanley Milgram (1974). In the basic version, a person is recruited as a subject for what is described to him or her as a learning experiment. The subject joins the experimenter and a supposed other subject who is actually working with the experimenter. A rigged drawing makes the real subject the teacher and the confederate the learner, and the experimenter explains that the teacher will ask questions and give an electric shock for each wrong answer, and then increase the shock level for each successive wrong answer. The other subject (confederate) proves a very bad learner and makes many mistakes. The surprising result of this experiment is that most subjects increase the shock, step by step, from 15 volts to 30 to 45 volts and so on up to 450 volts, a level that on the (fake) console carries a posted warning "Danger, Strong Shock, XXX." In other words, most subjects put in the position of using shock to try to teach a slow learner (actually an actor) are willing to apply increasing shocks at each wrong answer until the learner starts to scream with pain and even after the learner mentions a heart condition, falls silent, and stops responding. Approximately the same results are obtained with female as with male subjects as teachers, and with Australians, Japanese, Italians, and Germans, as well as Americans (Blass 1999).

Why do about two-thirds of all subjects agree to go all the way, to raise the shock level past the point where the learner's silence suggests injury or even death? (It should be noted that this was one of the psychological experiments that so distressed professional psychologists that rules were instituted in all universities and research labs that now prohibit placing this much psychic pressure on uninformed subjects.) Most discussions of the research emphasize the authority of the experimenter, who seems to be an official, responsible scientist, and who responds to any attempt to stop the shocks by saying that "the experiment demands it, you must go on." But there is a variation of the experiment that points in another direction.

In this variation, there are two confederates posing as subjects as well as a genuine subject. The rigged drawing as usual makes the real subject the "teacher" and one confederate the "learner," but the other confederate joins the real subject as a second "teacher." The second teacher (confederate) gets the job of determining whether the answer is correct or not, and the genuine subject gets the job of pulling the switch to deliver the shocks. The official-looking experimenter is called away on a pretext, and the confederate teacher comes up with the idea of raising the shock level with each wrong answer. In this alternative scenario, then, the genuine subject still gives the shocks, but it is a confederate teacher rather than the experimenter who says to raise the shock with each mistake. The result is that 20 percent of real subjects go all the way to deliver the 450-volt shock. One-fifth is considerably less than two-thirds, and the difference is a reflection of how much authority the "scientist" conducting the experiment actually carries. But a 20 percent compliance rate nevertheless represents a surprising level of inhumanity toward the supposed learner, especially when the one giving the orders to deliver potentially killing shocks is perceived to be just another random subject with no authority.

One way to explain this result is in terms of rationalization. According to dissonance theory, humans are likely to change their opinions to make sense of their behavior. Especially if we have done something stupid or dishonest, we are likely to come up with reasons that will justify or excuse us (Sabini 1995). The dissonance interpretation of why 20 percent of the subjects will administer 450 volts in the absence of authority goes as follows. The finely graded levels of shock are a slippery slope, in which the best reason to give the next, higher level of shock is that a slightly lesser shock has just been given. If the next level of shock is wrong, there must be something wrong with the previous level of shock already delivered. But if there is nothing wrong with giving the immediately preceding level of shock, the next level, only 15 volts higher, cannot be wrong either. Ultimately, then, 20 percent of the subjects never stop, and go from giving mild shocks to deadly ones, or at least think they are doing this. Having already given a number of shocks, some subjects feel a need to justify themselves and to preserve their self-image as decent people. The justification of the previous shock then rationalizes the next level of shock.

This is the psychology that reinforces desensitization and routinization of killing. Each additional killing makes the next one easier because each killing leads to changes in beliefs and values that justify the preceding one: I have been ordered to do this; those being killed are doing something wrong; they stand in my way; they deserve it; they are a threat to my own people; they are not quite human; they are polluting. Desensitization and routinization of killing thus occur in two ways. There is reduced emotional impact of originally disturbing stimuli associated with death, and there is increased cognitive and moral rationalization of the act. These mutually reinforce each other in supporting escalation once killing has begun. The killer's own behavior and rationalization, starting from the first occasion, become part of the pressure to kill more and to further reduce dissonance by legitimizing what is going on as something that is necessary.

The important point to understand here is that it is unnecessary, and even misleading, to think of those who engage in large-scale killing of civilians as somehow abnormal. Given the right circumstances, it is not too difficult to turn a significant proportion of humans into mass murderers. The disgust one may feel, the identification with the victims, the sense of unfairness can all be overcome and have routinely been overcome with training and experience.

Organization

Desensitizing the killers, however, is not enough; they must be organized if the killing is to go beyond occasional bloody episodes. The need for organization is most obvious in large-scale genocides. In *Death by Government* (1994) Rudolph Rummel estimates that in the twentieth century about 40 million people were killed in wars, but 140 million noncombatants died. A significant portion of these millions of civilians, well over half, were not killed as more or less accidental casualties of war but by deliberate actions—by being starved or worked to death, by outright slaughter, in concentration camps and in prisons, as helpless refugees fleeing persecution or cowering in their homes. Killing large numbers requires a high level of organization and a gross asymmetry of power in favor of the perpetrators.

More significant than this, the actual perpetrators function much more efficiently and can overcome their moral reservations if they are well organized and led. Membership in a group of killers creates powerful bonds of solidarity that can legitimize killing and reduce any dissonance felt by those who murder. The logic by which cohesion can be turned to killing is this: the group is assigned a difficult and dirty task, and any individual who does less than his share is putting an extra load on his buddies (Stouffer et al. 1949). Browning (1992b) repeatedly mentions the importance of group support to sustain Nazi police charged with murdering Jews. In Rwanda, many killings were perpetrated by locals on their neighbors; however, neighbors' turning on each other was not a sufficiently reliable or consistent method for carrying out mass genocides, so the Interahamwe, a Hutu youth group turned into a centrally directed, organized death squad, led the house-to-house searches for Tutsis and was sent to intervene in areas where the local population was loathe to participate (Mamdani 2001, 212). As with special elite German SS troops, they did not do all the killing but provided the "specialists" called in to direct the murders and stiffen the less-organized others who also participated. Organized, well-led groups with a sense of camaraderie are much better at performing such difficult tasks. Neighbors can commit mass murder, but without the background support and intervention by organized special killers, such genocidal acts are self-limiting.

It is precisely because rioting crowds are not as disciplined and organized for massacre that even deadly ethnic riots do not normally kill large numbers of people. They may commit atrocities, dismember and torture, rape and murder, but without organized, politically motivated cadres backed by the authorities, their killing power is relatively weak. In the 150 or so cases of deadly ethnic riots studied by Donald Horowitz, few approached genocidal proportions; riots that kill an entire targeted community, even at the local level, are very rare (2001, 22–23). Nevertheless, poorly organized, more spontaneous ethnic or religious riots that kill some members of a targeted group offer us an insight into the causes of larger killings, because many of the emotions that unleash such events are similar to those that lie behind genocides, namely, fear and hatred of those branded for destruction. In this sense, such deadly riots are indeed little "protogenocides."

Emotional Appeals: Leaders and Followers

To mention organization is to consider the role of leaders, and this entails thinking about the psychology of those who order, plan, and lead politically inspired mass murder. In most instances of mass killing it is the perceptions of the group's leaders that are the most important, and they typically perceive realistic personal threats that are more direct and immediate than those perceived by their followers. In Rwanda, for instance, the genocide was organized by Hutu leaders whose power was, indeed, threatened from without by invading Tutsis and threatened from within by moderate Hutus. This is why the power-sharing peace agreement worked out by the United Nations was the final element that provoked the genocide (Prunier 1997, 192–212). Similarly, the Armenian genocide was organized by Ottoman leaders from the Young Turk movement who saw their power threatened during World War I by a combination of Christian enemies abroad and Christian Armenians at home (Naimark 2001, 27–30). Leaders were able to mobilize followers by playing up threats and reminding their people of negative past experiences, making fear seem more realistic, and even provoking the enemy into acts that would confirm these fears.

Slobodan Milošević, for example, was a master at making Serbs fearful about what would happen to them if they failed to maintain an ethnically pure Greater Serbia, and his Croatian enemy and counterpart, President Franjo Tudjman, was just as clever. Whether, in fact, they both believed what they were saying became irrelevant as the fear they aroused not only provoked the Yugoslav massacres and wars of the 1990s, but also made these two warring leaders more popular and kept them in power. As has been noted quite often, war itself raises the danger of group annihilation and so greatly strengthens group solidarity. Russell Hardin emphasizes the Yugoslav example to support his theoretical conclusions about why serious threats reinforce group solidarity and the popularity of extremist leaders (1995, 142–53).

A rare example of mass killing that seemed to lack central leadership occurred in 1946 and 1947 when British India was partitioned. There, supposedly, ancient differences between Muslims, Sikhs, and Hindus resulted in spontaneous massacres that killed anywhere from 200,000 to 360,000 people. But even though the top leaders of the emergent Pakistani and Indian states did not order these killings, the massacres were far from spontaneous. Rather, local leaders among Muslims, Sikhs, and Hindus actively encouraged and armed gangs of assassins to spread fear in communities other than their own; the goal was ethnic cleansing. Once the killings had begun, the masses of affected people were swept up in the massacres, and in many instances men murdered their own families, especially women and children, in order to avoid the dishonor of having them defiled or forcibly converted by killers of the other religious groups. What motivated the local leaders, however, was primarily their belief that it would be easier to maintain control over their communities and territories if other groups were disposed of (Brass 2003).

Although simple cost-benefit analysis can explain some leadership behavior inciting genocide, there is much left unexplained. Leaders, like followers, are subject to emotions and sentiments that can produce killing far beyond what would seem to be rationally useful. Temporary fits of passion may result in unexpected, sometimes seemingly irrational violence, but large-scale genocidal acts are the result of planning and of long-lasting, not short-term passions and ideologies.

An obvious example is the single-minded determination of the Nazis to kill Jews. Only someone sharing Hitler's theories about race, pollution, and the danger posed by Jews can fully understand why genocide was such a high priority. There is little doubt that the treatment of the Jews, and of other captured people deemed racially inferior by the Germans, severely impeded their use as workers and damaged German war production. Alan Milward in his economic history of World War II points out that "the predominance of political dreams of the future over the realities of the economic present in Germany emerges with fearful clarity" (1979, 227).

The same is true of the way in which communist ideological visions that killed so many millions in the Soviet Union, China, and Cambodia also did immense economic harm. The Chinese Great Leap Forward of 1958–60 resulted in somewhere between 20 million and 40 million deaths from starvation and disease, all for the purpose of furthering Mao's ideological fantasies of making China a great industrial power while turning the countryside into what he called "a garden" populated by peasants living in ideal communes without old-fashioned notions of property or family (Dittmer 1987, 32; Lardy 1983, 41–43, 150–52; MacFarquhar 1983, 126–27, 154–55). As Jon Elster puts it in *Alchemies of the Mind,* "the short-lived passions undermine the theory of the ratio-nal actor, whereas the durable ones undermine the theory of *homo economicus*" (1999, 306). What are those "durable" passions that lead to so much horror?

FEAR

Fear is perhaps the key emotion for understanding genocide. Indeed fear can be found as an element in every case mentioned so far except in the crassest examples of ethnic cleansing for purely material reasons, when the targets offer no real threat to the perpetrators, except to their financial well-being. Removal of the Cherokee is such a limiting case, but the killings done for honor and revenge have at least some element of fear, and of course, the last two categories of genocidal acts, when the designated population is deemed dangerous or polluting, are very clearly based on fear. William the Conqueror, Genghis Khan, Julius Caesar, and Tsar Alexander II of Russia (who ordered the genocidal elimination of Circassians) all had something to fear from the resistance of those they killed, though these also were "genocides of convenience" based on cold calculations of benefits of action against the potential costs of inaction.

Similarly, genocides of revenge, such as the German killing of the Herero, usually have strategic aspects: if "they" (the Hereros in this case) get away with this attack, what else will they do, and who else will be encouraged to attack us? This is the kind of fear that undoubtedly lies behind the whole notion of killing to maintain honor. Vengeance is psychologically satisfying, but there is also the realistic fear that if it is not extracted, worse will follow because "we" will be perceived as weak. That is what lay behind Rome's foreign policy of always getting revenge for slights to its authority, no matter what the strategic impor-tance of particular cases, and it is the basis of the unending blood feuds in societies unprotected by state law and order (Hardin 1995, 117–23). It is also what underpins the rational calculus of deterrence displayed by reprisals against violations of agreements—though modern deterrence theory suggests that reprisals need to be limited in order to work; other-wise the target of retaliation will feel there is nothing to lose in resisting to the bitter end (Schelling 1966, esp. 169). In other words, if the killings go too far, they well may cease to have any deterrent effect at all, but certain kinds of fear overwhelm such cost-benefit analysis and do cross this line.

The most powerful fear is fear of extinction, the fear that "our" people, "our" cause, "our" culture, "our" history may not survive. This fear will elicit the most violent and extreme reactions. Group identification, caring about what happens to "our" group, is what makes intergroup conflict possible. Without such identification, individuals would be loathe to risk their own lives for the collective; yet, we know that people commonly do take risks, and sometimes invite almost certain death on behalf of their families, close friends, clans, tribes, religions, and nations. Those groups developing the most powerful common identification are those that promise some kind of immortality. Few are willing to die for their tennis club, but many are willing to die for a cause, religion, ethnic group, or nation in which the individual can continue after death through the survival and success of the group. Serbs in Kosovo facing an Albanian majority in the 1980s and 1990s, Turks facing the elimination of what they perceived to be their nation in 1915, or Mao's communists in China after the near-extinction of the Long March and a brutal civil war that lasted two decades—all of these groups have been capable of genocidal acts because they believed that their survival was at stake and that only the most ruthless measures could save them.

Fear of pollution or contamination is a particular kind of survival fear: the fear that the group as we know it will not survive even if many of its members do. The group will exist in the future only by losing what is most important and distinctive about it and by being amalgamated with some other group. The relevant emotion for this kind of survival concern combines fear with disgust. Fear of pollution is not so much a threat to the physical continuation of a group as to the essence or nature of the group. Hitler's obsession with the "Jewish disease" and race mixing, fantastic as it may seem to those who do not take such pseudoscience seriously, was a deep fear that his idealized Germanic race would not survive, combined with disgust for what he perceived to be the increasing Judaization of the world. In some instances the idea of marriage with outsiders creates the same kind of fear, that the group's identity will not survive, and so, exogamy (marrying outside the group) becomes the greatest of taboos, the ultimate, disgusting, evil act.

The disturbing story of Dinah, Jacob's daughter (Gen. 34) is a startling reminder of how deeply feared pollution by strangers can be when it seems to threaten the identity of a beleaguered group. Shechem the Hivite rapes Dinah and falls in love with her. He has his father ask for her in marriage, and Jacob insists that all the Hivite men be circumcised in order to mix and intermarry with the Israelites. They go ahead and all get themselves circumcised, but Jacob's sons sneak into the Hivite city and slaughter every man, and take all their flocks, women, and little ones as "prey." Jacob finds this genocidal act excessive, but his sons remonstrate by saying, "Should he [Shechem] treat our sister as a harlot?" As the biblical scholar James Kugel puts it, "Shechem's crime was particularly heinous because, as a foreigner, he was not to marry a daughter of Jacob's; any such union was a defilement. His offer to marry Dinah and have his kinsmen intermarry with Jacob's family thus only compounded his offense. . . . Jacob's sons were merely instruments of divine punishment" (Kugel 1997, 244). The story emphasizes this point, in that it is not Shechem alone who is killed for his transgressions, but all the males in his (presumably fairly small) tribe, because Shechem's family wanted to mix with Jacob's.

It is important to notice that the motivating fear that underlies genocide is not the same as the emotion usually studied by psychologists (Öhman 2000). As a basic emotion, fear has a biological expression that all of us recognize: pounding heart, sweating palms, hair standing up, dry mouth. These are the signs of arousal of the sympathetic nervous system, and they tend to disappear quickly unless, as under bombardment, the fear-arousing situation is long continued. But this fear reaction does not explain planned mass killings. The killers are no longer reacting with immediate fear to those they are slaughtering but to an abstract evaluation of the threat posed by the group to which the victims belong.

Polls of contemporary Israeli Jews find that personal fear of Palestinian attacks is unrelated to willingness to compromise with Palestinians (Maoz and McCauley 2006). It is not that all respondents are equally afraid, because there are individual differences in perceived danger from Palestinian attacks that are related to where respondents live. Nor are differences in personal fear related to differences in attitude toward two-state solutions to the Jewish-Palestinian conflict. Those who see themselves most threatened do not differ in their attitude toward compromise from those who see themselves least threatened. Instead, it is those Israeli Jews who see their group as threatened by an implacable and hate-filled enemy who are least willing to compromise, no matter whether they feel personally safe or highly endangered by suicide bombers. The best predictor of unwillingness to compromise is perception of a zero-sum relation between Jews and Palestinians. If Palestinians are seen as hating Jews and determined to evict Jews from Israel, then anything given up to compromise makes Jews less safe. In a zero-sum conflict where one side's gain is an automatic loss for the other side, only winning can make "our" group safe. Fear for the survival of one's group does not, of course, lead automatically to genocidal acts, but it certainly makes extreme measures that involve ethnic cleansing or large-scale killing more legitimate, and therefore, ultimately, more likely.

There is reason to believe that humans are particularly alert to pain and loss, far more than to success and gain, a tendency called *negativity bias*. Rozin and Royzman (2001) and Baumeister et al. (2001) have recently reviewed a wide array of studies indicating that we see losses as greater in magnitude than gains of the same size. (So, the distress of losing one thousand dollars is greater than the pleasure of gaining one thousand dollars.) We pay more attention to negative than to positive events, and we spend more time explaining the unhappy ones. In mixed situations we tend to weigh the negative parts more than the positive ones. This research will not surprise anyone who has noticed the prevalence of negative events in news reports or wondered why misdeeds by individuals are usually more newsworthy than good deeds.

Negativity bias accounts for our tendency to remember episodes of threat and fear more strongly than longer periods of calm and peaceful relations with other groups. This is a powerful source of intergroup violence, and it makes it easier to understand how perceptions of threat and the fear these provoke may be quite abstract and enduring. It also explains how leaders manipulate their groups' emotions by stressing negative images and acts by the enemy group, and why this so often works even though groups may have coexisted for long periods of time with only occasional problems and with relatively little past violence.

Finally, no one should underestimate the role of fear of fellow members of the in-group as an explanation of participating in genocide and ethnic cleansing. When one's own group is threatened by another group, certain reliable consequences ensue. Hostility toward the threatening group is an obvious result, as discussed in the next section. Less often recognized, however, are the consequences for in-group dynamics, the relations among members of the group facing a common threat. Any such group experiences an increased feeling of togetherness, which may be called cohesion, patriotism, or nationalism. Increased cohesion is associated with three other changes: increased respect for leaders, increased idealization of in-group values, and increased readiness to punish deviates from in-group norms. There is a large literature in social psychology focused on the consequences of out-group threat for in-group dynamics, but one need only recall the reaction of U.S. citizens after the attacks of September 11, 2001, in order to feel the force of the in-group response to out-group threat.

It is the increased willingness to punish deviates that is at issue here. Individuals who criticize group values or norms or who refuse to participate in group activities related to common defense are very likely to be punished. The punishment can vary in severity from disdain and ostracism to loss of occupation, a prison sentence, torture, or death. The extent to which a group feels threatened determines the level of cohesion and the strength of punishment for deviating from the norms supported by that cohesion. For a group feeling threatened enough to commit genocide on its enemies, the punishment for lack of enthusiasm in killing the enemy is likely to be death for the deviate and perhaps death extending to the deviate's family. This was the experience of Cambodians pressed to kill those with so-called Vietnamese minds, and of Hutus pressed to kill Tutsis. Fear of punishment is a motive for soldiers to follow orders (Keegan 1978). Fear of punishment is no less a motive to participate in genocide and ethnic cleansing.

ANGER

Perpetrators of massacres are often described as angry, or even enraged, against the group they are killing. What, exactly, does this mean? There are two main theories of anger. One is that anger is elicited by damage or disrespect aimed at me or those I care about; the other view is that anger is an automatic, biologically based response to pain or frustration.

The first view was advanced by Aristotle and emphasizes conditions that are necessary and collectively sufficient to make us angry: undeserved damage or disrespect has been inflicted on us or on those we care about, and those responsible should be punished. It is true that we can feel anger when there is no obvious perpetrator (the traffic stoplight that slows us down when we are in a hurry, "the system" that has failed people we care about), but these experiences elicit anger because they are experienced as generalized disrespect for our personal needs and rights by some abstract authority or system—"them," the ones in charge. In this view, anger is an emotion that follows upon a moral judgment of harm: Was the harm deserved? If not, we have a right to be angry. It is also a judgment about the presumed perpetrator who injured us: Was the harm intended? Could someone have done something to prevent it? This can be called *insult-anger* theory.

The second explanation of anger begins with the translation of Freudian ideas into animal learning experiments that became known as *frustration-aggression* theory (Dollard et al. 1939). In this view, frustration always leads to anger, an emotion that includes an impulse to aggression; but whether anger is actually expressed in aggressive behavior depends on the rewards and punishments that are anticipated in a particular situation. In more recent years, frustration-aggression theory has been expanded to become *pain-aggression* theory, in which frustration is just one of the sources of discomfort that can trigger anger (Berkowitz 1989).

These two views of anger differ chiefly in whether anger follows a cognitive appraisal of moral violation or is an automatic response to any painful experience. For insult-anger theory, there is no anger without a moral appraisal of the target of anger; whereas for pain-aggression theory, anger is a blind impulse seeking a target. In everyday examples, the target of anger is often obvious, and the two theories converge. If someone hurts or insults me or mine, both theories say I should be angry, whether in response to the perpetrator's moral violation or as a response to the pain I experience. Examples involving intergroup relations usually show a similar convergence. If your group insults or hurts mine, both theories say I should be angry and looking for retribution.

The distinction between theories becomes more important if the perceived harm to a group is long-term and diffuse, when it appears to be a whole system of social relations that is causing the damage rather than some specific individuals, and when the injury is not limited to a particular instance but to a whole set of circumstances. How much perceived inequity does there have to be to elicit anger and aggression? Does all injustice elicit anger? In the absence of immediate human perpetrators, moral violation theory (insult-anger) cannot easily explain anger unless generalized so far as to assert that all injustice is a source of anger (Homans 1974). The complex abstractions involved with this view make the other, the pain-aggression theory, more commonly accepted by psychologists dealing with large political issues. Ervin Staub (1989), for example, suggests that genocide is made more likely by economic frustrations and difficult life situations. It seems reasonable that those content with their situation are far less likely to engage in massacres, but economic frustrations and difficult life situations are common, and genocide is relatively rare. One possibility is that turning frustration into killing requires a moral construction. Humans are moralizing animals who need to justify their acts. Poverty, disaster, political turmoil, or other painful experiences may anger us, but we will not kill unless we have a specific target, and we must justify our anger toward that target by making its behavior appear to us as morally repugnant.

Crusaders setting out to liberate the Holy Land from Muslims killed Jews in German towns in 1096 because Jews were violating the law of God by not converting, and it was the Crusaders' increased religious fervor, not any sense of economic frustration that motivated them (Chazan 2000, 27). There was something wrong with the world, indeed, and one of the causes of what was wrong was the presence of Jews (as well as Muslims, who were slated for subsequent slaughter), but pain-aggression theory seems a far-fetched way of explaining the Crusaders' anger.

Rather, in their religious fervor, the very presence of Jews who had refused to convert to Christianity was a moral insult.

Interestingly, the subsequent Jewish explanation of the massacres of Jews in the Rhineland in 1096 also sees these events in a religious light. Unlike the Christian version, however, that blamed the Jews for the death of Christ and for not accepting Jesus, the Jewish *Solomon bar Simson Chronicle*, written shortly after the events, returns to the ancient biblical explanation for catastrophe. "The sin for which punishment was meted out in 1096 stretched back to the days of Moses in the wilderness; the Jerusalem of Jesus played no role in the divine retribution exacted in 1096" (Chazan 2000, 59). In other words, sins committed in the very distant past still explain more recent disasters.

Caesar's extermination of the Eburon, clearly carried out for quite practical reasons, is nevertheless explained by his chronicler as retribution for treachery (Harmand 1984, 92–93). Genghis Khan's entirely practical tactic of terrifying populations into submission by extermination of those cities that resisted, nevertheless, in the case of Herat, is explained by his outrage at the city's betrayal of a prior agreement (Morgan 1986, 73–83). This is not to minimize the fact that the Mongols also had considerable contempt for the highly civilized Persians they were conquering, just as Caesar had contempt for the barbarians he was conquering, and the Crusaders had for the Jews they were massacring. Looking at another group's habits and cultures as somehow contemptible also promotes a sense that "these people" are violating basic laws of decent human behavior and so deserve whatever awful fate they suffer.

In more modern genocides, anger is clearly evidenced, but whether in the Stalinist extermination of class enemies, the Khmer Rouge killing of one-quarter of their population, or the slaughter of Armenians by the Ottoman authorities, there is always an element of justification based on the unfairness, immorality, or perfidy of the targets. The genocide of the Herero is a particularly interesting example of how the logic of colonialism, often the source of genocides of convenience, can, when challenged, support an angry reaction. A cool appreciation of strategic and economic interest can turn quickly to angry retaliation for resistance to this interest. The von Trotha proclamation describes the

Herero as viciously uncivilized, thereby casting the German reprisals as a meting out of justice. (Dedering 1999, 211).

Despite the obvious importance of insult-anger theory, there is no reason to abandon the pain-aggression explanation, because, in fact, most mass political murder is also either a response to very specific, relatively recent acts, or at least is presented by leaders as such in order to deliberately anger and motivate their followers. Whatever the long-term causes of the Croat-Serb war in Yugoslavia in the early 1990s, there were a number of incidents staged by provocateurs on both sides specifically designed to outrage their publics and remind them of past fears. In one notorious case in May 1991, before the war really got under way, Croatian policemen were sent in to reestablish order in a Serb held area, probably with the knowledge that they were too weak to accomplish their task, and a few were killed and horribly mutilated by Serb paramilitaries in Borovo Selo. Pictures of the mutilated bodies were then held up by Croat officials as an example of what awaited Croats at the hands of Serbs, and Croats were publicly reminded of the horrors that had occurred during ethnic fighting during World War II, almost fifty years earlier. Thus, a sense of injustice among Croats, who felt that under Yugoslav communist rule Serbs had been unfairly favored, was turned into a very immediate sentiment of fear and anger provoked by these events (Glenny 1993, 75–77).

The worst massacre of African Americans in the twentieth century, the killing of up to three hundred (no one knows the exact number) by whites in Tulsa, Oklahoma, in 1921 began with an accusation of rape. A young white woman operating an elevator said a black man had assaulted her (he may have inadvertently touched her). Whites resolved to lynch him, blacks tried to protect him, and the incident turned into a mass assault on the prosperous, largely middle-class black district of Greenwood. In the end, about thirty-five blocks were burned down (many blacks died in their burning houses), national guard airplanes were called in to fire on blacks, and along with the killings, hundreds of African Americans were arrested. No one would claim that a supposed attempted rape alone caused this massacre, but it was the claim of rape, whipped up by local newspapers, that set off the incident as angry crowds of whites demanded revenge. Other, more fundamental, factors played a part as well: the jealousy and unease of many whites about the prosperity of this African American community; the social turmoil of the period, including changing mores and increasing self-assertion by blacks; and long-standing southern racism. Nevertheless, a specific incident, fabricated as it may have been, aroused the immediate anger of the whites and strengthened their sense that their women were directly threatened (Madigan 2001).

It is not surprising that accusations of rape have so commonly been the precipitating factor in such events. As Coleman Blease, onetime governor of North Carolina in the 1910s and a U.S. senator in the 1920s put it in his defense of lynching, "Whenever the Constitution comes between me and the virtue of white women of the South, I say to hell with the Constitution" (quoted in Reed and Reed 1996, 122). The fear of racial mixing as pollution, as we have already seen, has been a common source of ethnic and religious tension, and specific incidents have provoked extreme anger among those predisposed to mistrust or fear specific ethnic or religious groups.

In a sense, the distinction between the two kinds of psychological theories about anger resembles the common distinction made by historians between long-term and proximate causes of an event. To feel injustice has been committed, or that a moral wrong has occurred that justifies anger against a group blamed for this outrage, requires a historical perspective and a history of moral judgments. To feel anger in the face of a perceived hurt requires much less perspective. Typically, the two are combined to produce murderous killings. Donald Horowitz's work on deadly ethnic riots is full of examples of rumors about violent incidents that set off murderous riots. "The rumors," he writes, "are of aggressive behavior, often with but sometimes without a sexual element" (2001, 71). Sometimes, the excuse is a real event, but whether the incident is real or fabricated, it will arouse sufficient anger to produce mass killing and persecution only if the ground has been prepared by a sense among the perpetrators of the massacre that the targets are fundamentally immoral and potentially dangerous.

McCauley (2000) has gone so far as to argue that the final common pathway of intergroup violence is a moral judgment against the out-group targeted. Group conflict may be based on competition for material resources (realistic group conflict theory) or on competition for status and honor (relative deprivation theory). But whatever its origin, group conflict does not produce violence without a consensus among the in-group, or at least its leaders, that another group has done something both wrong and harmful, something dangerous to the in-group.

Ultimately, the difference between insult-anger and pain-aggression theories is artificial, because the two kinds of motives blend together in the minds of those who kill for political reasons. This is true of wars as well as of genocidal massacres and lesser cases of mass murder. The first of the hugely destructive wars of the twentieth century, World War I, had many complex diplomatic, military, economic, and social causes. But it did, after all, begin because of the murder of Archduke Franz Ferdinand and his wife Sophie in 1914 by conspirators backed by the Serbian secret services. The murder shocked and deeply distressed the Austro-Hungarian political elite, including the elderly emperor who was counting on his nephew to succeed him. They wanted to avenge this injustice, which they interpreted as the culmination of a long, unjust, and dangerous set of conspiracies against them, but their pain was just as important in pushing them into wanting revenge (S. Williamson 1989, 236).

The implication of this intertwining of fear and anger is that most intergroup violence, and in particular most cases that result in mass killings, will involve both feelings of fear and anger, both a sense of injustice and one or more specific affronts. That we may believe that the perpetrators have no right to feel this way, that the injustice and the pain are fabricated, or that they do not justify the horrors that follow should not blind us to the reality of the emotions and stress experienced by those who set off such events.

HATE

Ethnic and religious conflicts, especially those leading to extreme violence, are often attributed to intergroup hatreds, sometimes qualified as "ancient" or "historical," and if in Africa, "tribal." Hatred is usually cited along with anger as a source of the most horrific cases of violence.

In the case of class-based genocide, hatred is also given as a reason for mass murder. Pol Pot encouraged the rage of poor farmers against the city dwellers, both "foreigners" (that is, not ethnic Khmer) and Cambodians who lived well on the backs of the rural farmers. The Khmer Rouge propaganda line to explain why Cambodia's urban dwellers were expelled into the countryside, causing the deaths of hundreds of thousands from starvation and disease, was that the urbanites had enjoyed "an easy life," had "exploited the peasantry," were "immoral," and "shirked productive work." The Khmer Rouge had another reason for the expulsions, as they thought the war would continue and that the cities might slip out of their control, but that is not inconsistent with their hating urbanites (Kiernan 1996, 62–64).

The association of hatred with genocide and ethnic cleansing is so strong that it appears in the title of books on these topics even though the word *hate* is never defined (e.g., Kressel 1996, *Mass Hate*) or else does not appear in the book's index (e.g., Naimark 2001, *Fires of Hatred*; Kaufman 2001, *Modern Hatreds*). The common association of hatred with anger brings immediately the question of whether hatred means anything more than strong anger. Indeed some use hate to mean any strong antipathy, as in "I hate broccoli." Thus the first question about hatred is whether it is an emotion or a combination or emotions, or only a way of talking about strong dislike.

Although some psychoanalysts have written about hate (Gaylin 2003), systematic investigation of the subject is barely beginning. In particular, there is little empirical research to answer the question of how hate may be related to anger (but see Fitness and Fletcher 1993). Introspection and common language suggest, however, that there are important differences between anger and hatred. Anger is normally thought to be hot, reactive, and usually brief, whereas hatred is steady and can be cold. If anger is a response to insult or pain delivered by another, hatred is more a response to the character or nature or essence of the other. This is similar to the distinction made above between a reaction to proximate provocation versus one to a long series of perceived injustices, distrust, and moral condemnation of another group. The idea that hatred is focused on a bad essence, however, can improve our understanding of how hate works, because perception of essence is something distinct from the difference between "injustice" and "pain" as causes of conflict.

Even loose talk about "hating" something trivial, say, broccoli, includes an implication of essence. To hate broccoli is to suggest there is something inherently wrong with it, something that cannot be ameliorated or sauced over; in other words, the implication is that it would be better if broccoli did not exist. Donald Horowitz quotes Aristotle: "The angry man wishes the object of his anger to suffer in return; hatred wishes its object not to exist" (2001, 543). This suggests something much deeper than the arousal caused by immediate pain, injustice, or fear.

Psychologist Robert Sternberg (2003) has suggested a three-component theory of hate involving contempt, disgust, and a mixture of anger and fear. This approach would make hatred a derivative or blend of two or more basic emotions rather than a primary emotion in its own right. This is appealing in that it recognizes that hate is associated with a number of different sentiments. Not only anger or fear, but disgust and contempt are often mentioned as feelings toward a hated individual or group. Less often noted are positive feelings of joy, relief, or even pride when a hated individual or group fails or is punished. This kind of antipathetic feeling is commonly referred to in German as *schadenfreude*, the malicious enjoyment of others' misfortunes.

But if hate is associated with many different emotions, it does not follow that hate is nothing more than a blend of these emotions. Rather, hate seems to us best understood as an extreme form of negative identification (Royzman, McCauley, and Rozin 2006; Shand 1920; for a related conception, see Gaylin 2003, 171). When the target of hate prospers and succeeds, we feel negative emotions; when the target of hate fails and suffers, we feel positive emotions. Whatever combination of contempt, disgust, anger, and fear at are work, and however different various combinations might be, the origin is the same in that we have a persistent negative appraisal of the object. "This conceptualization of hatred has the advantage that it is consistent with modern research in which basic emotions are understood to be relatively brief and situational. Such basic reactions produce characteristic thoughts, feelings, and behavioral tendencies that result from distinctive appraisals of the situation" (Frijda 2000, 63–64).

Anger, as described above, is a reaction to appraisal of harm or imme-diate insult, and the reaction includes thoughts, feelings, and behav-ioral tendencies toward aggression. Similarly, fear is a reaction to ap-praisal of threat, and the fear reaction includes thoughts, feelings, and behavioral tendencies toward "flight or fight." If hatred is steady and enduring, it cannot be simply an emotion or combination of emotions but must be something more like an appraisal or attitude, that is, a stable evaluative reaction to some individual or group. That is why the notion of "essence" is important—we hate only what we have, over time, come to evaluate as being essentially bad. Though this hatred can be strengthened by immediate acts and provocations, or possibly slightly attenuated by what appear to be good acts, change can only occur slowly. If hate is strong enough, it may be virtually impossible to overcome it because the best of acts are interpreted as something the hated actor or group is doing to hide something that will hurt us even more. It is hard not to think of the biblical example provided above, when the Hivite men's willingness to get circumcised in order to inter-marry with Jacob's family (presumably a rather major concession and sacrifice for adult men in the days before anesthesia) only reinforces their negative image rather than improving it.

Love

Our conceptualization makes hate directly the opposite of love. Like hatred, love is associated with many different emotions, including joy, elevation, and pride when the loved one is well and prospering, and including fear, anger, and shame when the loved one is attacked or failing. But most would agree that love does not cease to exist when the lover is not experiencing any of these emotions. That is, love is as steady as hate and is better understood as something that goes beyond a mere blend of other feelings. Love implies a focusing of attention on the loved one as hate implies a similar focus on the hated individual or group; both may be extreme enough to be seen as obsessive. Love is an extreme form of positive identification, whereas hate is an extreme form of negative identification.

The core of identification is caring about what happens to others, but identification is more than an attitude. A positive attitude toward a particular kind of music or entertainment, for example, is unlikely to elicit the positive concern for well-being that is elicited by individuals or groups with whom we identify. Music and entertainment can be good or bad, pleasing or not pleasing, and they can evoke strong emotions, but they are not generally perceived as affecting our direct welfare. To be sure, certain kinds of music become symbolic representations of entire ethnic groups, of religions, or particular ways of life, and then we can identify with those who play that music, and feel strongly about their successes or failures. When Zubin Mehta was director of the Israeli Philharmonic and played a piece by Richard Wagner, the audience booed and stopped the performance. Wagner, a notorious anti-Semite, had been Hitler's favorite composer, and any reminder of his high standing in the musical world elicited rage with this particular audience. (Hitler reputedly could whistle all of the Wagner operas by heart. On Hitler's worship of Wagner, see Fest 1975, 47–57. On Wagner's anti-Semitism, see Wagner's own essay, "Jewry in Music" [1850], which explains why "repellent" Jews cannot be great musicians or poets, quoted in Mendes-Flohr and Reinharz 1980, 268–71.)

Positive or negative identification with a group thus means more than just a positive or negative attitude; identification means that our emotions are positively or negatively linked to the welfare or reputation of the group identified with. Concern with reputation extends to the symbols of a group we identify with. Flags, anthems, monuments, and sports teams can elicit strong reactions, and challenges or insults to such symbols can elicit anger.

Because group identification is the psychological foundation of intergroup conflict, our analysis of emotions that lead to political mass murder implies recognition that at the bottom of conflict and violence there is love. At the individual level it is love of self and individuals close to us, while at the group level it is love for a collectivity that can be as large as an ethnicity, religion, culture, or nation. Genocidal killings are associated with hate and fear, or at least, in the case of ethnic cleansing, with complete contempt for the welfare of other groups. But what motivates those who carry out these deeds is also solidarity and identification with their own group, which, they feel, benefits from such actions. Thus the obverse of genocide is identification with a loved group—friends, family, village, clan, tribe, class, nation, or religion on whose behalf the massacres are carried out (McCauley 2001).

A mundane appreciation of the power of love in relation to violence comes from everyday experience of differential reaction to threat, violence, and murder. We react much more strongly to violence visited on those with whom we positively identify and feel less involved when more distant others are killed. A bomb in India has to kill many more than a bomb in California to get the same column inches in U.S. newspapers. There is, however, no comprehensive theory about why we care more about threats to some than to others, or how we pick those with whom we identify. Sociobiological explanations tend to stress the fact that we are altruistically inclined toward those with whom we most likely share genes: that is, the more closely they are deemed related to us, the more we identify with and support them. In this explanation, those who look like us, or behave like us, are more likely to elicit sympathy from us, and we are more likely to identify with their suffering or come to their aid (Degler 1991, 270–92). Thus, for example, African Americans were more likely than white Americans to identify with the struggles of black South Africans against apartheid. While this sociobiological explanation may be useful for groups composed of closely related kin (but even in this case, there are exceptions), it is difficult to sustain for larger groups such as ethnicities, coreligionists, or nations. It may be that ethnicities and nations are perceived as kin groups, but the sociobiological explanation depends on actual relatedness, which must be low in groups as large and varied as African Americans.

Russell Hardin goes in the opposite direction and claims that adherence to and subjective identification with various groups is a matter of rational choice—we belong and identify because it is to our advantage to do so, and ultimately, we cease to identify if we do not feel we are gaining something (1995, 46–71). Here Jon Elster's comment, cited above, is apt. Long-term sentiments bring into doubt our willingness to act on pure cost-benefit calculations (1999, 306). Once we strongly identify with a group, to the point of loving or hating it, changing our minds for instrumental reason is rare. One need look no farther than at the persistent refusal of many (though hardly all) Jews to convert to Christianity during times of intense persecution in the Middle Ages, when conversion would have been the easy option. For them, religious belief, or more broadly, their conception of who they were, trumped individual survival. This behavior, of course, was also rational in some sense, given their ideological values, but at that point, anything can be explained as rational.

From an evolutionary point of view, the human capacity for love that can triumph over self-interest is the answer to the free-rider problem (Frank 1999). If we were simple economic machines, we would never spend resources or take risks for group projects that would bring benefits to all but no individual advantage for those who bear the costs of action. At best, we would be quick to abandon such projects if they threatened serious cost or harm to us as individuals. Indeed, many people do just that; they let others bear the costs and risks (they "free ride"). But many do not. Identification resolves this problem by making the welfare of others part of our hedonic calculations. We need not stop caring for our personal welfare to care also about the welfare of others; self-interest includes both personal welfare and the welfare of loved ones. In short, identification means that the interests of others are not opposed to self-interest but part of its calculation. Identification can make sacrifice for loved ones a rational choice and likewise can make the killing of those who in some way threaten the well-being of our group equally rational.

This perspective contrasts with the common association of genocide as a manifestation of irrational hatred. Hatred of targeted groups is no more irrational than love of groups with which we identify. Whether for sociobiological reasons, through material calculation, by imitation and familiarity, or more likely, through some combination of these, we identify strongly with some groups, and that identification becomes the basis of our own sense of self. Our hatreds are the reflection of our loves.

Shame and Humiliation

Shame and humiliation are often cited as causes of genocide. In Rwanda and Burundi, for instance, Hutu violence toward Tutsis has been described as a reaction to the shame and humiliation inflicted by years of Tutsi overlordship. René Lemarchand cites a common Hutu explanation of who they are and why they hate the Tutsi in Burundi: "In the past our proper name was Bantu. We are Bantus. 'Hutu' is no tribe, no nothing! . . . *Muhutu* is a Kihamite word which means 'servant.' [The Tutsi, in the racial mythology surrounding Rwanda and Burundi's genocidal wars, are "Hamites" and invaders from the north as opposed to native "Bantu."] . . . The name means 'slave.' We are not Hutu; we are *abantu*—human beings. It is a name that the Tutsi gave us" (1996, 20). Burundi, which has drawn somewhat less attention than Rwanda, had a similar colonial experience and precolonial social structure but remained under the control of the Tutsi after independence and has been the subject of fierce wars and massacres almost as bad as those in Rwanda.

There is little doubt that the humiliation of the Versailles Treaty contributed substantially to Germany's turn to genocidal extremism, though this is hardly the only explanation. For Hitler, the mortification of his beloved German nation was crucial, and the fact that he blamed the Jews, whom he thought delighted in humiliating Germany, was one of his key motives for genocide. Raul Hilberg, a noted historian of the Holocaust, has written: "In Hitler's eyes, the Jews were Germany's principal adversary. The battle he fought against them was a 'defense.' It was a settlement of accounts. . . . It was an answer to Jewry's laughter. Hitler was not going to be laughed at, belittled, or made the object of mockery. He saw Jews as deriding everything that was sacred to Germans. When he spoke on September 30, 1942, he said openly that the Jews would soon stop laughing everywhere" (1992, 10).

In many of the genocidal episodes listed so far—Roman exterminations of frontier tribes who had rebelled, German genocide of the Herero, or the Japanese massacres in Nanjing—the element of revenge follows a period in which the powerful perpetrators have felt humiliated by the temporary success of a treacherous and inferior enemy who should have been kept in line. Bernard Lewis notes that the majority of cases in the Middle Ages in which Muslims persecuted Jews (admittedly much rarer than the Christian persecution of Jews) were the result of what Muslims claimed to have been "arrogant" behavior by Jews who did not heed their accepted but inferior status. This "arrogance," of course, is precisely what led to a sense of dishonor, and then violent outbursts against the transgressors (1984, 45–57). One of the most severe massacres of Jews in Muslim Spain occurred in Granada in 1066 where, according eyewitness reports, the entire Jewish community was slaughtered because "both the common people and the nobles were disgusted by the cunning of the Jews, the notorious changes which they had brought about in the order of things, and positions which they occupied, in violation of their pact. God decreed their destruction" (Cohen 1994, 165). In other words, they had become too rich and powerful, and for the faithful this was humiliating. Indeed, in the long passages describing the history and position of the Jews in the Quran, one of main themes, along with their cupidity, is their arrogance in thinking they can get away with not accepting the true word of Muhammad, the holy prophet (surah 2:40–103, esp. 80–88 [King Fahd Holy Quran Printing, 1411 H.]) and the explanatory notes added in the official Saudi Arabian religious authorities' translation). Arrogance is degrading to those who are belittled by it and may, in extreme cases, enrage them.

There is a considerable psychological literature, including empirical research, on the emotion of shame, although the distinction between shame and humiliation is an issue of continuing controversy (Tangney and Dearing 2002). Both involve a public loss of esteem or status, but there seems to be an important distinction between status loss that is experienced as deserved and the same loss experienced as imposed and undeserved. Shame is the emotion experienced when one's inadequacy or failing is discovered by others. (Closely related is guilt, the emotion experienced when the failing, which may or may not be publicly known, is a moral violation.) Humiliation is the emotion experienced when a public loss of status is imposed by another. This imposition is usually perceived as unfair and undeserved. To the extent that it is more comfortable to attribute our failings to others than to ourselves, any particular instance of loss of status or honor is likely to be attributed to a humiliating other. Shame, therefore, is easily rationalized into humiliation. For understanding intergroup conflict and genocide, the difference between shame and humiliation is the difference between anger over status loss being directed inward, toward the failing self, versus anger directed toward those who imposed an undeserved loss of respect. It is humiliation, or the shame brought about by others whom we can blame, that may lead to revenge killings and massacres (Scheff 1994).

DISGUST

In most genocidal events the perpetrators devalue the humanity of their victims, often by referring to the victims as animals, diseased, or exceptionally filthy (Weitz 2003, 20). We have cited Hitler's categorization of Jews as a "virus" (Hitler [1941–43] 1973, 332). His disgust, he claims, began when he was a young man living in Vienna. "By their very exterior you could tell that these were no lovers of water, and, to your distress, you often knew it with your eyes closed. Later I often grew sick to my stomach from the smell of these caftan-wearers" (Hitler [1925–26] 1971, 57). Leo Kuper, in his pathbreaking study of genocide, cited the similar way Ibos were portrayed by northern Nigerians for years before they were subjected to massacres in 1966: "Educated Northerners spoke of the Ibos as vermin, criminals, money-grabbers, and sub-humans without genuine culture" (L. Kuper 1981, 85). Well before the massacres of Tutsis by the genocidal Hutu authorities in Rwanda in 1994, Tutsis had been described as cockroaches (C. Taylor 2002, 168), but Tutsi fighters in the invading army fighting to overthrow the Hutu regime were also pictured as "creatures from another world, with tails, horns, hooves, pointed ears, and red eyes that shone in the dark" (Prunier 1997, 142).

Paul Rozin and his associates have found that disgust is elicited by bodily products, culturally disapproved forms of eating and sex, and animals associated with death or offal (Rozin et al. 2000). Animals that elicit disgust notably include pigs, rats, maggots, cockroaches, and other vermin, though sometimes horror of the enemy is emphasized by also portraying him as monstrous. The relation between disgust and genocide in animal images of the enemy is reinforced by the peculiar importance of contamination as an aspect of disgust. A disgust-elicitor contacting a neutral object often has the power of making the neutral object disgusting in its turn. A piece of a dead body, a bit of blood or saliva, or a cockroach—any of these brought in contact with food will make it inedible. As bodies of Rwandan victims of the genocide were dumped into rivers that ran into Lake Victoria, people in Kenya, Uganda, and Tanzania who ate lake fish refused to do so, despite the reassurance of the authorities that commonly eaten fish did not eat human corpses (C. Taylor 2002, 160).

Contamination is not just a fear of germs and disease. Reassurance that eating Lake Victoria fish could carry no trace of human corpses, especially in parts of that huge lake far from the mouth of the river that flowed from Rwanda, did not allay fear of contamination, just as, at a trivial level, reassurance that a cockroach was sterilized before contacting a piece of food will not make it more palatable. Rather, contamination is a matter of history. The history of contact makes an object disgusting in the absence of any sensory trace of the contact—a cognitive accomplishment that is apparently limited to humans. The most natural interpretation of contagion phenomena is that objects have essences, and that essences are transferred by contact.

The idea of essence, then, turns out to be a key psychological concept in explaining violence against groups. Something about members of the targeted group is inherently disgusting—their habits, their animality, their appearance—and this justifies the violence against them because their disgusting characteristics threaten to pollute the environment and must be eliminated.

Essentializing Others

By definition, genocidal killing is killing by category, by membership in a group rather than by individual guilt or crime. It inevitably includes many who, no matter what the provocation, or imagined provocation, are noncombatants who could not directly hurt the perpetrators. What is the psychologically distinct quality of such categories that makes genocidal killing possible?

The first thing to note is the variety of categories that have been victims of genocide. We are likely to think first of ethnic, religious, and national categories: Jews, heretics, Armenians, Circassians, Hereros,

Eburons, Cherokees. The people of Yorkshire, however, were "cleansed" by William the Conqueror simply because their presence supported rebellious lords, not because of their ethnicity or religion. Genghis Khan's victims were residents of cities who resisted him, regardless of their ethnicity or religion. Stalin and Mao killed by Marxist categories of economic class: kulaks, landowners, and "capitalist roaders." Pol Pot's Khmer Rouge killed by ethnicity in targeting Vietnamese and various minorities, but the majority of victims were Cambodians said to have been infected with a foreign and capitalist culture that was seen as threatening the authentic rural Cambodian culture.

In short, it seems that almost any kind of social category will do, as long as it can be considered self-reproducing. Ethnic and national categories are seen as reproducing themselves in biological terms, but cities, cultures, and even economic classes can also be viewed as self-reproducing and imbued with some sort of shared personality, spirit, or nature. Categorization of victims can be based on both concrete and abstract commonalities ranging from directly observable traits such as skin color, physiognomy, and stature to abstract characteristics such as class, ideology, residence, and culture.

This capacity to see millions of diverse individuals as a single object is a remarkable feat of human cognition. Ethnic, economic, cultural, or political groups are never as objectively uniform as they seem to be in everyday discussion. Who are the Hutus, the Tutsis, the Jews, the Germans, the kulaks, the capitalist roaders, the authentic versus foreign-tainted Cambodians? No single observer has ever seen more than a small fraction of the millions of individuals who inhabit these categories, and modern scholarship has made it clear that such categories are both more diffuse and more fluid over time than they are generally made out to be. This point is the focus of Benedict Anderson's much cited book about the origins of nationalism, *Imagined Communities*.

Nations, once thought by romantic nineteenth- and twentieth-century historians to be clearly delineated cultural and biological groups, turn out to be no such thing (B. Anderson 1991; Geary 2002). Virtually no nation or ethnic group is "pure." Migration, acculturation, conquest, and secession together guarantee that membership in such groups is not fixed but fluctuates over time. Cultural exchanges guarantee that, on the ground, the borders of target categories are fuzzy. Indeed, in all modern genocides, identification is a key problem, because without identity papers or a resort to crude and unreliable stereotypes, it can be difficult to tell who, exactly, is "Jewish," "Croat," or "Tutsi," especially as intermarriage was not, in fact, all that rare. Gérard Prunier explains that in the Rwandan countryside, where "Hutu" and "Tutsi" were social categories and people knew who was which, escape for the Tutsi during the genocide was practically impossible. In the towns, especially the capital of Kigali, people did not know each other. "There the *Interahamwe* manning roadblocks asked people for their identity cards. To be identified on one's card as a Tutsi or to pretend to have lost one's papers meant certain death" (1997, 249). Those who were not stopped or who had fake IDs could escape.

What is to be made of the contradiction between expert opinion, which sees ethnic and national groups as imagined, changing, and porous, and everyday opinion, in which there is no doubt at all that Tutsis, Ibos, Vietnamese, and Jews are no less real and distinct than beagles and bulldogs? (For a wonderful recent discussion of the artificiality of European nations, see Geary's [2002] comparison of the realities of early medieval European ethnic migrations and mixtures with the mythologies developed about that history in the nineteenth century to justify modern nationalism.)

One way to make sense of the contradiction is to suggest that humans are biologically prepared to understand the world of living things in terms of essence (Gil-White 2001; Hirschfeld 1996). An essence is the hidden something that makes a living thing what it is. The closest example of essence is the self. My essence is whatever it is inside me that makes me the same person today as I was when I was five years old. I could not tell you what the something is—it is somehow more than history—but I am nonetheless confident that I am the same person despite radical change in my appearance. We credit others with essence also, each individual with a separate essence that is referred to in different times and places as character, personality, identity, soul, or spirit.

It is not only individuals who have essences. The living world is divided into essences. There is something inside a tiger that makes it a tiger, even if it is albino, toothless, and three-legged. Essence is not just another way of talking about genetics but an idea much older than any human knowledge about genes (Keil 1989). Before the age of four or five, American children say that an animal is what it looks like and can easily be fooled into thinking that, say, a raccoon with hair cut and dyed to look like a cat really is one, or that a cat that has undergone plastic surgery to look like a raccoon is indeed a raccoon. But older American children will say that a cat is a cat, and a skunk is a skunk, no matter how its appearance is changed. Some will offer a protobiological explanation, namely, that if the skunk had babies they would still be skunks. The same kind of experiment repeated in Africa records the same kind of transition at the same age, but the explanation is different. The dikdik remains a dikdik despite looking like a springbok because it still has the spirit of the dikdik (Keil 1989).

The idea of essence is the common denominator of "biology" and "spirit," the conceptually primitive notion that lies beneath both. There is reason to think that humans are biologically prepared to see people, as well as animals, divided according to essence. Cultural groups, in particular, may be understood in terms of essence because of the conceptual economies that result from assuming that the eccentricities (by in-group standards) of one member of another culture are likely to be repeated in most other members of the same culture (Gil-White 2001). Whatever the advantages of seeing human groups and group differences in terms of essence, there is one area in which the idea of essence is potentially disastrous. A group that is seen as having a different essence from ourselves is not quite human, and such a group can be used, abused, and eliminated as if it were another species of animal.

Observers of genocides have remarked on the importance of dehumanizing the enemy (Staub 1989; Waller 2002). Reference to the enemy in terms of disgusting animality or dangerous infection is an obvious marker of dehumanization. But the idea of essence makes this kind of reference more than metaphoric. Essentializing the out-group means that there is something bad about all of them, every one of them, and that badness goes deeper than the images used to describe them. Nazis knew perfectly well that Jews were not literally rats, and Hutus knew that Tutsis were not cockroaches, but they did believe that everyone in that category, old and young, strong and weak, threatening and

helpless—all must be exterminated, just as all vermin must be exterminated. Essentializing turns the enemy into a single dangerous and irre-
deemable character.

Liah Greenfeld quotes Ernst Arndt, an early proponent of German
nationalism, who wrote in 1802: "I hate all Frenchmen without distinction in the name of God and of my people, I teach this hatred to my
son, I teach it to the sons of my people. . . . I shall work all my life
that the contempt and hatred for this people strike the deepest roots in
German hearts" (Greenfeld 1992, 276). The composer Richard
Wagner, in his essay on why Jews were incapable of genuine artistic
feelings and were polluting German art, wrote in 1850 that "we" (presumably good Germans) have to understand why "we feel an instinctive
repugnance against the Jews' prime essence" so that "it must . . . become plain to us what we hate in that essence" (in Mendes-Flohr and
Reinharz 1980, 269).

It is not only the out-group that is essentialized; so also is the in-
group. The Turk, the German *volk*, the authentic Cambodian or Hutu,
the working class, each can be seen to have a positive essence that
makes it a superior class of people, a chosen people, deserving of respect
and priority. The Final Solution depended on essentializing both Germans and Jews, a perception that perseveres in the right of return offered today by both Germany and Israel to those who can show evidence of the right essence. This is the basis of what is sometimes called
"nationalism of blood" or "ethnic nationalism," as opposed to "civic"
or "liberal" nationalism. The former assigns citizenship by heredity, no
matter how distant. Where the presumed citizen was born or what her
cultural habits may be has no bearing. "Civic" nationalism, on the
other hand, agrees to accept outsiders willing to move to and become
integrated in a particular national culture (Brubaker 1992, 1996;
Greenfeld 1992).

It might be thought that culture is the opposite of nature, that an
ethnic nation can be essentialized but a civic nation cannot. Unfortunately, there is reason to believe that culture too can be essentialized.
The United States is generally agreed to have a civic rather than an
ethnic nationalism, but it is possible to see Americans as sharing an
essential character or spirit even if it is difficult to specify what this

essence is. An American essence is signaled by occasional public debates in which some individuals, groups, rituals, and beliefs are referred to as "un-American." Such references may be contested, but not by arguing that they are meaningless. No one says that denigration as "un-American" is just silly because there is no content to the idea of "American." In a clearer and more horrific case of essentializing cultures, Pol Pot and the Khmer Rouge essentialized the authentic Khmer culture in opposition to the Vietnamese essence that they contended had gotten into some Cambodian minds.

If both ethnic descent groups and cultural groups can be essentialized, then any in-group can be essentialized. We suspect that essentializing the enemy is linked strongly and perhaps even necessarily with essentializing the in-group. It is in that sense, as we suggested above, that the hate felt toward the out-group is so closely related to the love felt for the in-group. The result of this double essentializing is a battle of good and evil, of two incompatible essences in which love of the good means necessarily hate for the threatening out-group. This is what lies at the heart of the most extreme genocidal cases, where the fear of pollution can lead to what would otherwise seem to be incomprehensible mass murder. The out-group's essence must be kept from contaminating the in-group's essence. Indeed, the very ideas of pollution and contamination require the idea of essence, the unseen spirit or nature that is endangered by contact or infection. The German *volk* had to be protected from the foreign and degrading Jewish essence. Protestants and Catholics viewed each others' heresies as such an abomination that they had to be rooted out. Authentic rural Cambodian culture had to be protected from the foreign pollution of urban centers. The authentic proletarians in both the USSR and China had to be protected from the threat of spiritual pollution of their class enemies. Pollution can be expelled, but if that is impossible or risks eventual retaliation by the victimized group, it has to be obliterated.

Writing about the St. Bartholomew's Day massacre in 1572, when Catholics slaughtered thousands of Protestants in France, the historian Mack Holt explains:

Viewed by Catholics as threats to the social and political order, Huguenot [Protestants] not only had to be exterminated . . . they also had to be humiliated, dishonoured, and shamed as the inhuman beasts they were perceived to be. The victims had to be dehumanized—slaughtered like animals—since they had violated all sacred laws of humanity in Catholic culture. Moreover, death was followed by purification. . . . Many Protestant houses were burned, invoking the traditional purification by fire of all heretics. Many victims were also thrown into the Seine, invoking the purification by water of Catholic baptism. (1995, 87)

The Dangerous Similar Others

There is a special danger for those who are closest to the group essence but still outside it, as Christian Protestants were to Christian Catholics. Their superficial similarity makes them the most perilous source of pollution in the same sense that cancer—a disease of the body's own cells—is more treacherous than most infectious agents. The more these deviates look like members of the in-group, the more insidious they are. They must be attacked with special intensity.

For the Nazis, the special fear and disgust for Jews can be understood from the fact that the Jews were considered able to assimilate, and at least some German Jews lived among Germans "pretending" to be German. In Cambodia, where one-quarter of all Cambodians were killed by other Cambodians, the danger of pollution was particularly strong because so many Cambodians had become "infected" with foreign, particularly Vietnamese, thinking. In a remarkable interview in 1997, shortly before his death, Pol Pot, the deposed Khmer Rouge leader, blamed everything that had gone wrong on the Vietnamese, who had supposedly infiltrated Cambodia and caused the famine. Pol Pot asserted: "To say that millions died is too much. . . . Another aspect you have to know is that Vietnamese agents were there. There was rice, but they didn't give rice to the population." He continued: "My conscience is clear. . . . If we had not carried out our struggle, Cambodia would have become another Kampuchea Krom [the Mekong Delta, part of the ancient Khmer Empire conquered by Vietnam in the sixteenth century]" (quoted in Thayer 1997). But in fact, whatever political designs the Vietnamese may have had on their fellow communists in the Khmer Rouge, there were no Vietnamese left in Cambodia during Pol Pot's rule, as those who did not flee were all killed, along with those who were part Vietnamese, and Khmer who had been born in Vietnam, or all those suspected of being "Khmer bodies with Vietnamese minds" (Kiernan 1996, 423–25). The problem was, of course, that it was hard to tell who might have been tainted with Vietnamese blood or thoughts, and any trace of either was grounds for treachery and pollution of the "pure" Cambodians.

In religious wars, the heretics—Protestants for Catholics, Shiite for Sunni Muslims—are even more likely targets of mass violence than those of a completely different religion because they are a perversion of the truth, and being so close it, can pollute the true faith. (On how contemporary radical Sunni Muslims—the ones we call "fundamentalists"—feel about the Shiite heretics, see Sivan 1985, 115. More recently, Michael Doran has explained the genocidal intent of the most extremist Wahhabi Sunni Islamists in Saudi Arabia against Shiites. See Doran 2004, 46–49). Once a difference in essence is perceived, the smaller other differences are, the greater the pollution threat and the fiercer the hatred.

In explaining this phenomenon, Michael Ignatieff describes nationalism as a form of "narcissism," or completely absorbing self-love, in which minor differences between peoples are glorified into major ones in order to solidify national boundaries and strengthen national solidarity; this implies belittling the "other" who does not share these traits. He cites Sigmund Freud, who invented the term *narcissism of minor difference*, to the effect that there is a paradoxical relation between narcissism and aggression. "It is precisely because the differences between groups are minor," writes Ignatieff, "that they must be expressed aggressively. The less substantial the differences between two groups, the more they both struggle to portray those differences as absolute" (1997, 48–53, quote 50–51).

That is certainly not the case with all genocidal massacres, but it goes a long way toward understanding the particular viciousness of the killing and torturing of fellow communists by Stalin, Mao, Pol Pot, and other communist leaders. Many of Stalin's victims were portrayed as Trotskyites, but a close reading of the ideological positions taken by Leon Trotsky and Stalin show that there was not, after all, very much difference between them (Chirot 1996, 111–18; on Stalin's purges, see Werth 2003, 215–39).

What is at issue in the narcissism of minor differences is a competition of essences. Which of the two antagonistic groups possesses the "true and the good" essence, and which one is an "evil" impostor? It follows that the special destructiveness of modern communist and Nazi ideological genocides was not, as Zygmunt Bauman (1989) supposed, a function merely of bureaucratization or of their misuse of modern science and technology. Rather, the special destructiveness of the modern world is associated with the special threat posed by enemies, whether ideologically or ethnically defined, who could so often blend into the "good" in-group. It may be no coincidence, then, that some of the worst ethnic genocides of the twentieth century involved targeting groups that were difficult to differentiate on physical or cultural grounds from the perpetrators. The Jews were too similar to the Germans, and the Nazis had to begin with measures to identify and separate Jews, to issue identification cards, and to make group membership visible with armbands. Tutsis and Hutus, as we have seen, often could be identified only by their identity cards if they were not denounced by neighbors or others who knew them. The ideal physical types, tall, thin Tutsis and shorter, rounder Hutus, did not fit a very large proportion of the population because of centuries of mixing.

The greatest genocides of the twentieth century were more ideological than ethnic. Mao, Stalin, and Pol Pot killed their millions to eliminate threats to ideological purity, with no mercy accorded for ethnic similarity. Of course, the supposition that the Khmer Rouge killed mostly Vietnamese, as they claim, is patently absurd, especially given the records of torture and death for entire Cambodian families in notorious Tuol Sleng prison (Gottesman 2003, 30; Kiernan 1996, 335–36). Ideology, even more than ethnicity, is invisible, and members of the same movement who share similar views are even harder to unmask as traitors, so that ever more fantastic procedures must be used to do the job and justify genocidal massacres on a Stalinist, Maoist, or Khmer Rouge scale.

The Conditions of Genocide

The paths to genocide are many, and only a few of the conditions we have considered are necessary. Essentializing the enemy is crucial, but there are many ways in which that can be done, and, as many groups not involved in conflict are also essentialized (Haslam et al. 2000), essentializing the enemy may be necessary, but it is not sufficient for genocide.

If the motive is pure greed, as occurred in the destruction of many people by colonizers, notably in the cases of Native Americans and Aboriginal Australians, then the mere fact that these populations might fight back, or could logically be expected to resist, can be enough to engender some fear. In any case, the targeted populations were essentialized as being "lazy and incompetent" or "barbaric" and therefore in the way of progress. That was reason enough to dispose of them (Maybury-Lewis 2002, 43–53).

We know from social psychological experiments and actual experience with mass killing that it is possible to get ordinary people to commit horrific violence even when they have no strong negative emotions or negative sentiments about the victims. Tapping into prior prejudice, fear, anger, and hate can make killing even easier. We have emphasized the importance of organization in understanding genocide: the habits of obedience, the structure of everyday organizational incentives, and the specialization and routinization that undermine personal responsibility. These aspects of organization can support mass killing even in the absence of strong negative emotions or sentiments toward the victims. Fear of reprisals for not killing, including fear of death, is another part of what moves perpetrators.

Leaders who order genocidal killings are a different matter. They are the ones who create complex rationales for what is going on, particularly when those being targeted seem quite similar to those doing the killing. The sophisticated historical explanations of why it was necessary for Cambodians to kill Vietnamese, or why Trotskyites were objectively traitors rather than the devoted communists they claimed to be, or why "Hamitic" Tutsis were illegitimate invaders, or why, for that matter, Protestants were dangerous heretics even though their faith was so similar to that of Catholics—these explanations had to be justified by intellectuals who read and thought deeply about such matters. It is at the elite level that one sees most clearly the human predilection for historicizing our fears and angers, our hates and loves, and for nursing our past humiliations and errors in order to turn them into vengeful action.

Many recent scholars of genocide have emphasized the role of memory and deemed it a good thing to elicit trauma memories from surviving victims. Recovering the past is presumed to be a protection against repetition of such horrors, to be therapeutic for victims, and to be an advancement of justice (e.g., Hinton 2002, esp. pt. 4; Miller and Miller 1993). We ought not forget, however, that memory and historical reconstruction, often invented but nevertheless sincerely believed, are important contributors to demands for vengeance of past wrongs that in turn can lead to a new series of mass killings.

Comparison of leaders and perpetrators leads to the curious realization that negative emotions and sentiments about the enemy are often stronger in the leaders than in those who actually carry out the genocide. It is easy to think that those doing the dirtiest work must be those with the strongest motives for killing, but the reverse is nearer the facts. Mao talking about capitalist roaders, Stalin talking about kulaks, Hitler talking about Jews, Hutu leaders talking about Tutsis, Pol Pot talking about Cambodians with Vietnamese minds—here in the discourse of elites is where one finds the strongest evidence of anger, fear, humiliation, and disgust directed at the enemy. It is possible to imagine that this kind of rhetoric is entirely bogus, a cloak for the self-interest of elites in maintaining and strengthening their own power. We lean, however, to the view that successful leaders often believe or come to believe in their own rhetoric, and feel or come to feel the emotions they make so vivid. That is, we believe that hate is more an explanation of genocide for leaders than for followers.

In the now vast literature on genocide and mass murder, the largest part is about the motivation of those who organize, lead, legitimize, and are thus the chief perpetrators of the killings, or about the victims. It is far more difficult to find a good analysis of those who did the actual killing, and Christopher Browning's innovative *Ordinary Men* (1992b) is unusual in that respect. It is hard to find, as he did, the memoirs of such "ordinary" killers, for whom no well-kept files of their letters or actions exist. Very recent genocides, such as in Rwanda, have produced interviews with some of the rank-and-file killers (Mamdani, 2001, for example, cites some), but usually those who killed are less willing to talk and appear far less sympathetic to researchers than surviving victims. Furthermore, they tend to repeat stock phrases to excuse themselves or else claim that they really were insignificant pawns who had no choice or did not really know what was happening. Therefore, understanding the psychology of the ordinary killers seems to be more difficult than explaining the calculations, ideologies, fears, hatreds, and resentments of the leaders.

Perhaps the kind of genocidal killing most difficult to explain is when civilian perpetrators or temporary members of local militias murder their neighbors and fellow countrymen, especially when there seem to be no central authorities organizing and leading them. For in these cases the excuses made by those, like Browning's German police battalion killing Jews, that they were following orders, that they were military men bound by camaraderie operating in a foreign and hostile environment, do not work at all. These less-militarized killings—as in Rwanda, or in Indonesia in 1965–66, or in the many deadly ethnic riots studied by Horowitz (2001)—may have had leaders and were often backed by complicit armed forces or police, but they nevertheless were partly, often largely, perpetrated by eager volunteers.

One of the most notorious cases was brought to light by Jan Gross's disturbing and masterful book, *Neighbors*, about how in a Polish town that was half Jewish and half Christian, Jedwabne, the Christians slaughtered almost all of the 1,600 Jewish men, women, and children, in a most brutal and direct way (Gross 2001). This was not unique but occurred in some other Polish towns as well. In fact, without substantial Polish collaboration, the Nazis would not have been able to slaughter about 90 percent of Poland's three million Jews.

The events in Jedwabne took place shortly after the Germans occupied the region in 1941, taking it from the Soviets, who had divided up Poland with Germany from 1939 to 1941. The motives were complex, combining resentment over the welcome extended by some Jews to the Soviet occupation, long-standing anti-Semitism, cupidity, and in the background, the fact that the new German authorities clearly sanctioned such an event. What stands out, however, is that in the circumstances of wartime Poland, normal social conventions, law, and the scruples that most of us have about acting on our deepest prejudices, fears, and passions, were absent. The town and region had been traumatized by the collapse of the Polish state in 1939 and by the brutality of the Soviet occupation—Gross (1988) has also analyzed what happened in neighboring territories—but without previously restrained prejudice and recent resentments, the massacre would not have occurred. The Germans did not disapprove, but they had not ordered the killing in Jedwabne.

It turns out that mass killings of civilians by civilians under conditions of drastic political upheaval, when the authorities seem to approve, and when normal law and social restraints have broken down, are not an unusual part of genocides. In describing the slaughter of suspected communists in Indonesia in 1965–66, Robert Hefner makes the same point. In East Java, when word reached local Islamic youth groups that the army was killing communists (Muslim organizations had been involved in an increasingly bitter conflict with Indonesia's large Communist Party for years before this took place), they took it upon themselves to initiate a wave of killings that were particularly gruesome, uncoordinated, and indiscriminate. Gradually, as the army restored order, official commissions were set up, and while the killings continued, they were more precisely targeted at actual communists or leftist sympathizers. Also, it was only after this official takeover of the violence that it moved into more mountainous areas where there had been little earlier social tension, and almost no mass violence before the authorities imposed it (Hefner 1990, 209–15).

A similar set of events took place in Bali, another part of Indonesia, where about a hundred thousand people, 7 to 8 percent of the population, were killed in 1965–66. Again, it is clear that the Indonesia military, who had just taken power as part of a counterattack against what they saw as coup attempt by left-wing officers, was chiefly responsible for setting loose a wave of massacres (Robinson 1995). The army announced that communists were to be purged and that those who did not join in this "cleansing" would be considered enemies of the state. But what happened in the chaos, as the old order broke down in Bali and fear spread across the island, was that people turned on each other, often for personal reasons of jealousy and old hatreds. Leftists were singled out, and old conflicts about issues of property and caste played a role, but much of the killing was less precisely structured. In fact, some people committed suicide, fearing that a leftist taint would condemn them and their families; others turned themselves in; and villagers killed some suspected of leftism to escape punishment themselves. There were instances of relatives killing each other, and it seems that women's organizations were specifically targeted because of their leftist associations. Along with the killings, there were numerous rapes and public humiliations of activist women. In short, the entire social structure and the bonds that held people together broke down, abetted by an army that aimed precisely at this end, to reorder Balinese society (Dwyer and Santikarma 2003, 289–305).

Such examples can be multiplied. They do not diminish the role of official power, and they do not suggest that every society with internal division, jealousies, and competition between identifiable class, ethnic, religious, ideological, or regional groups is always on the edge of murderous mass violence. What they do suggest, however, is that the grievances and hostilities individuals and groups may have toward each other are normally restrained by countervailing social arrangements and psychological inhibitions. Once these have been broken down, by the political acts of the authorities, or by crises skillfully manipulated by leaders eager to initiate violence, the potential for mass killing rises quickly and can reach genocidal proportions.

Given the many paths that may lead to it, it is no wonder that genocides occur. Perhaps what is more surprising and needs explanation is that there are not more of them. Intergroup tensions and wars, overwhelming power differentials, periods of political chaos, ancient historical grievances, and political manipulation of tensions are common events throughout most of the world. Normal individuals can become capable of categorical killing in ways that are all too easy to understand and replicate. So, why are genocidal events not more common? The next chapter will discuss exactly that—how societies have devised ways of containing our genocidal impulses.

CHAPTER THREE

Why Is Limited Warfare More Common Than Genocide?

We marry those whom we fight.
—Tallensi proverb (Fortes 1969)

Most warfare, whether it is between nations or smaller groups, does not reach the level of genocide. Even the general slaughter of noncombatants is far less common than warfare itself. For that matter, most conflicts between social groups of any size do not lead to large-scale violence. Why is this? The answers are not immediately obvious. To be sure, as we suggested in the previous chapter, slaughtering others is an activity most people are loathe to engage in. Contact with dead bodies, body parts, and bodily products is the occasion of disgust unless conducted within the narrow confines of cultural rituals. It is difficult to kill without reminding ourselves that we are animals bound for death, and to massacre we need some way of ritualizing and distancing ourselves from what we are doing (Rozin et al. 2000).

On the other hand, every society has found ways of doing exactly that, legitimizing certain forms of killing and, if need be, ritualizing them to make warfare acceptable. There has been far too much bloodshed throughout history for us to think, somehow, that violence is either unusual or not properly human. Having explained what kinds of competition, emotions, and circumstances drive us occasionally to be genocidal, we need to explain what prevents these forces from causing even more havoc.

Looking at both ethnographic and historical evidence, we find that there are many ways in which societies have learned to limit conflict and make it less genocidal. There is, of course, the very obvious fact that warfare and extreme violence are costly and dangerous, so they are not entered upon lightly. Trying to kill all of one's enemies always runs the risk of failure that will result in catastrophic retaliation. That, however, is hardly a sufficient explanation, because violent conflicts will nevertheless occur, and controlling the victor's lust for immediate gain that can be obtained by wiping out competitors, or for revenge, is no easy task. When fear comes into play, restraining killing is even more difficult. Strategies and techniques for limiting mass murder, even after violence breaks out, therefore must be developed. There are three broad explanations of why most conflicts manage to be settled without catastrophic outcomes.

First, competing groups, be they families, clans, tribes, ethnicities, or nations, can work out rules of conflict and conciliation that dampen violence and make the complete destruction of any of the competing parties less likely. Codes of honor can reduce the scope of violence if they emphasize the importance of limiting violence to combatants; ritualized competitions can partly replace violence; and legal codes, setting boundaries, and international covenants to limit the ravages of war can be effective, even without the presence of an authority to strictly enforce the rules. Success, however, requires the parties in conflict to have enough experience with each other to know the rules and value them. Such codes, rituals, and conventions typically take time to develop, so that rapidly changing circumstances and the arrival of new competitors is often likely to make violent conflict much worse. We will see that there is a rich record of societies working out "rules of the game" to limit violence.

Second, exchanges are worked out between competing groups that give them an interest in maintaining rules of conflict to limit damage. Exogamous marriage rules, commercial exchanges, ritualized gift giving, and a host of related activities are part of this broad category of mitigating strategies. This is what led Enlightenment philosophers to suppose that mercantile societies were less likely to press war to its ultimate ends. (We will discuss this in considerable detail below.) The mechanisms for this were, after all, not so different from those developed long before capitalism by small-scale, pre-state societies in which exchanges of goods and marriage partners dampened conflicts without ever eliminating them.

Third, and most important today, is ideology. Some ideologies are highly conducive to genocide, and others are not. Moral codes are ideological, and some codes are more conducive to violence than others. That is one reason we have been citing biblical examples of calls to genocide. Whether or not the cases described occurred or not is not really relevant to our argument, because what matters is that these were ideological statements that justified, under certain circumstances, genocidal action. As the modern world's competing groups have become larger, and technologies of communication and destruction have rapidly improved, dangerous ideological currents have vastly increased the dangers of genocide. Anti-individualistic, strongly communitarian ideologies, when combined with utopian certitude and an exalted sense of mission, led to the worst genocidal conflicts of the twentieth century. Such ideologies could again support genocide in the future. If ruling ideologues believe that it is possible to purify their world and achieve perfection by force, and that it is necessary to rid themselves of all real and potential enemies, mass murder is only one crisis away.

We need to examine each of these approaches in some detail, always remembering that there is no single explanation, no magic formula for eliminating politically motivated mass murder, and that the best of arrangements have never brought perfect peace or provided permanent solutions. Conflicts continue, and as situations change, old customs, patterns of exchange, and moral codes have to be revised. Nevertheless, history shows that peaceful change is possible and that violence can be contained, even if there have been some catastrophic failures in both the past and present.

Weighing the Costs of Genocidal Conflicts

The simplest explanation of why genocidal conflicts are rare is that warfare and violence are costly, and extreme warfare runs the risk of being very costly. Killing others always entails the risk of being killed or injured oneself, but even more important, any nation, tribe, clan, village, or family engaging in warfare can never be absolutely sure of the outcome. Economists have recently applied cost-benefit analysis and rational expectations models to the study of war, and their findings are consistent with the notion that those who initiate violence must expect to win something, or else they are unlikely to break a peace or truce (see Collier and Hoeffler 1998, on contemporary civil wars). Political scientists James Fearon and David Laitin have argued that in the overwhelming majority of cases ethnic groups in contact with each other do not let their competitive conflicts escalate into violence because it is simply more efficient, that is, more rational, to compromise and live peacefully (1996).

Even in the face of great odds, however, rational calculations may not prevent violence if a group faces complete destruction and desperation alters the calculation to make extreme resistance seem the only alternative (Gross 1979). This helps explain why it is dangerous to back enemies into a situation where they are threatened with annihilation. Unless an absolute victory is certain, ruthlessly massacring some of the enemy's population hugely raises the risks of subsequent vicious retaliation.

If there are any expectations of living peacefully with enemies in the future, either on equal terms or by subordinating them and turning them into an exploitable resource, excessive killing is inherently wasteful and entails higher costs; but as we saw in the first chapter, the desire for revenge or honor, and fear, especially fear of pollution, may distort perception so much that groups miscalculate the risks involved, or their calculations are trumped by their emotions and ideology. Presumably, this is what the biblical injunctions to commit genocide against the Amalekites and Canaanites were meant to overcome: a kind of cost-benefit analysis by the Israelites that it would be more reasonable to enslave and use their enemies rather than to exterminate them. This the Lord did by insisting to the Israelites that He guaranteed them victory if they killed all their enemies, and that these foes were so polluting that sparing their useful members was absolutely forbidden.

More typically, groups of people of any size that engage in regular conflicts with others work out rules and rituals to limit the damage inflicted by warfare. Even when these do not bring peace, they reduce the danger of wholesale massacres. This can be seen at every level of human organization, from small, pre-state societies (those without formal rulers or permanent governing institutions living in small, self-regulating groups) to the largest contemporary states.

Limiting the Damage of Warfare

If the Dani of highland New Guinea (studied in the 1950s and 1960s before their culture had been heavily influenced by direct contact with the outside) were at all typical of warlike, pre-state, stone-age people, their pattern of warfare may illuminate an important aspect of why large-scale killing was rare in such pre-state societies. Land and other food resources were scarce in New Guinea, and competition created a climate of nearly permanent stress and conflict between neighboring villages. Despite this, violence usually took the form of highly ritualized combat with only occasional killings. Honor and the demand for vengeance required to pacify the ghosts of those killed in the past could be satisfied with very few deaths, sometimes a single one, and fighting was viewed more as a kind of sporting game that relieved tensions than as an opportunity to wipe out the enemy. Only in rare instances, perhaps once every decade or two, would warfare turn into massive combat between large alliances that could result in decisive victories and massacres of large numbers of men, women, and children on the losing side (Heider 1970, 104–23).

The most recent research about the Yanomami, an Amazonian pre-state people whose warfare has been the subject of great controversy, suggests that because of intense competition over scarce resources, there was certainly killing, but nothing approaching wars to the finish (Ferguson 1995; Harris 1996). Ferguson refutes Napoleon Chagnon's famous hypothesis that warlike Yanomami males reproduce more successfully and that this accounts for Yanomami bellicosity (Chagnon 1988, 1990). Competition for women occurs among men and often leads to violence, something common in many societies, modern as well as premodern; but such individual competition does not normally lead to intergroup war (Ferguson 1995, 358–62).

There is now good evidence that before the arrival of Western influence the Yanomami had a more stable social system with less violence than in more recent times, because when conflicts developed, antagonistic groups tended to fission or move apart from each other and establish neutral boundaries. New technologies from the outside, particularly metal tools, unbalanced the system of exchanges that had previously worked to keep their conflicts within bounds and made some (but not all) Yanomami groups far more violent than they had probably been before (Early and Peters 2000, 229–30; Ferguson 1995).

Even the most devoted followers of the theory that all humans, and particularly pre-state, stone-age horticulturalists (those who farm without plows or animal labor, like the Dani or Yanomami), are inherently warlike, do not claim that massacres are the usual outcomes of conflicts. If anything, there is a growing consensus among specialists that war became more serious and deadly with the emergence of socially stratified chiefdoms and states because it then became possible for a few leaders to make their subjects bear the costs of large-scale warfare. Only by maintaining permanent military forces could such leaders keep themselves in power, extract taxes from their subjects, and capture the resources, including slaves, needed to satisfy the elite's growing demands (Carneiro 1990).

This does not mean, however, that more politically stratified societies, even those most prone to war, frequently engaged in unlimited killings and massacres. Tamerlane (Timur-i-lang, or Timur the Lame), is remembered as one of the most bloodthirsty and ruthless Turko-Mongol nomadic conquerors in Eurasian history, renowned for his terrible massacres, for having captives cemented alive into towers to die slowly, for heaping up pyramids of prisoners' skulls, and for the indiscriminate massacres of inhabitants in some captured cities (Morgan 1986, 93; Prawdin 1967, 442–43, 469–73). Yet, this same Tamerlane built up his empire in the late fourteenth century by frequently forgiving rebels and tribes who had fought against him and by incorporating enemy dynasties of central Asian nomads into his own realm by seducing them with gifts and honors, including intermarriage. Only the most tenacious and dangerous of his enemies' leaders were killed, and often more pliant members of the same families replaced them. He was ruthless against cities, especially distant ones that resisted him, but avoided killing large numbers of nomads who could potentially be enrolled under his banner, even if they refused to submit (Manz 1989, 64–92).

The reason seems to have been a combination of steppe etiquette and Machiavellian practicality—it was bad form to pursue war too far against enemies who might someday be needed as allies, and dangerous to make permanent enemies who might one day strike back. Reasonable caution became a matter of honorable restraint, and if at all possible, it was better to intermarry one's sons and daughters with actual or potential enemies than to fight them to the death. So enemy nomadic rulers, Mongol and Turkic, were manipulated and seduced, but rarely eliminated, and their followers were easily forgiven after being defeated. But sedentaries in cities whom he viewed as soft aliens—Persians, for example, or Christians in the Caucasus—were generally deemed incapable of deeply threatening Timur and were therefore not beneficiaries of his particular code of chivalrous generosity.

In the European Middle Ages we also find that there were both codes of honor and practical reasons that limited the killing of defeated enemies, even though sieges did occasionally turn into massacres. Part of the European medieval code of honor was to spare noncombatants, though, as we have seen in such cases as William the Conqueror's brutality in Yorkshire, this was not always followed. A major Church Council at Charroux in 989 declared illegal the violation of churches, striking unarmed churchmen, and despoiling a "peasant or other poor man." There were many other similar decrees (Duby 1977, 125). Later, partly as a result of the wars of religion between Protestants and Catholics, where neither chivalric codes nor restraint in killing civilians was practiced, a whole set of military conventions were developed in the seventeenth and eighteenth centuries to limit warfare's damages, and these became part of the doctrine of "just wars" that specified what was legitimate or illegitimate violence (Johnson 1999, 121–24). Similar codes and restraints were very common in Hindu, Islamic, Chinese, and Japanese legal systems. They were particularly applicable in "cultures of honor," which glorified individual valor and the prestige of the noble warrior (Johnson 1999, 125). Killing was entirely acceptable, but rules were to be followed, and wantonly slaughtering innocents was dishonorable.

More important than the limitations on killing in warfare that were developed in many kinds of societies is the fact that large-scale warfare itself was the exception, not the rule. Even in supposedly endless wars, such as the Hundred Years War in western Europe from 1337 to 1453, actual warfare between France and England only occupied about one-fifth of that time. More destruction and killing of civilians were caused by bands of stateless mercenaries in times of truce—when they were not being paid and were essentially roving bandits operating under no rules or laws at all—than by the combatants during periods of active warfare (Fossier 1986, 59–63; see also Olson 2000, 3–14, on why "roving bandits" who do not expect to systematically exploit a region they control are so likely to plunder without restraint).

The elaborate regime of security measures and arms limitations treaties worked out between the Soviet Union and the United States during the Cold War resembles many other such sets of rules developed by fundamentally hostile competitors who have to adjust to the fact that genocidal war is too risky (Larson 1997). Despite the almost constant set of smaller wars fought on the periphery of the Soviet and American zones of influence, there was never a direct war between the two main participants in the area of greatest strategic value to both of them, Europe, and no nuclear war that would have killed hundreds of millions.

The many ways in which all kinds of societies have tried to limit the ravages of war, to find ways of not allowing killing to get out of hand, and to accept various forms of reconciliation show that we have long known techniques for reducing the likelihood of genocidal acts. By examining the ways in which conflicts and violence have been limited by different kinds of societies, we can develop some ideas about how to limit killing in the present. Some of these solutions can be applied to conflicts within societies as well as between societies, whether these conflicts are based on ethnicity, class, region, religion, or political ideology.

Working out rules and agreements to limit the loss of life in war are not the only ways in which genocidal killing has been controlled. A very common technique, particularly important in very early, pre-state societies, and of continuing importance until recently for some cultures, had to do with marriage rules.

Exogamy: Making the Enemy Part of the Family

For more than a century, one of the central concerns of anthropologists was to explain the widespread practice of exogamy—marrying outside one's group. In the most restricted sense, that included rules against incest, but more broadly, it raised the question of why so many premodern, stateless societies seemed to favor marriage patterns that obliged daughters and sons to exclude large numbers of relatives, even some very distant ones, from the acceptable marriage pool (A. Kuper 1994, 154–66). At the extreme, for example, the Nuer were not supposed to marry anyone in their patrilineal clan (anyone descended in the male line from a common male ancestor), thus excluding a large number of potential spouses who might be related only very tangentially (Evans-Pritchard 1940, 225–28).

All kinds of reasons have been advanced to explain exogamy. There are sociobiological explanations that say exogamy exists because inbreeding eventually leads to obvious genetic flaws. This may work well for the very widespread (though not absolutely universal) prohibition of brother-sister, and child-parent incest, but it cannot begin to explain broader kinds of exogamy such as those practiced by the Nuer and many other pre-state societies. There are psychoanalytic theories, which again refer mostly to incest taboos. And there are functionalist explanations that see in exogamy a useful way of cementing alliances that may have significant survival value (Shepher 1983, 1–6). Because there are so many different kinds of marriage rules around the world, and considerable differences between formally prescribed laws and actual marriage patterns within most societies, it has been impossible to establish a single, consistent theory to explain various degrees of exogamy (Barth 1973, 6).

Nevertheless, the functionalist view, stressed most prominently by Claude Lévi-Strauss, makes it clear that in some societies marriage be-

tween different groups contributes significantly to creating potential alliances and ways of resolving conflicts over resources, both internally
by reducing competition between men for women within the group,
and externally by making it possible to find common ground when
there are boundary or other disputes over control of productive and
reproductive resources. For Lévi-Strauss, all marriage is a form of exchange without which societies could not survive, though he recognizes
the multiplicity of forms the exchange can take. His main examples
were taken from studies of Australian Aborigines who relied on complex
forms of intermarriage to cement alliances with other tribes to secure
their foraging rights over widespread territories for food and water without risking perpetual warfare over resources with their neighbors
(A. Kuper 1994, 164–65; Lévi-Strauss 1969, 478–97).

One of the best-known instances in the ethnographic literature of
the importance of limiting conflict through exogamous marriage was
summarized in Meyer Fortes' reporting of the adage common among
the Tallensi (a northern Ghanaian, stateless people in the precolonial
era): "We marry those whom we fight." Fortes cites many other such
examples and explains them thus: "Kinship, amity, the regulation of
marriage and the restriction of serious fighting form a syndrome. . . .
Non-kin, whether or not they are territorially close or distant, regardless
of the social and cultural affinities of the parties, are very commonly
identified as being outside the range of prescriptive altruism and therefore marriageable as well as potentially hostile to the point of serious
fighting" (Fortes 1969, 234). Sending daughters to marry non-kin is a
way in which many pre-state people solved the problem of warfare with
potential enemies. Such exogamous rules reduced the chance of
wholesale massacres, as some of the enemy were in fact related, and,
as Fortes puts it, "enemies who marry can do so only if, in the last resort,
they accept some common norms of morality and jurality, together with
the corresponding procedures and sanctions for implementing them"
(Fortes 1969, 235). This proposition does not imply that violent conflict
ceases, or that war is always avoided; it means that violent conflict is
more likely to be conducted according to rules that limit destructiveness. Such rules do not end warfare; they reduce its deadliness.

An ethnographic comparative study found that the higher the level of exchange between groups, whether in trade goods or intermarriage, the higher the incidence of war (Tefft and Reinhart 1974). Of course, groups that have something to do with each other are more likely to be in conflict than those that have no relations at all, but that also makes it all the more likely that they will develop methods of limiting the damages from warfare—which is why Meyer Fortes' observation and the many empirical examples of this principle at work remain persuasive. The case cited above, of Tamerlane's treatment of enemy nomadic tribes and his habit of promoting elite intermarriage, is a particularly good illustration, as his accommodating policies neither prevented wars with neighboring tribes nor produced any lasting solidarities that survived his death. They did, however, serve Tamerlane's purposes and were a regularized part of the damage control worked out by neighboring warlike nomadic groups (Manz 1989, 128–31).

In a famous 1889 article, E. B. Tylor (whose theories influenced Lévi-Strauss) writes: "Again and again in the world's history, savage tribes must have had plainly before their minds the simple practical alternative between marrying-out and being killed out" (quoted in A. Kuper 1994, 164). This has often been interpreted as meaning that those who practiced endogamy, marrying only within the group, were more likely to be overcome by their enemies than those who married out because they would become isolated and have fewer allies on which to draw in dangerous times. Its more important implication, however, is the notion that limiting killing and destruction in war can play as important a role in self-preservation as forging alliances against enemies.

An illustrative case is found among the Amazonian Xingu, about one-third of whose men are forced to find mates in other settlements because of the existence of a strong incest taboo that limits their choice within their own village. As linguistic communities in the Amazon are very small, this often involves moving to a place with a different language. The Xingu do not consider it desirable to have to live in a village speaking a different language, but the fact that this happens often is a major source of peaceful contact between villages. Conflict between individuals in different locales therefore remains limited to those directly involved, as it is very difficult to get entire communities to join together against neighbors where many men are likely to have close kin. This greatly limits the potential for destructive war, though it hardly eliminates conflict (Gregor 1990, 113).

In Highland New Guinea there are many types of exogamy, some obliging men to take wives from other villages or political units, and almost all prohibiting marriage within the same patrilineal moiety, that is, within the half of the group related to an individual's relatives through the male line. As people in New Guinea (like the Dani, discussed above) were under heavy ecological stress from natural calamity and overcrowding, and frequently resorted to warfare to obtain more land and resources, and because this led to almost continual ritual warfare even when large-scale war was not being practiced, links established through marriage with outside groups were an important way of maintaining communications. Trade was facilitated, but war could also be mitigated, to the point, even, of creating rules whereby some groups who lost wars were allowed to take their possessions and emigrate to a different region rather than being annihilated (Berndt 1964; Heider 1970, 62–133; Morren 1984; Vayda 1971). Intermarriage did not stop wars, but it made mass slaughter less likely.

This principle is easily discerned in the practice of intermarriage among ruling elites in many agrarian states, where decisions about war and peace, and how to conduct violent conflict, were made by noble families and clans rather than by ordinary peasant communities. Marriage alliances among western European royal houses from about the eleventh to the nineteenth centuries show this pattern at its most extreme. Partnerships came to be made between royal and princely houses in order to cement relations, make peace, garner support for wars, or just to expand a particular house's prestige, power, and wealth. This was not so different from marriage arrangements at the level of commoners, except that it involved whole populations in shifting alliances, wars, and changes in rulers. But because the number of ruling houses was limited, they eventually all came to be related, and exogamy turned into a kind of high-level international endogamy. By the nineteenth century, almost all the ruling houses of Europe, and certainly all of the major ones, were part of the same family (Lamaison 1994).

That all the major rulers of Europe gradually came to be cousins and each other's in-laws neither guaranteed amicable relations nor ended warfare between the states over which they reigned. On the contrary, it would be easy to claim the opposite, as some major wars, such as the Hundred Years War between the French and English, were fought over what were essentially squabbles within families over inheritance. But over time it became increasingly accepted that such violent struggles over patrimonies should be limited and rule-bound. Only the wars of religion, in which ideological fundamentalism trumped existing rules of warfare, deeply violated these restrictions on brutal massacres.

There is a seeming contradiction here. Within royal families, it was sometimes necessary to slaughter all of a certain branch of the family (as did Ottoman sultans) in order to make sure that no surviving child could threaten the ruler by laying claim to the throne. And yet, these were kin, and in every stable monarchical system that evolved over time, the murder of whole branches of the family was replaced by softer methods. Rules of succession were sharpened to make competition less likely, and the practice of giving frustrated claimants to a throne minor but still lucrative, honorable positions always tended to become more common. By the second half of the nineteenth century and the early twentieth, the only kingdom in Europe (including the Ottoman Empire) that witnessed royal murders designed to install rival royal families was the relatively new kingdom of Serbia, whose two competing ruling houses were the only ones in Christian Europe not part of the extended family of "cousins" who made up the other European monarchies (Jelavich 1983, 32–33). The century that spanned the fall of Napoleon in 1815 to the start of World War I in 1914 was the most peaceful in European history after the collapse of Rome, though the Europeans did not practice such self-restraint in their colonial wars. Perhaps, then, the rise of democracy that made these royal familial alliances increasingly irrelevant by the late nineteenth century contributed to the European disasters of World Wars I and II? (We will return to this question later in this chapter.)

The principle that exogamy generally reduces the potential for unlimited killing can be looked at from the opposite side of the fence. Among competing groups that practice strict endogamy it stands to reason that the potential for bitter, highly murderous conflict with out-siders should be higher. Rules designed to enforce ethnic, class, and religious endogamy have been common for a long time. They serve to keep "pure" a group that views itself as an elite (whether realistically or not), either to preserve that group's identity against assimilation and disappearance or to reinforce the group's domination over others.

Nobles who consider it wrong to marry commoners or royals who will only marry other royals are the best-known examples of the latter type of endogamy, in which socially more powerful groups define mix-ing with lower orders, especially sexual contact between their women and men in the lower orders, as dangerously polluting. Indian caste rules that prohibit not only intermarriage but also any sexual defilement of women by lower caste men are generally interpreted as being in place to preserve very old social hierarchies (Douglas 1984, 126; L. Dumont 1980). Louis Dumont notes, however, that upper-caste men are often allowed to consort with and even in some cases to marry lower-caste women, whereas the reverse is very rare (1980, 109–29).

Rules prohibiting the mixing of blacks and whites in South Africa and the United States, until their civil rights revolutions, had the same purpose: to prevent the inclusion of mixed-race offspring into the domi-nant group and to make it less likely that the harsh conditions imposed on the dominated blacks would be eased. In all these cases, the more insecure the dominant stratum, the more fiercely its members tried to impose ethnic endogamy. This was particularly evident in the United States and South Africa, where such rules were actually tightened after the elimination of slavery. In contrast, in Brazil, where the racial order placing whites on top, mixed people in the middle, and blacks on the bottom was not openly challenged until very recently, formal rules against mixing were never established. There still exists in Brazil a myth of racial harmony quite different from that which prevails in the United States or South Africa, even though discrimination and sharp income differences between the groups are at least as strong as in the United States (A. Marx 1998, 65–79).

The kind of endogamy that tries to keep various layers within a soci-ety apart is not meant to create conflict but to ensure that social hierar-chies are maintained. In the long run, however, the creation of separate castes or ethnicities reinforces divisions that may have to be sustained by force. The problem becomes acute at times of social upheaval when dominant groups feel particularly threatened and there exists a legacy of endogamy reinforced by notions that mixing is pollution. That is when large-scale massacres become much more likely, as has happened from time to time in the United States when racial separation was strongly enforced but the old order seemed in danger because of rapid social change. The mass murder of some three hundred African Americans in Tulsa, Oklahoma, in 1921, discussed in the previous chapter, is a good example (Madigan 2001; Staples 1999, 64–69). The murder of thousands of Koreans in Japan right after the earthquake of 1923 is another case in point. It seemed to many Japanese, based on unfounded rumors, that the despised Koreans living in Japan (whom the Japanese, to this day, avoid intermarrying) might take advantage of the catastrophic earthquake to plunder and get even with their betters. This is what led to the massacres (Isiguro 1998, 331–33). In India, violent, often murderous, conflict between castes (hereditarily defined groups stratified according to levels of social prestige) has been steadily increasing and spreading throughout the country in recent decades as the traditional authority of the upper castes slowly crumbles. Yet the higher castes still struggle to maintain caste endogamy and prevent mixing with the lower groups (Brass 1997, 39–40).

In all these instances the perception that mixing between castes or ethnicities has become possible, thereby threatening the power of those who are dominant, raises fears and exacerbates tensions. But once caste or ethnic exogamy comes to be widely accepted, the opposite occurs, and tensions ease. This is, in fact, the secret of Brazil's seemingly harmonious race relations; Brazilians think that they mix easily and that they always have, even if this is somewhat a myth (A. Marx 1998, 72).

The biblical example of Joshua, cited in chapter 1 (Josh. 3–22) is a perfect example of how the holy injunction to avoid exogamy is associated with rules of pollution and demands genocidal acts to enforce it. The book of Judges and the laws given in Deuteronomy, written by the same author or authors as Joshua, were specifically aimed at keeping the Israelites separate from others by imposing distinctive dietary laws, prohibiting exogamy, and stressing their uniqueness. Revised during and after the Babylonian conquest and the exile of the Judean elite to Babylon in 587 B.C., the text further reinforces the command to remain apart and not intermarry, and explains the disaster by claiming it was the violation of cultural, religious, and marital exclusivity that had caused it (Finkelstein and Silberman 2001, 296–313).

All this worked to preserve the Jews and sustain them. It also created what may be the most eloquent legitimation in history of unlimited warfare and genocide, one of the most thorough calls for religious purity and the avoidance of pollution by outsiders, and perhaps the most influential text ever written opposed to ethnic and religious mixing. This is a tradition that has survived and influenced both Christianity and Islam to this day. Robin Lane Fox, the British biblical historian, cites Oliver Cromwell "who took Joshua as his model in his lethal campaign against Ireland's Catholics" (1992, 232). What would have happened had the Jewish people tolerated more widespread exogamy and acceptance of a kind of early multiculturalism? No doubt, as a distinct ethnicity and religion, they would have disappeared, and they never would have left us a religious tradition justifying total war.

What was almost certainly only an extended metaphor in praise of purity and intolerance of outsiders in the Bible remains a potential incitement to genocide when the metaphor is put into practice. Endogamy is, literally, the custom of restricting marriage within the group. Its opposite does not eliminate conflict, but it softens it, because it is not merely marriage and procreation that are at stake, but cultural mutual understanding and the establishment of rules of interaction that set bounds to violent conflict.

For weak and often persecuted stateless groups such as Jews or Gypsies living in states and nations where they are minorities, trying to remain endogamous can help them preserve their identity against overwhelming odds. Both these peoples have mixed widely while maintaining myths of purity, but without the myth and some enforcement of their endogamous rules, they would no longer exist as identifiable ethnocultures (on Gypsies, see Barany 2002, esp. 8–19, 52–64; Fraser 1995, 157–59, 239–46). It is easy to sympathize with a minority group's eagerness to survive. The corollary of this, however, is that when a dominant group enforces endogamy and carries the rules of purity to their logical extreme, the result can become racial apartheid, and at its most extreme, a justification for ethnic cleansing or genocide. It is difficult to avoid the impression that a devotion to endogamy is dangerous.

Establishing Codes of Warfare and Exchange to Limit Violence

Those who have studied modern genocides have noted that the major ones in the twentieth century took place after periods of great social and economic instability. The old rules no longer seemed applicable, and the level of general political insecurity was high. The Nazis came to power promising a revolutionary solution to the problems caused by World War I: inflation, depression, and the threat of bolshevism. Communist revolutionaries in Russia and China took power violently, after periods of world war and civil war. The Armenian genocide took place during World War I, and the Rwandan genocide happened during a bitter civil war. The genocidal episodes in Yugoslavia in the 1990s occurred during civil wars that were the culmination of a decade of political uncertainty and economic collapse. Eric Weitz's recent book on genocides emphasizes the revolutionary aspect of these genocides (except Rwanda, which he mentions but does not cover in detail). All these revolutionary episodes, in fact, created new situations with new rules of behavior in very uncertain times (Weitz 2003).

The principle that uncertain times are more likely to produce extreme violence than settled periods can be generalized to many situations beyond the famous modern revolutionary conditions that created such havoc. In any social setting, it takes time for competing groups to work out a somewhat stable social system of exchanges and rules to contain conflict within reasonable bounds. It may be to everyone's long-term advantage to do this, but the combination of greed, opportunism, pride, and fear that can lead to the most murderous massacres make it difficult to establish such rules. Sudden changes in ideology or material conditions that redefine the competitive situation, any change that greatly increases or decreases the power of one of the competing groups and gives it an unexpected advantage or reveals its weakness, the sudden collapse of resource bases, or the entry of entirely new actors who are unaware of the rules of competition will destabilize a situation and make violence more probable. We could call this "Tamerlane's Law," as Tamerlane's warlike relations with other Muslim nomadic Turko-Mongols, especially those close to his own base, tended to be restrained by codes of conduct, whereas his wars against complete outsiders to his system were far more destructive and ruthless. Beatrice Manz outlines the milieu from which Tamerlane came: "The Ulus Chagatay . . . was a society in balance and with a tradition which discouraged violence. Timur could not afford to flout this tradition. He therefore had to subvert, rather than to destroy, to balance rather than to build, and this may have been one reason for the insecurity which remained with him throughout his life" (Manz 1989, 151). These nomads were anything but peaceful, but they limited the damage they did to each other, much as European monarchs and nobles learned to limit the damage they inflicted on themselves in the Middle Ages.

Already in eleventh-century Europe there were codes of honor among noble knights meant to limit the destruction wrought by what was essentially a class of professional killers (Duby 1977, 86–87, 129–31). This system broke down to a considerable extent during the great crisis of the fourteenth and fifteenth centuries, and almost completely during the ideological wars of religion in the sixteenth and seventeenth, but returned, as we saw above, after those conflicts (Fossier 1986, 175–76, 445–48). Writing about European warfare, John Keegan notes that the deadly but rule-bound combat of a duel was long considered the ideal form of combat. It was both honorable and reserved for the nobility; but that kind of stylized fighting could not be sustained when large numbers of men were involved and the stakes became too high (1978, 322–23).

The infamous case of the killing of the French prisoners seized by the English at Agincourt in 1415 illustrates the problem. Henry V had to bring in archers, who were commoners, and therefore not bound by the rules of chivalry, to slaughter captured French knights. But even then, only a few French men-at-arms were killed. High-ranking ones were spared because they could be ransomed, and the killing of the others stopped once it became evident that the French would be unable to rally and regain the initiative, so that there was no longer any danger that the prisoners might play a role (Keegan 1978, 108–12).

That was why more formal laws of warfare within Europe were developed after the Middle Ages to control the devastation, because warfare was no longer under the tight control of noble knights. Even so, carrying over some notions of courtly limits into general rules had some effect until anachronistic codes of honor were completely subverted by the advent of modern weapons and ideologies. In the modern era, social change altered the nature of political governance by mobilizing masses for warfare, turned nations into huge tribes deeply hostile to each other, and invented ideologies that claimed to be able to reengineer society. This created divisions even deeper than those between Protestants and Catholics during the wars of religion and undid the rules of limited war that had prevailed within Europe in the nineteenth century.

In western Europe, the codes about just wars that prohibited the slaughter of civilians were substantially respected in the eighteenth and nineteenth centuries and into World War I. There were exceptions, of course, and frequent outright violations in colonial wars, but it was not until World War II that the mass murder of civilians again became routine in Europe itself. When the Germans bombarded Louvain in Belgium in 1914 and executed about eight hundred Belgian hostages in retaliation for the sabotage of roads they needed for their invasion of France, there was an international outcry, and these sins were long used to condemn Germany (Murray 1995, 268, 284). Compared with the genocide of the Herero in 1904–5 or of the Armenians in 1915, with the German and Japanese slaughter of millions of civilians in World War II, or with the massive number of casualties caused by bombings inflicted by all the participants on each other between 1937 and 1945, the German atrocities in Belgium in 1914 seem almost petty.

It was not just among aristocratic elites that war could be limited by codes of conduct and elaborate procedures to limit violence. An interesting example is the evolution of the potlatch among the American northwestern coastal people, most famously the Kwakiutl. Before widespread contact with the Europeans, warfare among the stateless societies of this region, ranging from Puget Sound through the coasts of British Columbia and into the Alaskan panhandle, was frequent and bloody, with exterminations of whole tribes, except for those taken as slaves, not uncommon. This was probably related to intense competition for fishing grounds and fur-bearing animals but was compounded by the fact that slavery nourished by war captives was widespread among them (Ferguson 1984). Archeological evidence in the form of males buried with fractures probably caused by fighting indicates that in some parts of this region, for example, around Prince Ruppert Harbor, up to 40 percent of the burials were of individuals killed or seriously wounded by violence. In the same areas that produced such high incidence of violence-related fractures in buried skeletons, burial practices indicate that a very high proportion of the females were slaves. In relatively more peaceful parts of the Pacific Northwest, for example, around the Strait of Georgia, both the incidence of fractures produced by violence and the proportion of females who were slaves were much lower (Donald 1997, 103–16, 202–5).

Sometime near the middle of the nineteenth century, among the Kwakiutl and some other northwest coastal Indians this way of life changed, and competitive ceremonial gift giving, the potlatch, replaced warfare as a way of resolving conflict. There were three reasons for this. First, contact with Europeans brought a smallpox epidemic that significantly reduced the population and so decreased the competition for resources. Second, the whites began to interfere and impose peace on "troublemaking" Indians (Ferguson 1984, 307). Finally, by the last quarter of the nineteenth century, both the Canadian and American authorities began to try to end the practice of slavery. The last recorded ritual killings of captive slaves (a previously common practice) took place in the 1870s and 1880s, though there were unsubstantiated rumors of such killings into the early twentieth century (Donald 1997, 235–45).

The potlatch ceremonies that replaced war involved intensely competitive gift-giving ceremonies that were planned with military rigor by the rival groups. They were replete with violent imagery, and in some potlatches fighting actually broke out, though it was usually contained (Donald 1997, 103–4). Helen Codere quotes Kwakiutl as saying that the potlatch was "fighting with property instead of with weapons" and calling them "wars of property instead of wars of blood" (Codere 1967). The whole point was that honor and prestige that had formerly been earned by war could be won by gift giving. This misled Codere into thinking that prior wars had been fought primarily for honor, revenge, and prestige, not over resources. While this was not correct, it is true that among the Kwakiutl, as among all people who engage in frequent warfare, the satisfaction of honor to avenge slights and maintain status plays an important role. Even with the material causes of their wars removed, or reduced, and strong external pressure on them to desist from warfare, honor still had to be satisfied. Had it not been, greater violence would have been expected; but there are other ways to satisfy honor than to slaughter large numbers of opponents.

Codes of honor that reduce the likelihood of massacres between enemies are very much like rules of exogamy that establish a system of rule-bound exchanges between various parts of a society, or even between groups that do not view themselves as part of the same social unit. They have two characteristics that are similar and that contribute to the easing of bloodshed, though not necessarily its elimination. One is that they establish a system of reciprocal exchange. Spouses, material goods, prestige, moral obligations, or some combination of these may be exchanged. It is the exchange itself that creates some sense of commonality, respect, and anticipation of future beneficial exchanges between conflicting groups (Axelrod 1984). The second is that for these exchanges to persist they have to be regulated, and the rules must be followed by both sides. Enforcement mechanisms may exist, and that makes the rules stronger, but even in the absence of an impartial enforcer of these sanctions (which would imply that the contending parties have become part of a single state), there must be enough trust between the parties to continue following them. Accepting a system of rules might be based simply on rational expectation that there are benefits to be gained by obeying them. Rules become stronger, however, if they also acquire moral power, a sense that they are legitimate and that it is therefore dishonorable or polluting to violate them. Rules recognized as legitimate become, in effect, durable laws, even if there is no enforcing power other than custom and belief.

Rules of exogamy and other kinds of exchanges, including goods, and codes of honor do not necessarily end serious conflict or violence, but they make genocidal slaughters much less likely.

Are Rules of Exogamy, Codes of Honor, and Potlatching Still Relevant?

Rules of exogamy, steppe nomadic etiquette, and knightly codes of conduct may today seem as irrelevant as potlatching. Still, these old codes have some modern analogues. The race to the moon by the Soviet Union and the United States in the 1960s can be interpreted as a spectacular destruction of resources for the sake of honorably defeating an enemy without war. International competitions for Olympic medals, soccer titles, and Nobel prizes may be seen in the same light, as also may the piling up of missiles and atomic warheads in the Cold War. The cost of this display contributed to the demise of the Soviet Union's empire.

Similarly, urging hostile ethnic groups to fission, move off into another part of the forest, and set up neutral zones between them hardly seems very useful, but green lines (in Cyprus) or green walls (between Catholic and Protestant Belfast) may now serve similar functions, as do international boundaries established through treaties after wars. The specific details of ancient practices may seem irrelevant, but it is social structures that have changed, not basic human psychology. Therefore, we should expect to find contemporary analogues to these practices that serve to limit conflict and prevent catastrophic outcomes in most cases.

One of the most obvious limitations on internal warfare within modern societies is the existence of strong states that inhibit violence. In asking why white southerners in the United States never seriously contemplated committing genocide against African Americans during the Civil Rights revolution of the 1960s, John Reed notes that the federal government simply would not tolerate massacres and that the death rate was very low given the intensity of feelings (Reed 2001). A similar conclusion can be drawn in Northern Ireland, where the British army, for all its errors and inability to stop the killing has, nevertheless, prevented the widespread massacres that would surely have taken place if the country had been left to its own devices (Gallagher 2001). States enforce systems of law and rules that constrain conflict. Only when the state either wanted to commit genocide or when it broke down did the twentieth century's major genocides take place. The latter kinds of massacres were less systematic but could still be very bloody. The killings of Muslims and Hindus during the partition of India in 1947, or the deaths of millions in the Congo in the late 1990s and early 2000s, are not state-sponsored, but result from the partial, or in the case of the Congo, complete breakdown of state control and the collapse of prior systems of rules regulating conflict between communities (Horowitz 2001, 333; Orogun 2002; Sengupta 2003).

It may seem far-fetched to think of the rule of law as something analogous to rules of exogamy in technologically primitive, pre-state societies, but in fact, any system of exchange between groups bound by morally legitimate laws can serve to reduce the intensity of conflict. In modern societies, exogamy no longer follows prescribed laws (except to restrict marriages between very close relatives), but it can still be highly effective in dampening and ritualizing rivalries to make them less dangerous. Though it is difficult for some contemporary Americans to remember this, in the early part of the twentieth century there was little mixing between various categories of European immigrants in the United States, and those from southern and eastern Europe were not considered truly "white." In fact, the restrictive immigration laws passed in the United States in the 1920s were explicitly based on the assumption that there were inferior "races," particularly Jews and Italians, but also Poles and Irish.

In recent decades, close to three-quarters of those with English, Irish, and Polish backgrounds in the United States have married outside their ethnic communities, as have about half of all Jews. Even the intermarriage rate between what Orlando Patterson labels "Euro-Americans" and "Afro-Americans" has quadrupled, such that among young newlyweds in the 1990s about 12 percent of Afro-Americans married outside their ethnic community. The same pattern applies to descendants of Asian immigrants (Hall and Lindholm 1999, 130–31; Handlin 1973, 258–61; Patterson 1998, 190–91; Waters 1990). No one who has lived in the United States could claim that this has eliminated ethnic and racial tensions or political competition between ethnic groups, but it has made ethnic conflict more benign than it was in the late nineteenth and early twentieth centuries. On the other hand, keeping ethnicities distinct and pure can only exacerbate racial and ethnic antagonism. Endogamy preserves and enhances the probability of violent conflict; exogamy reduces it. Endogamy contributes to the perception of group essence, which we have already noted can contribute to in-group glorification and out-group dehumanization.

Peter Skerry has rightly pointed out that assimilation, which is the end point of intermarriage, is a complex process, and that in the United States it can intensify competition between groups because it is accompanied by increased residential mixing and heightened competition for jobs. In a modern, urban society, such mixing can produce a backlash, such as the one he found among assimilated Mexican Americans who do not speak Spanish but who try to recapture their lost identity (Skerry 1993). Again, however, intermarriage does not eliminate conflicts but helps to surround conflicts with rules and limitations that lessen the probability of acute, deadly conflict because there are so many ties binding groups together. It is difficult to view "those whom some of us marry" as inherently fearsome or polluting, whereas those who are deadly competitors with whom we exchange nothing easily come to be viewed in such extreme terms.

During the Yugoslav wars of the 1990s, some observers pointed to the relatively high rate of intermarriage between ethnic groups in parts of that country as proof that this did not diminish the intensity of warfare or prevent a number of terrible massacres. Careful research, however, shows that the rate of intermarriage was not high across the major cultural boundaries that separated Catholics, Eastern Orthodox, and Muslims. This was particularly true in rural areas and helps to explain a seeming contradiction of the sort discussed by Skerry. Ethnic competition was higher in urban areas where diverse ethnoreligious groups competed for housing and jobs, but where intermarriage was somewhat more likely; and it was lower in more rural areas where there was no mixing. In the end, however, especially in Bosnia, rural young men with little cross-cultural experience formed the bulk of the armed bands doing the most brutal killing. It was, as Misha Glenny puts it, "a struggle, above all, between the rural and the urban, the primitive and the cosmopolitan" (Glenny 1993, 164). Although urban intellectuals and politicians were largely responsible for deliberately increasing tensions in order to gain and hold power, the many-sided conflicts in Yugoslavia would not have ended in genocide and ethnic cleansing had there been more intermarriage to begin with, and a smaller rural population on which to draw in order to carry out the most brutal fighting and massacres (Botev 1994; Hodson, Sekulic, and Massey 1994; Massey, Hodson, and Sekulic 1999).

Just as there is a contemporary equivalent to ancient rules of exogamy, there are also modern ways of applying codes of honor to mitigate international conflict. The first Geneva Convention attempting to regulate the treatment of war's victims was drawn up in 1863 and signed by the European powers, the United States, and some Asian and Latin American states. It was expanded and amended in 1906, 1929, 1949, and 1977, and now covers the protection of civilians and the treatment of prisoners, wounded, and refugees. The 1977 version attempted to set rules for civil wars as well as international ones, but major states have not ratified that part. Since the collapse of European communism in 1989–91, the way has been cleared for the Western powers to try to bring notions of basic human rights to international law controlling war (Johnson 1999, 96–101). A cursory glance at the history of warfare, the frequency of genocides and ethnic cleansings, and the abysmal condition of human rights in many parts of the world since the first Geneva Convention would suggest that the entire exercise has been, at best, futile, and perhaps, even, a sinister fraud. But international law should not be dismissed as long as we remember that "codes of honor" are most likely to be effective if they are applied for a long time to a set of actors who regularly interact with each other, and as long as we are reminded that such codes are supposed to limit the ravages of violent conflict, not eliminate it.

A good example of a set of codes worked out to limit genocidal warfare is the set of understandings, treaties, and exchanges of information (including the "hot line" between Washington and Moscow) that eventually evolved between the United States and the Soviet Union during the Cold War, though it took a near nuclear catastrophe, the Cuban missile crisis of 1962, to get the process of under way (Hilsman 1996).

We have already noted that even during World War I most combatants, including the Germans, rarely engaged in the massacre of civilians, and prisoners of war were relatively well treated (Weinberg 1994, 896–97). World War II, beginning with the Japanese invasion of China in 1937 (some would say it began with the invasion of Manchuria by Japan in 1931), saw the near complete breakdown of such codes. Not only did the Japanese engage in massacres of civilians, despite the fact that their military code of honor was supposed to prohibit this, but the Americans also seem to have slaughtered substantial numbers of Japanese prisoners (Dower 1986, 71–73). In Europe, the Germans initiated the Holocaust of Jews; systematically abused and killed millions of Slavs, including totally innocent civilians and Soviet prisoners of war; and slaughtered Gypsies.

Toward the end of World War II the Anglo-American air forces incinerated hundreds of thousands of civilians in bombing raids, the most notorious of which targeted Dresden and Hamburg. These probably had more of a military purpose than has been generally recognized, though they do not seem to have turned Germans against the Nazis, which was one of their purposes. (Pape 1995 takes the conventional view that the Dresden bombing was pure revenge and had no military goal, whereas F. Taylor 2004 takes the opposite position.) Of course, the same fate was visited on Japanese cities (Walzer 1977, 160, 261). Yet, after World War II, just as after the terrible wars of religion in western Europe, attempts were made to strengthen the Geneva Convention and institute laws against genocide, as we saw at the start of chapter 1.

As long as the Western powers, specifically the United States and western Europe, dominate the world, their increasing sensitivity to human rights and to the need to honor codes of conduct that limit killing creates an international environment that can and does provide some such standards. The international war crimes tribunals on Yugoslavia and Rwanda are more than mere window dressing and suggest that slowly, painfully, some new rules, applicable to modern conditions, are being drawn up (Johnson 1999, 198–207). On the other hand, the obstacles to establishing a new world order genuinely devoted to human rights are formidable and would require an enforcing police power that simply does not exist (Blackburn 2000; Rieff 2000, 2002).

Exchanges between groups and sets of rules that regularize their competition can mitigate the degree of violence they visit on each other, but to get a more complete explanation of what has dampened conflicts in the past, and continues to do so in the present, we need to turn to the beneficial effects of commercial exchanges, which have always played an important role in this respect, and which exert an even more important influence today.

The Mercantile Compulsion

In a brilliant essay on the intellectual history of the idea of capitalism published in 1977, Albert Hirschman argues that Enlightenment philosophers seeking a way to tame the passions that had led to such bloody religious wars in the sixteenth and seventeenth centuries concluded that if men would only pursue their material interests, they would be more peaceful. His book, *The Passions and the Interests*, opens with a quote from Montesquieu's *The Spirit of Laws* (1748) worth repeating: "And it is men's good fortune that they are in a situation where, at the same time that their passions make them think mean thoughts, they nevertheless have an interest in not being nasty" (quoted in A. Hirschman 1977, v).

This, according to Hirschman, became the theory that legitimized the pursuit of gain, and eventually capitalism, in the eighteenth century. Whereas developed agrarian societies had previously considered the pursuit of wealth ignoble, and the satisfaction of honor virtuous, the Enlightenment reversed this. Not only did the search for gain (interests) counterbalance other passions and thus weaken them, but eventually eighteenth-century moral philosophers came to believe that material interests were inherently more peaceful than religiously inspired passions or the demand for honor, both of which led to endless violence.

Those acting to pursue material gain behave more predictably than those governed by other passions—that is to say, more rationally. For David Hume, the "love of gain" even turned into something benign, calming, and inherently peaceful (A. Hirschman 1977, 9–66).

In the work of James Steuart, economic interests became a safeguard against tyranny and its attendant irrational pursuit of personal glory and power. Albert Hirschman quotes Steuart: "A modern oeconomy, therefore, is the most effective bridle ever was invented against the folly of despotism" (1977, 85). The idea, adopted later by those who promote the idea that democracies are inherently more peaceful than autocracies or dictatorships, is that the interests of the many minimize the effects of war because majorities of people tend to want to just go about their ordinary business with as little disruption as possible, and if their will prevails, there will be fewer major conflicts (Fukuyama 1992, 262–64). Adam Smith went farther, insisting that if economic interests could dominate society, the result would be far more harmonious than when state political interference created ". . . a hundred impertinent obstructions with which the folly of human laws too often encumbers its [the economy's] operations" (quoted in Hirschman 1977, 103).

This vision did not remain unchallenged in the nineteenth century. On the contrary, the greed of capitalists came to be viewed as a leading cause of conflict, war, and violence, not only by Karl Marx and his followers, but by many others too. It is only in the early-twentieth-century writings of Joseph Schumpeter that we can find a reassertion of the Enlightenment theory of capitalism as something inherently peaceful (A. Hirschman 1977, 117–35). For Schumpeter, the persistence of cruel wars and of aggressive imperialism into modern times was an anachronism caused by the survival of precapitalist, premodern passions, while capitalism itself, he believed, was inherently peaceful and more interested in strengthening market forces and conducting peaceful trade than in conquest or nationalistic honor (Schumpeter [1919] 1955).

How valid is the contention that mercantile interests may indeed diminish the intensity and murderous potential of violent conflict between interest groups within and between societies? There is a simple argument for this contention. Markets are not zero-sum games; both parties, buyers and sellers, can walk away from the transaction feeling they have gained something, whereas war is almost always zero-sum. There are winners and losers, and anyone's gain is someone else's loss.

On the other hand, modern capitalist societies engaged in large-scale trading—the United States, Great Britain, France, and the Netherlands, for example—have been involved in numerous wars from the seventeenth to the twentieth centuries. In the past, mercantile states such as Venice and Genoa, or long before them, Carthage and other Phoenician city-states, frequently engaged in wars to protect or expand their markets and trade routes, raise tribute, seize raw materials, or defeat their rivals. The British in Australia, as in Tasmania, and the Americans, as against the Cherokee, even committed some kinds of ethnic cleansing that resulted in what would today be defined as genocide. The English treatment of the Irish during the potato famine in the midnineteenth century, while not deliberately genocidal, was cruel and uncaring enough to raise questions about the morality of practical capitalists (on Ireland, see Ó Gráda 1999). Despite those, such as Herbert Spencer (1897, pt. 5, nos. 567, 608), who have theorized that modern industrial societies have no reason to be as warlike as agrarian or pre-state societies, the record has not been reassuring.

Nevertheless, if war is approached as a practical, commercial matter rather than one of honor, revenge, or ridding the world of pollution, and if there is a way to profit from eventual exchanges with the enemy, then genocide is self-defeating. If, furthermore, some form of compromise in a conflict seems available, then practicality would dictate that it be taken to avoid the further costs of conflict. Finally, just as the exchange of brides or of ritualistic gifts allows a better understanding of potential enemies and creates a set of rules that limit the severity of conflict, frequent trade should do the same.

It all depends on the kind of commercial interest of the parties in a conflict. Max Weber noted that the more the economy of classical Athens came to rely on slave-based production, the more ruthless its wars of conquest; every city that was conquered had part of its population slaughtered and the rest enslaved (M. Weber [1922] 1968, 1,362). Even Carthage, whose links in the western Mediterranean were originally based on trade, turned into a harsh empire as the spoils of conquest, and then the revenues to be derived from enslaving local populations, made free trade less important (M. Weber [1922] 1968, 914). In contrast, inland medieval cities in Italy that counted more on their own production and commerce than on the exploitation of conquered territories tended to have much more limited war goals. The great thalassocracies of Venice and Genoa, cities that depended on colonial conquests and the exploitation of plantations in their Mediterranean islands, were more ruthless because they also needed slaves or serfs to work their holdings. In most of medieval Europe "military strength might be a support for the economic activities of the city burghers, but in land-locked areas it could not serve as the foundation for these endeavors . . . [so] the medieval burgher was forced to rely for the pursuit of his economic interests on rational economic means" (M. Weber [1922] 1968, 1,362–63).

Yet, even an imperial, militarized, mercantile state such as Venice had a quite different outlook on war from a state whose martial motives were a combination of ideology and desire for plunder rather than trade. In the long series of wars between Catholics and the Ottoman Empire in the sixteenth century, for example, booty and territorial gain were important considerations for Spain, but its militantly crusading ideology was also fundamental. The Spanish political elite did not see itself as primarily oriented to mercantile interests at all. The Venetians, on the other hand, considered themselves to be good Christians but were overwhelmingly motivated by commercial considerations. Venice knew that it was impossible to eliminate the Ottomans, so it was always more ready to compromise than were the Spaniards (Guilmartin 1989, 171). As Fernand Braudel put it, describing the power of the Ottoman fleet throughout the Mediterranean in the 1540s, all Christian powers "had to move in fear; unless, that is, they had come to terms with the Turk, as had his French allies, his Ragusan subjects [a trading city on the Adriatic that paid tribute to but was not directly ruled by the Ottomans], and the Venetian businessmen who favored neutrality in all circumstances" (1973, 906). Venice, in fact, was fruitfully engaged in peaceful trade with the Ottomans from 1540 to 1570 during a time of great Christian-Muslim hostility. It was only when the Ottomans threatened and then captured Cyprus, a Venetian island of cotton and sugar plantations and of salt mines worked by Greek Orthodox serfs and captured slaves, that Venice rejoined a "holy alliance" with Spain against the Ottomans. As it was, the Spaniards only agreed to join with the "perfidious" (or perhaps more rationally calculating) Venetians at the urging of Pope Pius V, who wanted to wage a crusade; and they never trusted their allies, who indeed turned out to be much more eager to find a compromise peace (Braudel 1973, 1,078–87).

The Dutch Republic, the most capitalist of early modern European societies, was engaged in more or less constant warfare from the late sixteenth to the late seventeenth century and by 1675 had an army larger than Spain's or England's and almost as large as France's and Russia's—two monarchies that were roughly ten times more populated than the republic (Parker 1980, 204). It was able to do this because of the wealth generated by its economic success, and it was during this period that it became a great world empire. Its wars, however, were anything but total. In the eighty-year war from 1568 to 1648 to rid itself of Spanish Habsburg domination, the republic "strove, through thick and thin, to nurture economic ties with Iberia that were essential to the viability of their trade with the Baltic as well as to their many ventures in the seventeenth century" (de Vries and van der Woude 1997, 370). Both sides continued to trade with each other throughout these wars, particularly through the unstable border between the remaining Habsburg possessions in the Low Countries (now called Belgium) and the Dutch Republic (now called the Netherlands). This was so even though much of the fighting took place along this border. The Spaniards needed the trade to supplement their war effort and obtain needed technology, and the Dutch did it to make money.

The Dutch historian Henk van Nierop recently asked why the wars of religion between Protestants and Catholics played out so differently in France and the Netherlands. In France, as we have seen, the sixteenth century wars degenerated into large-scale, cruel massacres. In the Netherlands, though there was much fighting, there were few outright massacres, and in fact, within the Dutch Republic, the Catholics, though in the majority, hardly fought back against growing Calvinism. Rather, many were so appalled by the extremism of the Spaniards who were sent by the Habsburgs to reclaim their rebellious lands that they actively or tacitly joined the Protestants fighting against the Habsburgs (van Nierop 1995, 38–44). The main difference between France and what would become the independent Dutch Republic was that the latter was much more urbanized and dependent on industry and commerce than the former. The Dutch urban elites were more independent and powerful, and far more resistant to being turned into religious extremists, than were the landed aristocracy, which still held dear to principles of honor and loyalty to a centralizing monarchy (Habsburg in the Netherlands and Valois in France) and which sided with the Catholic Church. This urban, merchant preponderance and the prevalence of a developed money economy had the further advantage of insuring that the Dutch military and naval officers were more likely to be appointed on the basis of merit than degree of nobility. It also made it easier to finance the army, which largely explains why such a small country could raise such a large military force (Hart 1995, 57–76; van Nierop 1995, 50–53).

Among the many consequences that followed from the uniquely mercantile character of the Dutch Republic is that it emerged from the terrible wars of religion that ended in 1648 as the only genuinely religiously tolerant and openly diverse state in western Europe at that time. Its Calvinism was more tolerant than that in Germany or Geneva, and its large Catholic population had no interest in siding with the Counter-Reformation policies of the Habsburgs or of Louis XIV in the second half of the seventeenth century (Bergsma 1995, 197–213). The Dutch went to war often, but fanatical purification of territories was not part of their agenda. Charles Wilson's classic history of the Dutch Republic stresses the same point by contrasting the more businesslike and successful Dutch East India Company with the more religiously oriented, stricter Calvinist Dutch West India Company. The former succeeded, while the latter engaged in series of overly ambitious, partly ideological wars and failed to keep its control over most Dutch conquests in the Americas (C. Wilson 1977, 207–12).

None of this is meant to suggest that this most commercially minded of European nations in the seventeenth century was gentle, that it conducted its trading relations fairly, or that it was in any sense in favor of free trade. Along the coasts of Asia the Dutch used their naval superiority to brutally crush native commerce and take it over; they massacred, enslaved, and banished 90 percent of the population of the Banda Islands, for instance, for daring to trade nutmeg to the English (Lape 2000). Along the African coasts, the Dutch engaged in large-scale slaving, and in the Americas they attempted to seize sugar plantations, monopolize the slave trade, and wrest as much commerce as they could from the Spaniards, Portuguese, French, and English. A Chinese seventeenth-century chronicler describes the Dutch in Asia thus: "The people we call Red-hairs or Red Barbarians are identical with the Hollanders. . . . They are covetous and cunning, very knowledgeable concerning valuable merchandise, and are very clever in the pursuit of gain. They will risk their lives in search of profit, and no place is too remote for them to frequent. Their ships are very large, strong, well built. . . . These people are also very resourceful and inventive. . . . If one falls in with them at sea, one is certain to be robbed by them" (Boxer 1965, 236).

It was largely because they coveted Dutch trading wealth that the English attacked the independent Netherlands and waged three wars against it from 1652 to 1674. These naval wars were in some ways the first modern large-scale naval wars, but their goals were limited and ended when the English decided that the costs outweighed the benefits. English merchants realized that even successful war could not bring automatic prosperity because commercial success needed good organization and efficiency as much or more than brute force (Jones 1996, 25–37, 221–23; C. Wilson 1977, 194–205). The Dutch Republic and England were so close to each other in their mercantile aspirations, their dominant Protestant cultures, and their advanced economies that they continued to exchange people, investments, and ideas, and in 1689, only fifteen years after the end of the third war between them, the Dutch prince, William of Orange, became King William III of England (Hamilton 2000, 1).

England, the second European nation to develop an advanced capitalist economy, was also frequently at war. In the seventeenth century, aside from its foreign wars, it also engaged in some bloody civil wars in England itself, in Scotland, and in Ireland. Of these, however, the one that witnessed the most massacres and atrocities by far was the war in

Ireland. What began as a rebellion by Catholic Irish lords to ensure control over their lands in opposition to Protestant immigrant lords, in 1641 turned into large-scale expulsions and killings of English Protestants. This, in turn, resulted in the spread of horrible tales in England about the massacres and a call for revenge. The killings escalated, and when Oliver Cromwell seized power in England, he turned the reconquest of Ireland into a religious crusade, sent a large punitive army that massacred Catholics in several towns, purged certain districts of their Catholic elite, and confiscated close to half of all Irish lands to distribute to Protestant immigrants. By way of comparison, historians estimate that in the English civil wars of the 1640s between the monarchy and Parliament, some 4.5 percent of the population were killed or died of disease and hardship caused by the conflict, whereas in Ireland 19 percent died, a death rate comparable to that suffered by the most brutalized lands in World War II: the Soviet Union, Yugoslavia, and Poland. Ultimately, the rest of the Irish population was not massacred because English lords needed their labor, but they were reduced to virtual serfdom (Clifton 1999, 107–26). The subsequent victory of the Protestant English led by William III (of Orange, the formerly Dutch prince) in the 1690s against a new Irish rebellion backing the deposed Catholic king, James Stuart, consolidated the power of the Protestant Scotch and English settlers and lords in Ireland, sealed the results of the terrible Cromwellian wars, and set the pattern for the future of Anglo-Irish relations that continues to this day in the ethnoreligious conflict troubling Northern Ireland (Canny 1989, 116–33). The hatreds between the participants of the seventeenth-century civil war in England were soon overcome; those in Ireland, where the killing took on aspects of a religious war of purification, never were.

This returns us to the question of whether practical, commercially minded, modern capitalist societies are less likely to commit genocides, large political massacres, or ethnic cleansings than are other kinds of societies. The answer so far would seem to be a qualified yes, but further elaboration is necessary, because in the nineteenth century capitalist England and the United States of America committed acts that are today considered genocidal, or at least brutal ethnic cleansing.

From 1845 to 1852, about one million Irish, one-eighth of the population, died because of the failure of the potato crop that had provided a large part of the nourishment of the rural peasantry. The cause was the spread of the potato blight. As a result of the famine, another million left Ireland, mostly for the United States. The famine greatly weakened much of the remaining population and greatly accelerated a migratory flow that further reduced its numbers. As a result, Ireland's present population of about five and a half million (Northern Ireland and the Republic combined) remains lower to this day than it was in 1841, the only such case in Europe (Ó Gráda 1999, 110, 226–32).

No serious historian claims that the famine was deliberate or that the English and the Protestant landlords who dominated Ireland had genocidal plans to reduce the Irish population. In fact, poor rural Protestants in Ulster also suffered, though Ulster's death rate was lower than that of the other Irish provinces — one in twelve rather than one in eight (Kinealy 1997, 10–11; Ó Gráda 1999, 110). Nevertheless, the British government reacted so callously and so much of informed English public opinion declared that this was just punishment for the "lazy" and "inferior" Irish that a plausible case can be made that this was a genocide of sorts. An 1847 article in the *Times* of London, then Britain's most important newspaper, summarized widely held English opinion: "Before our merciful intervention, the Irish nation were a wretched, indolent, half-starved tribe of savages and . . . notwithstanding a gradual improvement upon the naked savagery, they have never approached the standard of the civilized world" (quoted in Kinealy 1997, 133). Advocates of free trade, especially the Whig Party that was then in power, and the militantly free-trade magazine, the *Economist* (the same one that still exists) sternly opposed government intervention or the curbing of free markets, so that relief efforts were completely inadequate even though the means and money were available for a much more humane policy. The prevailing English interpretation was that the famine would teach the Irish to be more prudent and hard-working, and that the market would hasten eventual progress better if there was no intervention. This led Horace Townsend to utter the famous phrase that the Irish victims had "died from an overdose of political economy administered by quacks" (quoted in Kinealy 1997, 66–70, 132).

Was this a genocide conducted by a mercantile, capitalist society guided by an explicitly free-market trading mentality? The Irish economic historian Cormac Ó Gráda believes it was more a case of "doctrinaire neglect" than of deliberate genocide. Perhaps enough aid could not have been marshaled to save everyone, but much more was available than was delivered. In that sense, Ó Gráda compares this to the famine of the Chinese Great Leap Forward, in which more than 20 million Chinese peasants died in 1959–60. In some Chinese provinces more than one-eighth of the population perished because Mao Zedong refused to admit that his agrarian policies were producing a disaster (Chirot 1996, 195–96; Lardy 1983, 41–43, 150–52; Ó Gráda 1999, 10, 82–83).

If we make an analogy with murder, this was certainly not first-degree murder, planned ahead of time, as was the genocide of Jews by the Nazis, but it was *negligent manslaughter*, an accident that should have been avoided or could have been remedied if the responsible party had taken due precautions and behaved in a moral way. This kind of murder carries substantial penalties in most legal systems, even if these are usually lower than for deliberate, planned murder or killings carried out during the commission of other crimes.

Prejudicial ideologies about race and religion that shape the actions of those with economic interests, such as those widely held about the Irish in England, are not automatically eradicated by capitalism or a mercantile orientation. Dogmatic adherence to any theory, even one supposedly based on economics, remains a form of ideological prejudice that becomes more a matter of emotions than of rational calculation. The story of the ethnic cleansing and the resulting death of thousands of Native Americans in the eastern United States in the 1830s and 1840s, discussed in chapter 1, is another example of what mercantile interests can lead to if accompanied by utter contempt and dehumanization of others and a consequent sense that their survival could be of no conceivable use in the future.

Surely, then, whatever restraint mercantile interests may exert in conducting wars rationally and for limited ends, when a weak population is deemed to stand in the way of economic gain, then massacres and brutal ethnic cleansings may well occur. This was precisely the fate of the Tasmanian Aborigines at the hands of the Australian whites. It also explains the atrocious treatment of the Congolese under Belgian rule in the 1890s and early 1900s, where perhaps as many as half of its ten million people were killed or died of disease caused by forced labor, slavery, large-scale torture, mutilation, murder, and the destruction of villages. All this was done while the Congo was under the direct rule of King Leopold II of Belgium, whose only aim was to extract as much rubber and ivory as quickly as possible, with no concern for the future (Hochschild 1999, pt. 1).

All along, there were protests against these most egregious cases of slaughter resulting from greed. Tocqueville's prediction, that the natives would be entirely exterminated in North America, proved to be exaggerated. Even in the 1830s, there were moral American voices raised against the awful mistreatment of the Cherokee. The Supreme Court ruled that the State of Georgia had no right to impose its laws on the Cherokee lands that were theirs by treaty rights. Many, especially New England politicians and intellectuals such as Daniel Webster and Ralph Waldo Emerson, protested and tried to stop the ethnic cleansing, and almost all of New England's congressional delegation was opposed to what was happening. In the end, it was to no avail, largely because the southern states supported Georgia and made this issue, as well as the question of tariffs and slavery, grounds for potential secession if the federal government dared to protect the Cherokee (McLoughlin 1986, 428–47; Satz 1991, 42). President Andrew Jackson famously announced that as the Supreme Court had made the decision, let the Court enforce it.

It would take many more decades, but eventually the policy of the United States changed, though not for economic reasons. By the turn of the century, the inhumane treatment of Native American populations was being reconsidered, and some of their surviving war chiefs who had been among the last to surrender, such as the Apache Geronimo and the brilliant guerrilla warrior Chief Joseph of the northwestern Nez Perce, were lionized heroes invited to meet with Presidents McKinley and Roosevelt. This change had little to do with commercial or other material interests. Partly, it was a matter of the closing of the frontier and the end of any conceivable Indian threat. The transformation of former enemies into heroes certainly had something to do with growing nostalgia for a now lost past. Added to this, however, was the recognition that these people had been terribly mistreated and that as human beings they were owed something. In a real sense, the prevailing morality changed as it came to be more widely accepted that Native Americans were fully human, but until that happened, the fact that white America was a trading, capitalist enterprise was of little help for the natives (Beal 1966, esp. 290–302, for how this affected the Nez Perce).

The Boer War fought between whites in South Africa can provide another insight into the nature of capitalist colonial wars. This confrontation was provoked by English gold mining interests led by Cecil Rhodes, who persuaded the British to invade the white-ruled, Afrikaans (Dutch-speaking) Boer Republics of South Africa, where gold had been found. It was a brutal conflict. From 1899 to 1902, the British lost twenty-two thousand men (three-quarters from wounds and disease), and the Boers lost more than seven thousand. Some twenty thousand to twenty-eight thousand white Boer women, children, and old people died in British concentration camps set up to stop the Boers from conducting guerrilla warfare. Some twelve thousand to fourteen thousand of the Boers' African servants died in these camps as well. Most of the Boers' farms were burned and their livestock killed to deprive the guerrillas of supplies. The Boers themselves were vicious with Africans whom they suspected of being pro-British, slaughtering whole villages (Pakenham 1979, 518; Warwick 1980, 58–61).

Yet, as Eric Hobsbawm observes, "Whatever the ideology, the motive for the Boer War was gold" (1987, 66). Once the British won, the chief concern was to get the South African mining economy back on its feet, not to take revenge, much less to wipe out the Boers. Also, the Boers were, unlike other colonial people, white Protestants, and despite their defeat, they still constituted the majority of the 1.2 million whites in South Africa out of a total population of 5.5 million. Within a few years, the British accommodated themselves to this fact, completely forgave the Boers, and allowed them to form their own political parties and regain power. They also let the Boers maintain their unjust racist practices against black Africans, because the British viewed them as a people with whom it was possible to do business, and no thought was given to massive retribution, killing, or ethnic cleansing (Pakenham 1979, 572–78).

The nearly simultaneous war of conquest waged by the Americans in the Philippines bears some resemblance to the Boer War. It cost up to a quarter of a million Filipino lives. In that particular case, however, the Americans had no intention of replacing the natives with settlers, and after winning the war, they quickly made their peace with local elites who continued to dominate the country until it achieved independence, and do so to this day (B. Anderson 1998, 272–78). Here it was not that the local elite were whites or Protestants (they were Catholics), but simply that it was more practical to follow a conciliatory policy than to utterly destroy Filipino society.

These and other cases show that it is impossible to claim that the search for profits and the rise of capitalism somehow made humans gentler or less prone to engage in mass killing when this suited them. But mercantile interests did, under some circumstances, mitigate killing. Trade and industry involve exchange. It is necessary to sell to and buy from others, to engage others as laborers, and to maintain markets. On a very large scale, this is much like the exchanges of spouses seen in technologically primitive, small societies. Any form of exchange moderates conflict by creating an incentive to avoid killing too much for fear of losing potential buyers and sellers of labor and commodities. Furthermore, any continuing, stable system of exchange leads to the development of rules that regulate, even if they do not eliminate, conflict. What was true in the past, even in pre-state societies, has remained true for modern capitalist states. All forms of long-term exchange create the possibility of mitigating conflict, encouraging conciliation, and reducing the probability of mass murder. This, again, is the conclusion reached by game theorists such as Axelrod (1984), and it is borne out by historical experience.

In circumstances where capitalist societies believed that those against whom they made war were human enough, and advanced enough, that long-lasting, mutually beneficial economic relations were possible, the Enlightenment philosophers were right, and commerce could dampen the passions for killing, in the same way that in agrarian societies or warlike nomadic ones, wiping out entire enemy populations was counterproductive because it could eliminate future sources of revenue and potential allies. But if the population with whom Western capitalist powers dealt was considered subhuman, or unable to engage in trade and labor under market conditions, or incapable of costly resistance, there was nothing inherent in the search for gain to make Europeans restrain themselves. Obstructions to gain could then easily turn into genocide or, as in the case of the Irish, callous contempt with murderous consequences.

The history of the twentieth century shows that the palliative effect of world trade, growing commercialization, and widespread exchange may help but is not sufficient to stop the retribalization of societies into nations; to counteract ideological utopias that demand purification through the extermination of ethnic, religious, or class enemies; or to block the most extreme forms of internal conflict within very troubled societies. Economic growth, international trade, and globalized population migrations reached unparalleled levels, yet genocidal wars and ethnic cleansings became, if anything, more severe and common. To explain this turn for the worse—and to understand why, at the same time, new standards of human decency arose that condemn the kinds of atrocities so carelessly carried out by Europeans in colonial situations— we have to turn to the influence of ideology. Ideology is the basis of morality; together these influence the way in which different societies and groups approach conflict.

Morality and Modesty: Rejecting Certitude

Europe's twentieth-century history is the starkest reminder possible that scientific progress, growing wealth, and increased levels of exchange between and within societies are in no sense protections against genocidal violence. Though ideological currents were already present in the late nineteenth century that mocked the trend toward gradual democratization in Europe, and that were increasingly hostile to capitalist industrialization, World War I was the turning point that let loose the worst aspects of Western modernity.

Yet, World War I should not have happened. Theobald von Bethmann Hollweg, the German chancellor at the start of the war, was not lying when, asked to explain how it had all happened, sighed, "If only I knew" (quoted in Maier 1989, 279). Unlike World War II, there were no major ideological differences between the principal parties, except for competing nationalisms. The Germans, French, and British were different European tribes, but they shared similar cultures, economic organizations, and even their forms of government—partial democracy for males, but domination by well-established elites—were not terribly different. Austria-Hungary, or certainly the Austrian half, was also quite similar. Among the major powers, only Russia was still a backward autocracy, but World War I was not fought over its obsolete autocratic system.

Europe in the first decade of the twentieth century was at the center of an increasingly globalized economy. Foreign trade as a percentage of gross domestic products was higher in the western European economies than it had ever been before, and higher than it would be again until the 1970s; higher for the United States than it would be until the 1980s; and higher for Japan than it is even today. The fantastic revolution in communications—the telegraph, railroads, steamships—had created a global market. World financial and investment markets were more integrated than ever, and more so than they would be again until roughly the 1980s. Labor markets were more open, with proportionately higher levels of migration, than they are to this day (Rodrik 1997, 7–9; more generally, J. Williamson 1996). Rising prosperity had made living conditions better than ever for the populations of the advanced Western nations, with sharply falling death rates and rapidly growing levels of consumption. Even political representation for the poor and working classes was improving, as socialist parties were becoming accepted and successfully pushing for reforms.

Eric Hobsbawm has correctly pointed out that these agreeable conditions and trends were not present outside the wealthy Western countries and that growing instability and inequality in Russia, the Balkans, the Ottoman Empire, Persia, and China augured poorly for the future.

Nevertheless, in the end, had Germany, France, and the United Kingdom avoided war with each other, there would have been no World War. Furthermore, as Hobsbawm claims, "It is absolutely certain that no government of a great power before 1914 wanted either a general European war or even—unlike the 1850s and 1860s—a limited military conflict with another European great power" (1987, 276–79, 310–11). The Serbs provoked the Austro-Hungarians by tolerating and protecting the secret society that murdered the heir to the Habsburg throne, Franz Ferdinand, and his wife Sophie in Sarajevo in 1914, but how could a minor state at the edge of Europe with no significant resources create such havoc with one act of terror? (S. Williamson 1989, 234–35).

To understand what happened may help us perceive both the risks and the benefits of living in our own contemporary globalized, increasingly democratized, and for an even larger portion of the globe, prosperous era. More than nine million men were killed, which in France and Germany translated into about one-eighth of all men between the ages of eighteen and forty-nine during the war. The number of injured was even higher, and many of those were maimed for life (Murray 1995, 295; Winter 1985, 75).

Many miscalculations and blunders were made by leading statesmen and military planners, but there also had been such a long buildup of armaments (for at least two decades); such an alignment of alliances, splitting Europe into two hostile camps; and so much competition between the European powers for overseas colonies that the European international atmosphere was dangerously tense. Analysis of this background is the mainstay of scholarship on the causes of World War I, and the military planning that turned a minor crisis into a catastrophic war was well described in Barbara Tuchman's popular account, *The Guns of August* (1962). In contrast, David Welch has recently suggested that we go back to the emotions felt by the leaders who brought on this disaster. We should not forget that the French felt that theirs was a just cause because Germany had stolen Alsace and Lorraine in 1871, that the Serbs felt that theirs was a just cause because brother Slavs were being ruled by the oppressive Habsburgs, that the British thought justice was on their side because little, neutral Belgium had been invaded by Germany, that the Germans believed theirs was a just cause because they were being encircled by a hostile alliance, that Russia felt justified in coming to the aid of its little Slavic brother, and that the Habsburg monarchy thought itself on the side of justice because Slavic nationalists were plotting to destroy it (Welch 1995, 95–126 and 251–270 for citations of the literature on this topic).

What makes the case for this sense of aggrieved justice so powerful is that if the war had been merely a matter of costs and benefits, hostilities could have been stopped once it had become clear that no one could win without enormous, absurdly disproportionate costs. But in fact, this was the moment when the retribalization of Europe into ethnically cohesive nations that had come to consider themselves as distinct races became the determining factor in a large conflict. To maintain such huge armies, everyone had to be mobilized, and that was possible only by creating a sense of tribal solidarity. Once that had been accomplished by decades of nationalist education and patriotic enthusiasm, however, it was no longer easy to cynically bargain for peace by giving up the sacred principles for which such huge sacrifices had been asked. Samuel Williamson is right to conclude his review of the causes of what was once called "the Great War" with this observation: "Nationalism and ethnic arrogance can never be underestimated. The powerful, emotive forces of prestige and survival press statesmen to take chances that ostensibly rational actors might not take" (1989, 247).

Taking a more sociological approach, Joseph Schumpeter wrote in 1919 that aggressive imperialism, which he blamed for the war, had been primarily caused by the fact that the nations of Europe were still disproportionately influenced by a military class composed of members of the old aristocracy, or at least men modeling themselves on that class. The old autocratic state from which modern states had emerged embarked on destructive imperialist adventures because it had a heritage that ". . . included the war machine, together with its psychological aura and aggressive bent, and because a class oriented toward war maintained itself in the ruling position" (Schumpeter [1919] 1955, 97). He overlooked the changing ideological environment that contributed to the war, but he was right about the fact that it was led by honor-obsessed aristocratic military castes. The other side of this aristocratic ethos, of course, was that its rules of behavior kept this bloody war from becoming genocidal because the mass slaughter of civilians was not part of the old, vanishing code of honorable conduct. The anomaly of a World War conducted by officers imbued with an aristocratic, antimercantile, snobbish warrior ethic, leading masses of commoners whose mobilization on behalf of the nation signaled a democratization of political life, was superbly captured by Jean Renoir's 1937 film, *La Grande Illusion*. It was, indeed, a great illusion to imagine that these two clashing worldviews might continue to coexist.

Destructive as it was, this war failed to reverse the trends toward retribalization, growing ethnic solidarity and arrogance, or the proliferation of deeply ideological conflicts. It did, however, end the day when aristocratic limitations on mass violence would ever again be effective. Out of World War I there emerged two revolutionary, radical populist movements, fascism and communism, that were even less concerned with the petty gains and losses of mercantile transactions than the European leaders who had led their nations into catastrophe in 1914, and for whom the issue of "honor" was no longer relevant because they had history on their side and a vision of an ideal world to justify ruthless violence.

The European Revolt against Capitalism and Individualism

Even before 1914, an intellectual revolt against the spread of capitalist mores had been developing in the advanced European societies, a precursor to the antiglobalization movement exactly a century later. This was based on a sense that the modern industrial world was somehow not "authentic," that people were no longer "rooted" in community, that crass materialism was rampantly destructive of sound values, and that the forces of unchecked markets were destroying everything that was genuinely human and natural. Both the Right and the Left agreed about this.

For the radical Right, international Jewry, a contemptible, greedy, weak bourgeoisie, and mass democracy were responsible. For the radical Left, it was international finance, a rapacious bourgeoisie, and the corrupting influence of political parties that acted solely in the interests of their rich paymasters. For the Right, community and authenticity would be recovered only by creating a new tribal solidarity through the nation, to be led by a heroic elite who would embody national cultural virtues. For the revolutionary Left, proletarian solidarity would create a new sense of community, end inequality and injustice, and be led by an elite of political activists able to represent the true will of the working class.

World War I's carnage confirmed both the rightist and leftist views that the bourgeois order was a filthy, hypocritical mess that had to be overthrown. The far Left got its chance in Russia in 1917 when the ravages of the war caused its government to collapse, and the far Right took power first in Italy in 1922 as a result of the social conflicts and gloom that pervaded much of postwar Europe. The Great Depression that began in 1929 and 1930 did the rest and vastly increased the attraction of both communism and fascism. It brought the Nazis to power in Germany in 1933 (Schapiro 1987, 192–96, 214–19, 321–43; Sorel 1941; Sternhell 1994, 1996). Aside from Russia, the far Left did not gain lasting power anywhere after World War I, but the far Right did, gradually, throughout much of Europe and Japan, thus setting the stage for World War II and the genocidal frenzy that occurred between 1939 and 1945. Even before then, Stalinist communism perpetrated mass murder on a colossal scale in the Soviet Union in the 1930s.

The total number of deaths from World War II was on the order of 40 million, of which at least half were noncombatants who were deliberately murdered or starved to death. Jews and Slavs, who were the particular target of the Nazis, suffered more than half of these total deaths (Milward 1979, 208–15). What needs to be explained is why whole categories of civilians defined by race, ethnicity, religion, or in the case of Stalin's Soviet Union, by economic class, were exterminated even when they were not combatants. The three ideological principles behind these slaughters are clear, and it is by understanding them that we can explain why the constraints limiting mass slaughter broke down so badly.

THE IMPORTANCE OF ENLIGHTENMENT INDIVIDUALISM

In all these massacres, individual distinctions were not made. A Jew was a Jew, whether old or young, male or female, civilian or soldier. Jews were a disease that had to be eliminated. But kulaks in the Soviet Union in the early 1930s, and Chinese during the rape of Nanjing were also undifferentiated "others" to be wiped out. This was not the same as killing civilians during interstate wars as a means of breaking the enemy's will to resist; this was deliberately seeking to exterminate whole categories of enemies because all of them are presumed to be part of a united enemy collectivity. This can be attributed partly to the essentializing we discussed in chapter 2, but there was also an ideological explanation.

The search for community, for authentic roots, for relief from the supposed alienation of modern life caused by Western capitalism was generally perceived as a struggle to overcome modern Western societies' excessive respect for individualism. German Nazism sought to remedy this by creating a united, racially pure, national community, the *volksgemeinschaft* (Mosse 1964). Japanese doctrine was the same. In 1937, the Japanese Ministry of Education published an official explanation of what Japan stood for, "The Unique National Policy" ("Kokutai no Hongi"). This document decried the importation of the foreign ideology of the European Enlightenment that stressed individualism. It claimed that even the Europeans had recognized the harm done by individualism and were turning to fascism and communism to overcome it. Japan was doing this, too, as should the entire human race. Individualism had to be replaced by national harmony, patriotism, and loyalty to the emperor. The Japanese had taken useful elements from other cultures to create a unique and superior one, the document went on to explain, but it was now time to reject harmful elements from the West that risked corrupting and weakening Japanese unity, starting with a rejection of individualism (Japanese Ministry of Education 1937).

To accept the Enlightenment notion that the individual is important and has autonomy apart from any family, community, tribe, or nation is to abandon the principle of collective guilt and to reject collective punishment. To believe, on the contrary, that a group, however defined, consists of a single, hostile will with a single, united character is to open the way to genocidal acts. If all of "them," be they Tutsis in Rwanda, Cambodians with "Vietnamese minds" in Cambodia, Catholics or Protestants in Northern Ireland, Jews, Bahais in Iran, rotten landlord families, or whatever category, are but a single enemy entity, then mass killing becomes acceptable, or even prescribed in case of violent conflict. Essentializing by any criteria, combined with grouping that eliminates the individual as a meaningful actor, makes any conflict potentially much more deadly.

When the United States, or Great Britain, or any other post-Enlightenment Western nation committed genocidal acts on populations, it did so by rejecting Enlightenment political philosophy. When, as in the United States, this happened to Native Americans, it was a rejection of the fundamental Lockian defense of individual rights on which the state and nation were supposed to be based (Hartz 1955). There were protests about such acts, about slavery, about murdering aborigines to get them out of the way, throughout the nineteenth century. As the twentieth century progressed, growing portions of humanity were incorporated into the category in which individual responsibilities and rights had to be recognized, and this made such acts seem ever more immoral to the point of being criminal. The ideal has not always been followed—far from it—but it is an ideal that continues to animate political ideology in Western societies, that has become immensely stronger in continental Europe than it was in the early twentieth century, and has spread to some, though hardly all, of the rest of the world (Hunt 2000). Had fascism or communism triumphed in the midtwentieth century, however, these Enlightenment principles would have died.

The murderous acts of World War II were committed by regimes that blamed Enlightenment individualism for the ills of modernity, and in so doing, committed atrocities far greater than those supposedly brought on by the version of modernity they condemned. At the end of World War II, the victors, led by the United States, did not engage in mass killings or revenge but chose instead to arraign a symbolic few, very few, in the enemy countries. Only in territories controlled by the Soviet armies were there mass deportations and ethnic cleansings (Naimark 2001, 85–138).

In the modern world, literacy, ease of communication, and the ability of states to mobilize vast resources in case of conflict mean that there is a far stronger tendency than ever before to view huge categories of potential enemies as united, malevolent tribes. This was less of a problem when conflicts were local, between groups that regularly exchanged goods or spouses. Later, when wars were more a matter of elite competition, masses did not play a crucial role and could be ignored. In a world of intense nationalism, of self-conscious, organized ethnic and religious groups competing for control of states, and of competing ideological movements with strong views about how societies should be run, the old limitations on violence are less adequate. The modern world, in other words, has been retribalized, but on a larger scale than before. This is why the Enlightenment's glorification of the individual and individual rights is more important than ever, and necessary to restrain genocidal impulses.

THE IMPORTANCE OF IDEOLOGICAL MODESTY AND DOUBT

If the refusal to recognize individual differences within groups defined as enemies was one of the common characteristics of the murderous totalitarian regimes in the twentieth century, another one was a very high level of ideological certitude. The notion that "our" doctrine— communism, Nazism, racial or national superiority, more recently some extreme forms of Islam—is completely and unquestionably right gives moral legitimacy to the slaughtering of opponents. This is not new. The wars of religion in Europe also were fought partly as ideological struggles between opponents who believed that their faith required them to purge heresy in order to reestablish God's domain. The many Bible passages cited earlier show that such theories have been around for at least 2,600 years, so it should not shock us that they persist. In the twentieth century, utopian doctrines of a racially pure nation or of a classless and perfectly egalitarian society claimed to have bypassed the old religions, but in fact, they were as dependent on their own gods as any of the more traditional utopian religions. Hitler, Lenin, Stalin, Mao, Enver Hoxha, Ceauşescu, Kim Il Song, Emperor Hirohito, and the others were all deified and presented as the one true prophet to their people (Chirot 1996).

Marxist eschatology actually mimicked Christian doctrine. In the beginning, there was a perfect world with no private property, no classes, no exploitation, and no alienation—the Garden of Eden. Then came sin, the discovery of private property, and the creation of exploiters.

Humanity was cast from the Garden to suffer inequality and want. Humans then experimented with a series of modes of production, from the slave, to the feudal, to the capitalist modes, always seeking the solution and not finding it. Finally there came a true prophet with a message of salvation, Karl Marx, who preached the truth of Science. He promised redemption but was not heeded, except by his close disciples who carried the truth forward. Eventually, however, the proletariat, the carriers of the true faith, will be converted by the religious elect, the leaders of the Party, and join to create a more perfect world. A final, terrible revolution will wipe out capitalism, alienation, exploitation, and inequality. After that, history will end because there will be perfection on earth, and the true believers will have been saved. Whether one attributes such chiliastic revelations to St. John or to Karl Marx, the end is remarkably similar (Aron 1951).

> And he who sat upon the throne said, "Behold, I make all things new." . . . And he said to me, "It is done! I am the Alpha and the Omega, the beginning and the end. To the thirsty I will give water without price from the fountain of the water of life. He who conquers shall have this heritage, and I will be his God and he shall be my son. But as for the cowardly, the faithless, the polluted, as for murderers, fornicators, sorcerers, idolaters, all liars, their lot shall be in the lake that burns with fire and brimstone, which is the second death. (Rev. 21:5)

In the Marxist version the cowardly, the faithless, the polluted, the murderers, fornicators, sorcerers, and liars are the bourgeoisie, who will be cast into hell. In 1848, Marx wrote: "The abolition of bourgeois individuality, bourgeois independence, and bourgeois freedom is undoubtedly aimed at." The proletariat will organize itself as a class, and

> by means of a revolution, it makes itself the ruling class, and as such sweeps away by force the old conditions of production. . . . In place of the old bourgeois society, with its classes and class antagonism, we shall have an association, in which the free development of each is the condition for the free development of all. . . . Let the ruling classes tremble at a Communistic Revolution. The

proletarians have nothing to lose but their chains. They have a world to win. (K. Marx [1848] 1977, 233, 237–38, 246)

Though eloquent, Marx does not quite match old-fashioned biblical prophecy, but he comes close with the same message. There will come a day when virtue will triumph, when all evil will be purged from this earth, and an idyllic Eden will be recovered in Paradise. In fact, the great communist murderers all prophesized, too, and promised marvelous utopias. Mao Zedong said in a speech in August 1958, upon unleashing the Great Leap Forward in which tens of millions starved to death:

> Yesterday, I could not sleep. I have something to tell you all. In the past, whoever dreamed that a *mu* [one-sixth of an acre] of farmland could produce ten thousand catties of grain [five metric tons!]. . . . Our 1.5 billion *mu* of farmland will be too much. Planting one-third of them is enough; another one-third may be turned into grassland; and let the remaining one-third lie fallow. The whole country will thus become a garden. (Quoted in Salisbury 1992, 130–31)

Pol Pot's imaginary agrarian utopia created out of a combination of bad history, nostalgia for a mythological Khmer past, and Marxist-Maoist theory caused, proportionately, even more deaths (Kiernan 1985, 1996).

It was not an accident that Hitler promised a Thousand Year Reich, a millennium of perfection, similar to the thousand-year reign of goodness promised in Revelation before the return of evil, the great battle between good and evil, and the final triumph of God over Satan. The entire imagery of his Nazi Party and regime was deeply mystical, suffused with religious, often Christian, liturgical symbolism, and it appealed to a higher law, to a mission decreed by fate and entrusted to the prophet Hitler. There could be no doubt, no hesitation, and no compromise in carrying out this destiny (Fest 1975, 376–78; Mosse 1964, 207–16).

The Enlightenment's vision of ideology has generally been quite different. Skeptical, searching for incremental improvements in knowledge, rejecting religious dogma, and intent only on trying to remain objective, Enlightenment thinkers were necessarily more tolerant of diversity because they recognized that no one could know the absolute truth. There was always the possibility of new discoveries, of falsifying past knowledge, so that the only total moral imperative was to remain open-minded. This has become the philosophical basis of Western tolerance and is what is most hated by the many varieties of absolutist ideology, be they secular or revealed religions (Gellner 1992, 74–96).

As an ideology of government, Enlightenment philosophy takes the form of promoting checks and balances, such as those proposed by Montesquieu. As there cannot be human perfection, the perfect ruler is impossible. Only by limiting and taming power can there be a just government (Manent 1995, 53–64). It is not necessary to doubt the justice of one's cause to be tolerant; but it is necessary to doubt that any doctrine is so absolutely valid as to justify the slaughter of those who oppose it.

THE DANGER OF EXTREME PURITY

The bloodiest war in the nineteenth century, the only one that approached World War II in casualty rates, was the Taiping (Great Peace) Rebellion from 1850 to 1864 that left some 20 million to 30 million Chinese dead. The rebellion, which was really an attempted religious revolution supposed to convert China to a perfect, though highly idiosyncratic form of Chinese Christianity, was founded by a visionary, Hong Xiuquan, who presented himself as a brother of Jesus Christ able to speak directly with God. According to his vision, he had been commissioned by God to "restore" Christianity to China, where it had supposedly originated. In order to do this, he had to rid China of the barbarian devils, the Manchus, a northern people who had conquered China in the seventeenth century and were still ruling it. Then he would create his "Heavenly Kingdom of the Great Peace." This he proceeded to do, rallying vast numbers of discontented officials and peasants against the Chinese Empire.

The Taiping Empire that ruled a large portion of central China for a few years was meant to be a puritanical, holy utopia free of sin or conflict. In fact, it came as close to becoming a totalitarian nightmare as anything ever attempted before the twentieth century on such a large scale. It finally fell because of internal divisions and because Hong seems to have gone mad, believing in his own prophecies even as his entourage became increasingly corrupt and ineffective. It should not surprise us, then, that when the Heavenly Kingdom of the Great Peace began to experience serious problems, there were massive purges of those held responsible for having betrayed the cause. Thousands of families were exterminated. In the end, as millions starved, the "brother of Christ" wrote divinely inspired poetry, as Mao would do in similar circumstances a century later. The two visions, Mao's communist one and Hong's heavenly "Christian" peace, were in fact astonishingly similar (Spence 1997, esp. 242–44; Wakeman 1975, 143–56). About Mao's catastrophic vision in 1958, Jonathan Spence's wry comment seems apt: "It does not belittle the vision—which was as rich or richer than anything expressed in China since the Taiping Heavenly King, Hong Xiuquan, ruled over Nanjing just over a century before—to say that it did not coincide with reality" (Spence 1990, 580).

This kind of murderous frenzy is quite typical of violent utopian movements that believe in purifying society to transform it but then blame failure on insufficient zeal in carrying out this cleansing. From biblical injunctions to exterminate the Canaanites, to Hitler's genocidal racial obsession and Stalin's unending drive to eliminate class enemies and traitors, to Pol Pot's reign of terror or that of the Taliban in Afghanistan, the story is much the same (on the latter, see Goodson 2001, 104–32). Perfect purity imposed by force on a less than perfect world is an invitation to genocidal mass murder. The reverse is equally true. Accepting the imperfections, the impurities, the fallibilities of human beings and their societies is a necessary if not sufficient condition for compromising with internal as well as external enemies.

The compulsion to purify society by violently eradicating the impure in order to create a better world is the most extreme, the most severe, and the most demanding version of the kind of absolute moral certitude that can lead to genocidal acts. When purification is combined with a complete sense of righteousness and an utter disregard for individual differences among enemy ethnicities, classes, religions, tribes, or nations, all the pieces are in place for widespread persecutions and killings. The enemy becomes a single, unified Satan.

The desire for purity breeds puritan asceticism as well as a wish to cleanse the world. This was somewhat true of Oliver Cromwell, but truer yet of Adolf Hitler. It applies as well to today's Islamic fundamentalists who are prepared to slaughter Westerners, not just to change Western policies toward Muslim peoples and states, but to bring about a godly society. What they object to (and in this respect Muslim extremists are at one with Jewish and Christian fundamentalists) is the " 'American-style' traits of individualism, the abuse of alcohol, and sexy movies" (Juergensmeyer 2000, 180, 195–201). To this list one could add the toleration of homosexuality, giving equal rights to women, and religious pluralism that does not privilege the one true God, whichever one that may be.

It would be going too far to say that the sinners are always more gentle than the pure, but it is reasonable to say that those who are not terrified by sinners, who are secure but modest enough in their own morality to admit the imperfections of human beings, are not likely to command a genocide to rid the world of sin. Fortunately, extreme ideological puritanism is not easily sustained and does not usually dominate political life except in particularly troubled times. That is one reason genocides have been rare. But in troubled times, we will always have prophets who demand genocidal purification.

Yearning for Solutions

In every era, some humans so yearn for peace that they are willing to believe in miracles. In 1971, the "peaceful Tasaday," a supposedly stone-age people "were discovered" living in a remote part of the Philippines in perfect peace. Though there remains some controversy about whether or not they were completely invented by some anthropologists or were a partly isolated group that had split off in the nineteenth century from their farming neighbors, the original claim about their perfect, peaceful nature and its attribution to their "stone-age" origins was certainly a fabrication (J-P. Dumont 1987; Hemley 2003; Nance 1975; Walker 1995). Alas, there never were any "noble savages" (Ellingson 2001, 343–44; Konner 1990). Yet, at the height of a Cold War that threatened to turn into a nuclear nightmare, with a major war raging in Vietnam, and many others elsewhere, so many people deeply wanted to believe in some kind of prehistoric purity and peace that the Tasaday were quickly idealized and made an icon of human origin without original sin. Our willingness to accept such a story should not be interpreted as evidence of our foolishness, however, but of our eternal ability to retain some optimism that after all, we can find solutions to uncontrolled violence.

It is clear that violence is ubiquitous, but the very fact that so many societies, not just our own, have had myths of perfect peace and tranquillity shows that this, too, is part of our makeup. To counter violence every society also has ways of mitigating the destructive, frequently murderous aspect of competition, and of inventing protocols that try to avoid genocidal mass murders between competing groups. As a species we have a dual nature. We are competitive and warlike to the point of being murderous, sometimes even genocidal, but we also long for peace and are conciliatory and cooperative.

After the fact, we can always find explanations for the great massacres in the past, but the pessimism about the human condition that such analysis generates is actually excessive, given that these events are much less frequent than conflicts that end in less bloody ways. We have seen that human societies have usually found ways of controlling and mitigating competitive conflicts and the emotions that ensue. Such strategies include exchanges between groups, codes of conduct to regulate conflicts, and moral prescriptions against mass murder. That these can fail catastrophically is clear, and in the twentieth century, there have been such dramatic failures that we can wonder whether modernity has so unbalanced us that old remedies no longer work. Yet, antidotes based on old models but adapted to today's circumstances do exist. It is these we will explore in our next chapter.

CHAPTER FOUR

Strategies to Decrease the Chances of Mass Political Murder in Our Time

Fight in the Cause of Allah
Those who fight you
But do not transgress limits;
For Allah loveth not transgressors.
—QURAN, SURAH 2:190

There is an interpretative footnote added to the above quotation by the Quran's editors, a committee of official scholars acting on behalf of the "Custodian of the Two Holy Mosques, King Fahd ibn Abdul Aziz of Saudi Arabia." The note explains: "War is permissible in self-defence, and under well-defined limits. When undertaken, it must be pushed with vigour, but not relentlessly, but only to restore peace and freedom for the worship of Allah. In any case, strict limits must not be transgressed: women, children, old and infirm men should not be molested, nor trees and crops cut down, nor peace withheld when the enemy comes to terms" (surah 2:190). That this admirable restraint, which parallels the received wisdom in most holy texts and philosophical commentaries about war, has been violated often, and that it leaves quite a bit of room for interpretation about what "freedom for the worship of Allah" might really mean, does not negate its message. War is legitimate, but it should be as limited as possible.

Only some extreme or perhaps naive optimists can look at humanity's history and believe that somehow violent conflict can be eliminated. Nothing in today's world, or in the grim history of the preceding century, suggests that we are moving closer to such an ideal. Yet, longing for conflict reduction is so widespread that many approaches have been tried to limit violence. These strategies may often break down, but more often than not they do succeed in mitigating damage. We discussed some of them in the previous chapter.

Now we need to consider methods of reducing the viciousness of conflicts in today's world, policies that might be applied to avoid or ameliorate the kind of violently competitive situations that can lead to mass political murder. There is a growing literature on conflict resolution that suggests some ways of doing this, though there is little consensus on what the best approach might be, or even if it is more desirable to stop all violence or to just try to contain it. Generally, the idealistic impetus behind both scholarly and practical work in this area leans more toward eliminating violence rather than setting bounds that reduce the dangers of mass murder, but that does not prevent it from offering useful ideas. A larger problem is directly connected to the fact that there is no single reason that explains all genocidal acts, and therefore no single solution. On the contrary, almost all episodes of violent conflict that lead to mass murder have multiple causes and so need to be addressed with solutions that combine different approaches.

We will therefore present many kinds of proposals, some aimed at a high international and elite national political level, some at the very basic, local kinds of problems that create dangerous tensions, and yet others that offer suggestions for reshaping ideologies and morality. None of these promises ultimate answers, because what is most likely to work is some combination. The particular kind of mix that is best will depend on actual situations, and each particular strategy has serious pitfalls as well as holding out some promise.

The kinds of strategies we will propose can be grouped into four categories. First are those aimed at the leaders of governments, and these include both international involvement and suggestions for restructuring states to limit conflict within them. Second, we will discuss the growing pressure to impose some kind of global justice on those who are accused of having committed atrocities. This has both positive and negative consequences, and we will suggest that some unexpected, unpleasant consequences may result from pushing this kind of approach too far. Nevertheless, it is a process that can often help. Third, we will look at much more modest, local proposals that can defuse the kinds of competitive tensions likely to feed extreme conflict. These fall broadly under the rubric of "constructing civil society." But these kinds of proposals merge into another growing movement to encourage greater democratization. Democratization is not the ultimate answer, because democracies do engage in violent war—even occasional civil wars—and have committed genocidal acts, as we have seen. But like other offered solutions, it is one that certainly improves the chances of limiting mayhem. Without both institutions and social habits to support it, however, democratization is merely an abstraction, and this is what connects any such project with both civil society building and structural reform at the level of the state. Finally, we will pick up the theme first discussed in the previous chapter, the role of ideology in shaping morality. We will conclude by suggesting that there are ways of promoting certain ideologies that can significantly reduce the likelihood of mass political murder.

A recent example of genocidal war, the ethnic cleansing and mass murder occurring in Darfur, the western province of Sudan, at the time this book was being completed, illustrates the complexities of addressing such problems and shows why they have to be tackled at many different levels. By mid-2004, international estimates of non-Arab people of Darfur killed by the state-supported Janjaweed Arab militias ran into the many tens of thousands, and the number of fugitives starving in refugee camps had reached more than one million, with at least ten thousand dying of hardship and disease each month. The crisis was continuing unabated in late 2005 as our book was going into press. Grotesque stories of rapes and mutilations, of Sudanese military bombings of villages followed by cavalry militias galloping in to finish off the population, and of vast depopulated regions made this case a center of international attention. Colin Powell, the U.S. secretary of state, and Kofi Annan, the secretary general of the United Nations, visited Sudan in the early summer of 2004 to demand that this nightmare be stopped, but with little immediate effect (International Crisis Group 2004; Lacey 2004; Power 2004).

The background of this catastrophe shows that it had many of the same causes as genocidal events in the past. The government of Sudan had long been beset by civil war, mostly in the southern, black and non-Muslim part of the country. The northern, Arab and Muslim part of the population has always dominated and been resented for its subjugation of southerners. Southerners were treated as inferiors, were captured as slaves for generations in the past, and at least until very recently were still prone to being seized and enslaved (Keller 1998, 279–81). As agreement was being reached in 2003 and 2004 to finally end this stalemated war with a compromise between north and south, it was replaced by increased tensions and the new war in Darfur.

In 2003, a rebellion began in Darfur by black Muslim (but not Arab) sedentary farmers suffering from increasing droughts and land shortages. The region felt disinherited by the Sudanese government. At the same time, repeated droughts had severely hurt Arab Muslim herders in Darfur, who were also suffering from a shortage of pastureland and were in a desperate competition with the non-Arab farmers for land. Other similar herders had been migrating into the area from drought-stricken Chad and Niger as well, increasing the pressure on the land. Violent clashes had occurred between the Arab herders and non-Arab peasants even before the start of the rebellion, and these encounters helped to spark it. The government of Sudan then took advantage of this situation to arm the Arabs and help them with its own military to crush the revolt. These militias, the Janjaweed, had as their agenda driving out the sedentary cultivators in order to steal their cattle and use their land. The government concurred, as ethnic cleansing would certainly destroy the basis of the rebel movement (International Crisis Group 2004; Power 2004; Taban 2004).

Of the four main causes of genocidal ethnic cleansing laid out in this book's first chapter, at least the first three are present in this situation: purely instrumental conflict over resources and control, a desire for revenge against foes who are deemed to have transgressed, and fear of what will happen if the enemy is not eliminated as a threat. The competition for resources in Darfur between local inhabitants produced a rebellion that threatens the fragile hold on power of a Sudanese government that cannot afford to seem weak for fear of losing control of the entire country. Like William the Conqueror in Yorkshire in 1069, or Caesar in Gaul, this government has chosen to solve the problem with a strategy of ethnic cleansing. The government's local instrument, the Janjaweed, are herders whose people are locked in a deadly battle over resources with the non-Arab tribes they are destroying, and they must fear for their own survival if they lose. Needless to say, in a conflict that predates the rebellion and massive ethnic cleansing, but that has become far worse, there are deep resentments on both sides. The fact that the Janjaweed have used mass rape to humiliate and dishonor their enemies raises the likelihood that if the tables are turned, they will be subjected to brutal vengeance (Lacey 2004). What turned this from an endemic low-level civil conflict between competing groups that had long been living with each other into a major killing ground is the insertion of modern arms and the desire of the Sudanese government to rid itself of rebels, but now there is the added fear for both sides that to lose could mean extermination.

This did not begin as a Nazi-like attempt to purge the earth of a particular polluting ethnic group but as a kind of genocide of convenience such as those that have occurred over and over again. Yet, not only have the next elements, the desire for revenge and fear increasingly come into play, but even the fourth element—the pursuit of purity by eliminating a polluting race—is not entirely absent. When questioned by the *Economist*'s reporter, the leader of the Janjaweed, Musa Hilal, denied that he was conducting such operations. He claimed to be protecting his Arabs from rebels. "Things happen in wars," he said. "A bullet can miss its mark." Denying that his men engaged in the rape of black women (a bald-faced lie according to all reputable accounts) he said, "Why would we rape them? They disgust us." The *Economist* goes on to cite him to the effect that "African tribeswomen are barely Muslim and have such wanton sexual habits, as seen from the way they dance that force would hardly be necessary" (*Economist* 2004b). Perhaps their being "barely Muslim" excuses the blatant violation of Quranic law about "transgressing limits."

Francis Deng, a distinguished social scientist from Sudan has written that

the northern Sudanese . . . respects the Arab-Islamic identity and disdains the negroid African non-Muslim. But since certain African racial and cultural elements are still visible in the assimilated Sudanese Arabs, it does not require a professional social psychologist to presume that such a disdain for elements visible in one's own physiognomy must at some degree of consciousness be a source of tension and disorientation. Indeed . . . the tendency to look down on the negroid races as slaves could well be the result of a deep-seated inferiority complex. (Deng 1995)

Evidently, "negroid African" southerners are deemed inferior by negroid northerners. Inveighing against the cruelty of these events, sending in United Nations or other diplomats, and having international non-governmental organizations (NGOs) spearhead protests may do some good, but such measures overlook the desperation of the contending parties on the ground and the deep-seated prejudices that long predate the events of 2003–5. There is little question that the Janjaweed represent a group of Arabs who feel deeply threatened, both materially and psychologically, and however evil their response, telling them to stop neither resolves their problems nor reassures the government of Sudan that it can be secure if there is a truce, especially because after such awful persecutions, it is certain that the black non-Arabs will want to avenge themselves, in addition to demanding security of land tenure and economic help (Prunier 2005).

Could this conflict be turned into something less than a life and death struggle in which both sides come to fear that losing will mean their utter destruction? What might have been done at an earlier stage to lessen the likelihood of unrestrained warfare? Why, in desperate situations, do religious exhortations like the one cited above in the Quran have so little effect—explained away as not applicable or not violated, or as Janjaweed leader Musa Hilal suggests, both at the same time? As we now proceed to propose ways of addressing conflicts of this sort and the many others that beset the world, we will refer to Darfur as well as to many other situations to see how the large menu of suggestions we will make can be applied.

We will start with what might be called modern "macro" approaches that directly address state policies, either through initiatives that come from within the state or through the international system. It is the latter that the United Nations and the United States were trying to use in the Sudan to stop the killing in Darfur. In this case, as in others, however, we will see that no single approach is likely to solve long-term problems or stop the danger of recurring, extreme violence but that, rather, a mixture of solutions is necessary.

State Policies That Reduce Hostility between Groups

Bitter warfare between various competing groups over resources and power may be based on a variable combination of identities held by the contending groups. Ethnicity is the most commonly cited one, but as we have seen, religion, the region in which people live, or class (that is, economic) interests may be at the heart of conflict. Often, these get confused because rival groups interpret and legitimize their positions with whatever ideological tools are at hand. These, in turn, depend largely on the ideological bases of the main actors and their leaders. For Hitler, it was the Jewish race, that is, a biological construct, that was the enemy. For Stalin, kulaks were a hostile class. This was also the case when a Ming emperor in China set out to exterminate much of the Confucian bureaucracy and their families, a distinct class in the early fifteenth century. In Rwanda, Tutsis had previously been characterized by higher social prestige but were gradually transformed into a kind of almost hereditary caste and eventually into an ethnic group. When Protestants and Catholics fought each other in Europe in the sixteenth and seventeenth centuries, the main issue was religion. Regional location was the basis of William's destruction of Yorkshire in the eleventh century. In Sudan in 2003–5, ethnic cleansing is a combination of class (the economic competition between sedentaries and herders) and ethnicity (Arabs versus black non-Arabs), but the older and equally brutal war between the Arab Muslims in the north and the largely Christian and Animist southerners has been a combination of regional, religious, and ethnic warfare over political power and the control of resources, especially exportable oil.

All of these categories may be treated together because in practice they often overlap, and too scrupulous attention to definitions that make them completely distinct obscures the realities of intergroup conflict. Because the most common source of intergroup rivalries in the modern world is widely believed to be ethnicity, we can start with a discussion of different policy options that may be applied in multiethnic societies to deal with potential conflict. The conclusions drawn can then be applied to other situations where ethnicity is a less important source of identity between competing groups.

POLICIES DESIGNED TO DEAL WITH POTENTIAL ETHNIC COMPETITION WITHIN STATES

To begin, what are ethnic groups? Social scientists sometimes prefer to refer to *ethnies*, but leaving this terminological twist aside, Anthony Smith's definition is workable (he prefers *ethnie* to ethnic group). An ethnic group has a name for itself (we are the Irish, the Basques, the Han Chinese, the Cherokees). In other words, an ethnic group is composed of individuals who recognize one another as group members. It has a myth of common ancestry (we believe we originally all came from a small number of common ancestors). The group shares memories (we have struggled and survived throughout history), though these may be largely legendary. Specific cultural habits distinguish the group from others (often but not always a language; sometimes a religion; usually preferences for certain foods, arts, music, or other activities at which group members are thought to excel; or any number and combination of such attributes, attitudes, and ways of doing things). Finally, the ethnic group's members believe they have a link with a common homeland (which may be real or mythical), and some solidarity exists between elites within the group. The notion of a common heredity is often at least partly fictitious, but over time endogamy may reinforce biological commonality. Ethnic histories are practically always exaggerations, but they provide a basis for solidarity, particularly between leading members of the community (Geary 2002; A. Smith 2001, 13).

Ethnic groups are close to being what we now call nations, except that they do not always have their own state. Almost every modern state, however, contains some groups who are identified as different ethnicities. Some states explicitly are based on the notion that they are or should be a single ethnic group (Japan and Korea are the large modern nations closest to being monoethnic), whereas others have a far broader sense of what holds them together. In the United States, for example, a variety of different ethnic groups are considered legitimately "American" by virtue of sharing a common name, a common history, a common public culture that does not conflict with private or family cultural habits that may vary, and a common sense of obligation and loyalty to the nation. Some states are clearly not very united, and their various ethnic, religious, and regional groups share little common loyalty. This was very much the case in premodern agrarian states and remains true in most of Africa and parts of Asia today (A. Smith 2001, 21–42).

In the very effort to define ethnicity and nation we can see one of the common tensions that arise in almost every state. How can loyalty be assured? Can different, self-conscious ethnic groups be united to form a common nation? If not, how much will the state be weakened? Will it be split and destroyed? In the modern world, when central governments dispose of enormous resources and powers, any person's life chances are shaped by educational, economic, and political opportunities dispensed by the state, so if some groups are excluded from benefiting or see themselves as benefiting less than others, they are likely to be increasingly disloyal. Modern states and economies cannot survive very well unless there are at least some shared loyalties and habits, so any state has a strong interest in creating a common nationalism, or somehow dealing with those it does not fully incorporate to lessen the danger of disunity (Gellner 1983). It is precisely because it has few states with genuine national unity that Africa is so beset by many civil wars. Most African states are weak but still control enough resources so that those ethnic groups who do not have access to the resources dispensed by the state are likely in difficult times to rebel and try to seize power for their own group (Herbst 2000). Indeed, the competition to control African states is particularly desperate because non-state resources tend to be scarce.

There is very widespread agreement among academic specialists that both ethnicity and nation are flexible categories with boundaries that are subject to change. Italian immigrants who came to the United States in the nineteenth century rarely identified with the Italian state that was still very new, unlike the Italian elites at home who did share a common nationalism. In the United States, however, they became Italians because they were all lumped together as a category that was considered not quite white, particularly in the American South where they were placed somewhere in the social hierarchy between blacks and whites. A hundred years later their descendants are "Italian Americans" and part of what Americans seem to consider a common "white" or "Caucasian" race (Fenton 2003, 30–31; Handlin 1973, 166–67).

Throwing in the concept of "race" further complicates matters, because in some cases it means the same thing as ethnicity, though in some societies, such as the United States, it is associated with skin color. Surprisingly, the definition of skin color itself is also somewhat subjective. Most Sudanese Arabs are dark-skinned, but distinguish themselves from "black" non-Arabs, and this is one of the bases of the genocidal ethnic cleansing in Sudan. Tutsis and Hutus who had long intermarried and spoke the same language developed historical myths that identified themselves as difference races, though of course, in the United States, Brazil, or Sudan they would both be considered equally black and of the same race. Race is best treated as a variant of ethnicity as long as we keep in mind the fact that definitions do vary over time. What matters most is how groups identify themselves and how they are defined by their neighbors with whom they live and may compete for resources.

Michael Hechter, synthesizing the received wisdom of the best nineteenth- and twentieth-century scholarship on nationalism emphasizes the subjective element of nations and ethnic groups. "Nations," he writes, "constitute a subset of ethnic groups. They are territorially concentrated ethnic groups" (2000, 14). No set of completely objective criteria can ever define either nations or ethnicity, though in all cases members of each can point to strong commonalties among themselves. What are called tribes in Africa are ethnic groups that, if they are large and concentrated enough, fit the definition of what we would call nations. Nations, ultimately, are ethnic groups that make some claim to having a state of their own and consist of substantial majorities of people who agree that it is in their interest and a part of their ultimate destiny to have their own sovereign state. Of course, once a state is formed, it usually tries to convince as many of its people as possible that they form a natural nation (A. Smith 2001, 22).

Strategies for Dealing with Minorities within the State

	Inclusion	*Distinction*	*Exclusion*
Tolerant	Gentle assimilation	Multiculturalism	Voluntary separation or emigration
Intolerant	Forced assimilation	Segregation	Ethnic cleansing or genocide

Given the fact that almost all modern states contain various mixtures of ethnic groups, some of whom are themselves numerous and concentrated enough to potentially lay claim to nationhood, what are the methods employed to handle divergent group interests in order to hold the state together? The various policies toward different ethnicities within a state dominated by a particular nationality are summarized in the accompanying table, which is an adaptation of the ideas put forward by McGarry and O'Leary (1995) and summarized by Brendan O'Leary in his own chart (in Chirot and Seligman 2001, 44). Our schema proposes that there are either tolerant or intolerant styles of dealing with minorities, and three distinct kinds of strategies, each of which may be on the more tolerant or intolerant side. These strategies are inclusion, distinction (the maintenance of characteristic identities through a kind of compromise), or attempts at exclusion.

When we consider examples of each of these approaches, it is quite clear that the more intolerant and the more exclusive a strategy used, the more likely it is to lead to violence and mass political murder. Looking at just one national history, that of the United States, we can observe all of these approaches being used at one time or another, though to very different degrees. With respect to immigrants from Europe, American policies have generally been ones of tolerant inclusion, and these have worked to produce, if not a perfect melting pot, at least some considerable unity of customs, a common national identity, and quite strong political loyalty. But this assimilation was not always entirely tolerant, and it was based, as Anthony Smith puts it, on the assumption that others would have to assimilate to, that is, adapt to, the "cultural base of a Protestant English ethnie" (2001, 42). Others could continue to worship where they wished, eat whatever foods they wanted, and claim some sort of affinity with the people in their ancestral homes, but they had to send their children to American schools, behave increasingly like English Protestants, and limit their ethnic distinctiveness to superficial or symbolic behavior. At the same time, African Americans, even after being liberated from slavery, were maintained in the South as a distinctive, unassimilated ethnic group by legal segregation. Outside the South, segregation remained the rule as well, though not usually through legal discrimination.

With respect to African Americans, however, there was also a movement even before the Civil War to encourage voluntary emigration back to Africa, that is, tolerant exclusion. This policy option was actually favored by Abraham Lincoln before he became president, though the numbers who ever emigrated to Liberia, which was established for this purpose, remained very small (A. Marx 1998, 59). The United States has also practiced genocidal ethnic cleansing of some of its Native American populations, as we saw in the preceding chapters. Finally, in the past several decades, the United States has become much more of a genuinely multicultural society that accepts different ethnic identities without insisting as much on assimilation. Whether that will work or not, or whether it is really something that will lead to a new kind of tolerant assimilation remains to be seen, but it is yet one more strategy meant to deal with ethnic and cultural diversity. On the whole, given the success of tolerant assimilation in its past, it is likely that continuing this approach, broadening it to include all the various ethnic groups in America, and mixing in a dose of toleration for some multiculturalism will keep competition between ethnic groups nonviolent. There are, however, serious voices, such as that of noted political scientist Samuel Huntington, who claim that multiculturalism cannot work and that if the United States is unwilling to enforce assimilation, it should consider excluding further immigrants, especially from Latin America (2004). This is a kind of relatively benign exclusion that is far from being an expulsion, but would nevertheless be an admission that neither multiculturalism nor assimilation work in this case to preserve national unity and America's democratic, relatively tolerant political culture.

France is frequently held up as the European nation that has for centuries most successfully practiced cultural assimilation in order to create a common culture. Beginning with an assortment of Germanic tribes, Gallic remnants, and immigrants from throughout the Roman Empire, its monarchy forged an aristocracy that became French, then a bourgeoisie that considered itself French emerged, and finally, with the French Revolution, this identification was gradually spread to the masses. In the nineteenth century, widespread education and the military draft of all young men for several years finally produced the French nation we know today, one that is willing to assimilate some immigrants but that is not highly tolerant of those who refuse to become "French" (Geary 2002, 5–6; A. Smith 1986, 90–91; and more generally, E. Weber 1976).

Premodern empires typically practiced something close to the tolerant maintenance of distinction, that is, a kind of genuine multiculturalism that did not force different ethnic groups, (or usually, different religions) to assimilate to the dominant linguistic, cultural, or religious elite. This tolerance, however, was limited to the internal affairs of communities and excluded them from participating in state affairs. Writing about Jews, Greeks, and Armenians in the seventeenth century Ottoman Empire, Karen Barkey points out that they were ". . . established as communities, with internal jurisdiction for their affairs. . . . [But] they were never given autonomy for more than internal issues of community government." They could maintain their religion and internal customs, but the imperial government made sure that did not affect other groups in the society, much less the state's own power (Barkey 1994, 43). To the extent that this suited minority communities, the practice could not be called segregation, but it was not what modern Americans mean by multiculturalism.

Nevertheless, this was a situation far more tolerant and peaceful than what emerged as the Ottoman Empire tried to modernize and turn itself into a united national state. Following the model of the successful European nation-states, starting with France, that had become sufficiently culturally homogeneous to create united national economies and populations that could be mobilized for war, the Ottoman Empire turned to a policy that abandoned toleration. After weak and largely unsuccessful attempts to force assimilation into a common Ottoman identity, in the early twentieth century it turned to religion and ethnicity to insist that the Ottoman Empire was to be Turkish and Muslim. Those who could not fit into this mold, particularly the large non-Muslim minorities, were eventually cleaned out by forcible expulsion and genocide, such that within fifty years, what was left was an almost entirely Muslim society with a large majority that identified itself as Turkish (Bozdoğan and Kasaba 1997, 28–30).

This particular strategy worked, though at the cost of more than a million Greek and Armenian lives and mass deportations of Christians from Turkey and Muslims from Greece (which itself followed a very similar nationalizing policy in favor of Greek Christians). As the preferred nationalizing strategy of the Turkish state, however, this method has left that country in a difficult position toward its minority Kurdish population. The Muslim Kurds have resisted forcible and highly intolerant assimilationist policies, and this led Turkey into a civil war in the 1990s that resulted in tens of thousands of deaths. Contemporary Turkey has no plan to exterminate or expel Kurds, but it is clear that harshly intolerant, forced assimilation policies that denied even the existence of a Kurdish ethnicity and language, combined with continuing poverty in largely Kurdish southeastern Turkey, have not worked. Only a more tolerant policy, combining elements of assimilation with an acceptance of at least some multiculturalism, is more likely to lead to a peaceful resolution of this situation (McDowall 1997, 395–444).

Federalism is a particular form of multiculturalism that amounts to a kind of regional division of power. Federalism can also promote relatively peaceful accommodation by providing regions with distinctive ethnic minorities a substantial amount of self-government. This was the Swiss path to national unity in a state split along both religious (Catholic-Protestant) and linguistic (French-German-Italian) lines. (The fourth official language, Romansch, is spoken in a few isolated mountain regions of the southeast by less than 1 percent of the population.) As Jonathan Steinberg explains in the foreword of his book on that country, Switzerland is ". . . the Europe that did not happen, the Europe that escaped the centralization of state and economy associated with the modern world" (1996). In the twentieth century, what had been a loose confederation of virtually self-governing cantons became a self-consciously unified nation in which there is more centralization than in the past, but where cultural diversity has been maintained. Even today, few in or out of Switzerland care who the Swiss president is; he does not wield much power.

Canada has had a somewhat similar experience. In Quebec, the entrenched historical resentment of its French speakers against the dominant Canadian English speakers has created a strong separatist movement. Because Canada is a federation that gives its provinces considerable power, French-speaking Quebec rules itself with its own language. There are periodic moves to secede, but none has succeeded so far, and if one did, by referendum, few think that would produce any violence. The continuing resentment of the Quebecois has for decades been absorbed by Canada's federalist system and by the protection given to the French language that makes it legally the equal of English. A discussion by Quebecois intellectuals about the situation yields unending threats and gloomy predictions, but the fact is that in Canada even a separation would shift the situation from one of tolerant multiculturalism to one of tolerant separation (Bothwell 1995).

A much more contentious example is India, which has maintained itself as a functioning, highly diverse state since independence, despite continuing secessionist civil wars in some of its parts. Its success, despite a high degree of ethnic and religious violence in some of its provinces, shows that it is possible for a federal solution to work in a poor country, too. Because it is both democratic and federal, it allows opposition to express itself and gives locally dominant ethnic and religious regional groups who are minorities within India itself the right to substantially govern themselves even if they are not part of the dominant northern Hindu culture. India survives and has managed to create a sense of nationhood. Rearranging provincial boundaries to satisfy the linguistic and religious demands of minorities clamoring for—and sometimes fighting wars for—self-rule has contributed immensely to holding India together (Seton-Watson 1977, 296–303).

India's success so far in containing its separatist civil wars, some of which have involved quite horrible massacres of civilians, is much harder to explain than the simpler situation in wealthy Switzerland or

Canada. Allowing local ethnic groups power is part of the answer, but it is more complicated than that. Ashutosh Varshney writes that whenever Indian politics have seemed to veer toward the kind of religious or ethnic extremism that might turn its internal struggles into bloody chaos, it has turned back. In large part he ascribes this to the persistence of democracy and the need of regional, often ethnic or religiously based parties who control their province, to compromise in order to gain a share of national power. He observes that "India has a dispersed, not a centrally focused ethnic configuration. Since independence no single Indian identity or cleavage—religious, linguistic, caste—has had the power to override all other identities at the national level. . . . To come to power in Delhi, politicians must build bridges and coalitions across cleavages. In short, because of India's multicultural diversity, its politics is oriented towards ideological centrism" (Varshney 2002, 73–74, 85). Therefore, though there have been bloody local wars, no central Indian government has ever contemplated either genocide or ethnic cleansing to maintain control. To do so would alienate so many ethnicities and religions in the various provinces that it would spell the doom of India as a unified country. Instead, it has continued to be ruled as a multicultural democracy.

Multicultural federalism does not always work. In Yugoslavia, as we have seen in previous chapters, it led to the domination of two regions, Serbia and Croatia, by hypernationalist leaders prepared to use xenophobia as a way to obtain and stay in power, and that, in turn, led to civil war, genocidal ethnic cleansing, and the destruction of the state. The fact that when it was unified Yugoslavia had not been a democracy and that bargaining between regionally powerful ethnic groups had not involved electoral and parliamentary coalitions and compromises certainly played a role in this collapse. On the other hand, in federal Czechoslovakia, democracy brought increased ethnic tensions between Czechs and Slovaks, and this resulted in a peaceful separation of the federation, not in war. This was a solution that amounts to tolerant exclusion, as the majority Czechs permitted a Slovak divorce to create a more unified and more smoothly functioning national state of their own (Janos 1997). We do not need a complete explanation of the difference between Czechoslovakia and Yugoslavia to note the obvious. Tolerant, peaceful divorce is a better way to settle what seems to be an irreconcilable ethnic split than war and attempted ethnic cleansing, and such a divorce is a good way of keeping conflict at a reasonable level. It is interesting to note that separatist Quebecois now cite the Czechoslovak example as a peaceful model they could follow if Quebec ever became independent (Bothwell 1995, 244–48). If federalism does not work, tolerant, benign exclusion is the next step, but that requires political elites to forgo war as a way of settling boundaries.

One final, closely related variation of the multicultural and federal solution is what has been called by political scientist Arend Lijphart *consociationalism.* This is drawn from the Dutch example of a plural society originally designed to accommodate Catholic-Protestant conflicts by creating parallel systems, or "pillars" that allowed the two religions to function separately, draw equally from state resources, but remain together as members of one nation. What the Dutch call "pillarization" has been extended to include those who are not religious, and there is discussion about including an Islamic "pillar" to incorporate immigrants (Lijphart 1977; Zijderveld 1998). Lijphart, however, takes the notion much further and examines a number of multiethnic countries that have tried to remain united through multicultural toleration enforced by a division of power between different groups, as in the Swiss, Indian, and Canadian cases.

An interesting and successful example of relatively tolerant consociationalism, also cited by Lijphart, has been used to hold Malaysia together. There, the main ethnoreligious issue was that the large Chinese non-Muslim minority held dominant positions in the economy, but the poorer and on average less-educated Muslim majority controlled the political process. As in many other cases, the mixture of ethnicities is quite complex and has varied significantly over time, not only because of differential birth and migration rates, but also because of changing definitions of who belonged to what group (C. Hirschman 1987). At independence from British colonial rule in 1957, peninsular Malaysia, the main part of the country, probably had more ethnic Chinese than Malays until the peaceful expulsion of Singapore that created a distinct Malay plurality. Then, over time, the greater birthrate of Malays gave them a majority, while the Chinese proportion of the population shrank. The situation is complicated by the presence of a large number of people of Indian descent and of non-Muslim natives in the parts of Malaysia on the (nonpeninsular) island of Borneo. By the early 1990s, some 57 percent of peninsular Malaysia (which holds the large majority of the state's population and economy) was Malay, 29 percent was Chinese, and about 10 percent was Indian (Lee 2000, 29).

Rather than setting out on a policy of expropriation and perhaps expulsion, or of brutal subordination of the Chinese, the Malay government created an affirmative action policy that promoted Malays and gave Malay entrepreneurs special advantages. Chinese cultural expression was somewhat limited until about 1990, but never suppressed, and since 1991 it has been quite free. Chinese political parties were permitted, and the strongest one was brought into an alliance with the dominant Malay party, where it was able to defend Chinese interests. Here the existence of democracy, however imperfect, played a key role. Chinese schools continued to be allowed, and though public universities discriminated heavily in favor of Malays, private ones were allowed to cater to the Chinese (Lee 2000).

Perhaps most important, private entrepreneurship was accepted, along with significant foreign investment. This enabled spectacular economic growth for three decades and enriched every group (Lim and Gosling 1997, 285). In 1965, with British interests still predominant, the Chinese owned about 23 percent of corporate shares in Malaysia, the Malays less than 2 percent, the Indians less than 1 percent, and foreigners, mostly British, about 62 percent. The remainder were state-owned, so therefore under Malay control, but even taking that into account, Malays owned no more that 14 percent. By 1995, the British share had shrunk dramatically, though new Japanese investment had made great inroads in the now much larger economy. The Malay share (including state companies and special trusts run by Malays) had increased to about 29 percent, the Chinese share to almost 41 percent, the Indian share to 1.5 percent, and the foreign share was only about 28 percent (Jomo 1997, 245).

Malaysia has hardly been a model of perfect toleration, but it has combined a relatively accommodating policy toward the more entrepreneurial minority, affirmative action for the poorer majority, and acceptance of multiculturalism. In conjunction with rapid economic growth that has enriched all communities and created a powerful Malay middle class, this combination has significantly eased ethnic tensions. In 1969, there were serious ethnic riots between Chinese and Malays, with hundreds of dead. The prognosis seemed to be that Malaysia was heading for a deadly ethnic war. A third of a century later, the different communities continue to coexist and to have distinct interests and identities, but there has been almost no violence since then. From 1970 to 1995, the per capita Malay income grew by 830 percent while the per capita Chinese income grew by 635 percent. Thus, whereas the Chinese on average had incomes 2.29 times that of average Malays in 1970, that number had fallen somewhat to a multiple of 1.81 by 1995 (Lee 2000, 18, 25–26).

It should be evident from the examples just presented that what works for easing ethnic conflict is essentially the same as what can work when communities identify themselves on religious grounds. In practice, the line between religious and ethnic identification is often close to being the same. Most Malays (but not all) are Muslims. Most Chinese in Malaysia (but not all) are Christians or Buddhists. Most Croats are Catholics, and most Serbs are Orthodox Christians. Regional identifications also tend to become something close to ethnic ones. Of the major dividing lines, economic class is different, but it can be accommodated by somewhat analogous strategies.

What should be noted is that when class identifications are strong but class interests cut across ethnic, religious, or regional lines, the prospects for toleration and conflict resolution strategies are high. Thus, middle-class and entrepreneurial Malays share common interests in Malaysia with middle-class Chinese, and this lessens ethnic conflict. In fact, recent research in Malaysia shows that economic growth has created cross-ethnic alliances but has also produced splits within each ethnic community (Lee 2000, 26). This may exacerbate class conflict but makes ethnic warfare less likely.

Unfortunately, not all attempts to fashion a division of power succeed. Consociationalism is no more of a guarantee than federalism that either toleration or peace will survive a crisis, even in cases where a genuine democratic process exists. The most notorious failure of consociationalism has been in Lebanon, where a careful balancing of power between its various Orthodox and Catholic Christian, Muslim Sunni and Shiite, and Druze groups devolved into a vicious civil war that lasted from 1975 to 1991 (El-Khazen 2000; Khalidi 1986). To be sure, much of the problem had to do with outside interference from Palestinian militias as well as direct Syrian and Israeli military involvement. Also, as the Muslim population grew much faster than the Christians, it demanded more power, something that the original arrangement had not envisioned. The breakdown occurred, however, because the division of power among various ethnoreligious groups in this case could produce moments of peace but could never create a Lebanese national identity capable of uniting these groups against outside interference or able to overcome the suspicions and hostilities among themselves.

Tolerant assimilation, tolerant multiculturalism under various structural forms, and even peaceful exclusion in the form of splitting off parts of the state can greatly diminish the probability of violent conflict, and if there is violence, make it easier to control and limit. This can take the form of giving various communities a measure of self-rule, respecting their cultures, absorbing and co-opting their elites into a central political structure, or some combination of these. But how does one promote that kind of tolerance in order to avoid Lebanese or Yugoslav kinds of intolerance that have repeatedly led to ethnic cleansing and genocide? No structural adjustment can entirely guarantee tolerance.

Returning to a kind of Ottoman imperial maintenance of distinctive communities with internal autonomy is highly impractical in today's world, as it involves living with a state that provides very few services, is relatively undemanding of resources, and is content to leave communities alone as long as they pay enough taxes to support the central power and do not themselves pretend to be the equals of their political masters. The days of these kinds of agrarian empires are long over. States are expected to have and deliver more resources, so that control by one community or another is far more critical than in the past. Thus, the kinds of power inequalities that characterized the relatively tolerant empires of the past are no longer acceptable; most minority communities demand a greater share of those state resources. If they do not get them, and if they believe they are suffering as a consequence, conflict is likely. Without some mechanism to channel this in manageable ways, the possibility of murderous violence increases.

Returning to the Sudanese example, federalism with a considerable degree of local autonomy would create a system in which local problems and demands could be handled without attempts at genocidal ethnic cleansing. The central government, however, would have to remain tolerant of cultural and economic differences, as has the government of India, and not try to impose a single ethnic or religious hegemony. Conflicts over scarce resources would continue, but their consequences would be less dire. It was just such an arrangement that led to a period of peace in the Sudan between 1972 and 1983. What shattered this peace was the Sudanese government's attempt to maintain itself in power by catering to the ideological program of the northern Arab Muslim fundamentalists. As most of the south was not Muslim, war between the north and the south resumed, and the Muslim Arabs dramatically failed to follow Quranic prescriptions about limited warfare. The religious intolerance of the fundamentalist Muslims combined with their political power made structural adjustments fail, and that ended the peace. In discussing this history of Sudan, Donald Rothchild stresses the fact that interests can be negotiated, but not principles (1997, 229–39).

In 2004, the shift in bloody warfare to Darfur indicates that the Sudanese government, for all its willingness to negotiate with the south out of necessity, still considers total warfare a solution for problems in regions where those who protest central government policies are too weak to fight the center to a stalemate. Needless to say, this augurs poorly for maintaining the truce in the south, too, and the prospects that a unified sense of Sudanese nationhood will emerge to bind together the country are extremely low. Though it is not on the international agenda, and would be resisted by the dominant Arab northerners who want to maintain control over oil and other potential resources throughout this land, splitting this giant, unmanageable state is probably the only way to achieve long-term peace.

The international system that exists in the early twenty-first century, and has dominated since the end of World War II, does not favor splitting supposedly sovereign nations. This is probably why so many civil wars now last longer than they would have in the past (Hironaka 2005). In Africa, only the Eritrean-Ethiopian split has been internationally recognized, though clearly in some other cases it is warranted. Barring a split, another solution proposed for Sudan, and sometimes applied in other cases, most notably in Bosnia since 1995, is to have international forces try to impose a more tolerant model involving some sort of federalism or consociationalism on an internally divided and potentially or actually genocidal state. This strategy, difficult to apply and offering very mixed results, has to be looked at more carefully. It, too, can sometimes help but is both expensive and sometimes impractical because it does not address the deep-seated problems that led to mass killing in the first place.

INTERNATIONALLY IMPOSED SOLUTIONS TO DEAL WITH CONFLICT WITHIN STATES

International rules have long existed concerning how to conduct warfare in a decent way, predated by religious rules about just and unjust war. It has been only relatively recently, however, that forceful occupations of territories and sovereign nations for the avowed purpose of stopping mass murder, ethnic cleansing, or massive violation of human rights have been undertaken. Christian Europe's interventions in Ottoman affairs in the nineteenth century were in some ways humanitarian efforts to resolve deadly ethnic conflicts, but it was only Christian minorities that benefited from such attention (Kaiser 2000, 308–10). In fact, along with their intercessions on behalf of Christian minorities, the European powers had quite selfish trading and economic interests when they did involve themselves in that region. When the newly independent Christian Balkan states carved out of the Ottoman Empire in the nineteenth and early twentieth centuries massacred each other in dreadful wars, western European powers did not seek to intervene for humanitarian purposes but rather favored their own clients and pursued broader strategic alliances (Glenny 2000).

Much the same can be said of the U.S. interventions against Spain in 1898 that claimed to be on behalf of the Cuban people being abused by their colonial government, and to liberate the Philippines. Cuba was indeed revolting against Spanish rule and being harshly suppressed, but the U.S. intrusion quickly turned into an imperialist war that subjected Cuba to indirect rule and simply seized the Philippines from Spain. Filipinos who had wanted independence from Spain fought bitterly against the U.S. occupation, and this resulted in a three-year war of repression. Between one hundred thousand and two hundred thousand Filipinos died as a result of the brutal tactics used against them, including the large-scale slaughter of civilians by the Americans (Valentino 2004, 83, 201–4; Walzer 1977, 102–4; Zakaria 1998, 159). As humanitarian interventions, these were not models to be emulated.

World War II's horrors changed the way in which wartime mass murder was viewed. The Nazi's genocidal program was too extreme to be passed off as just the unpleasant side effects of battle, and war crime tribunals were established, the most important of which were the Nuremburg trials of German war criminals. The Nuremburg trials, and to a much lesser extent the Tokyo trials, set the basis for the adoption of the United Nations antigenocide convention in 1948 and have served as a precedent for late-twentieth- and early-twenty-first-century international interventions and tribunals for the crime of genocide (Weitz 2003, 253). There is no evidence, however, that the British, Americans, or Soviet Union originally entered the war against the Germans and Japanese to stop the terrible acts being committed by those regimes. As Yehuda Bauer has movingly argued, even in the face of persuasive evidence about the genocide of Jews in Europe by the Germans, American and British authorities had a hard time believing that this was going on. Nor did they want to appear to act primarily to save Jews, because this risked diminishing the legitimacy of their own war efforts. Anti-Semitism was still widespread, and in any case, they were not in a position to do much about the problem until they had actually defeated Germany (Bauer 2002, 213–24). Rather, the allies fought the war to save themselves, but once they had defeated the Axis powers, and particularly after liberating the ghastly Nazi death camps, perceptions changed.

Partly because knowledge of what happened during that war shocked public opinion in the Western democracies, a precedent was set for military intervention on humanitarian grounds. But this measure has been used very rarely because it is so costly, and also because there is usually little agreement about the nature or reasons for mass killing while it is going on. There is no evidence that international discussion and exposure of abuses on ethnic, religious, or political grounds has much effect on governments that engage in such behavior. The most brutal regimes, in fact, are the ones least likely to be swayed by moral arguments. Ultimately, a resort to force remains necessary if the most terrible mass killings are to be stopped. The principal reason for this is that massive political murder and ethnic cleansing are typically the result of a breakdown between communities. The perpetrators and soon the victims come to see what is happening as a struggle for survival with no rules. What may have begun as something planned and encouraged by political elites becomes a mass affair. Mere exhortation under these conditions does nothing to change the circumstances that led to the genocidal behavior, and calling the perpetrators criminals does little to stop them because they are already likely to be afraid that failure will cost them their lives. This is why two years of debate about the killings and ethnic cleansing in Darfur from 2003 to 2005 did so little to help.

Still, a few forceful international interventions have occurred, and some have stopped genocides in the making, even if they have rarely succeeded in creating a benign climate of trust between hostile communities. In 1971, East Pakistan (now Bangladesh) revolted against rule by West Pakistan. The West Pakistani army launched a brutal war of repression. Estimates of the number of people killed varies wildly, as it generally does in such cases because records are not kept, but the range is somewhere between a half million and three million (Valentino 2004, 77). If one takes into account the high death rate among refugees driven into camps, however, it seems likely that at least a million died. The main issue was that East Pakistani Bengalis wanted self-rule and had won an overwhelming majority of seats from their region in a relatively free election. Rather than bargaining in good faith, the dominant West Pakistanis, whose cultures and languages were different from that of the Bengalis, despite their shared Islamic religion, set about to repress dissent. They used West Pakistanis living in East Pakistan (called Biharis, though most did not come from the Indian province of Bihar) and the powerful Pakistani army to initiate a series of massacres, village burnings, rapes, and assassinations of Bengali elites. The Bengalis organized a resistance and in their turn committed atrocities against Biharis and immigrants from India, some of whom remain to this day as impoverished refugees in India and Bangladesh (Horowitz 2001, 164, 174; L. Kuper 1981, 76–80).

There is no telling how many more would have died had this war continued. Given the concentrated, large population of Bangladesh, the hostility aroused by the slaughters, and the distance separating West from East Pakistan, it is unlikely that the West Pakistanis could have prevailed indefinitely. As it was, however, India, the enemy of Pakistan, invaded East Pakistan, and the Pakistanis were quickly defeated. Bangladesh became independent, and the Indians withdrew. This was unquestionably a humanitarian intervention that put an end to a genocidal war that might have killed millions more. That India saw an opportunity to dismember its enemy Pakistan does not negate the fact that after assuring a Bangladeshi victory, it quickly pulled out. In this respect, the Indian action was, in Michael Walzer's terms, a "just war" (Walzer 1977, 105–7). It should be noted that international hand-wringing and exhortation did not put a stop to the massacres; military action by a major power did. Flawed as such interventions may be, in extreme cases they may be the only way to prevent genocide.

More recently, and for less obviously self-interested reasons, the United States intervened militarily twice in Yugoslavia, once to help defeat the Serbs in Bosnia in 1995, and the second time to stop the expulsion of Albanians from Kosovo by the Serbs in 1999. The first action was the culmination of a process through which NATO, led by the United States, helped build up a strong Croatian army capable of defeating the Serbs. In July 1995, after United Nations troops had stood by while Serbs massacred eight thousand Muslims in Srebrenica, the United States finally threatened a more direct involvement and actually used its air force to bomb Serb positions. Slobodan Milošević, realizing he would be unable to defeat the largely American NATO military effort, dropped his support for the Bosnian Serbs and agreed to a complex treaty, the Dayton Accords, which guaranteed a multicultural, tolerant, federalized Bosnia. Unfortunately, as Misha Glenny noted, and as remains true to this day, the peace in Bosnia is tenuous (2000, 642–52). There are some signs of progress, and there is no war; but after ten years of European supervision and the presence of a large peacekeeping force, the agreements between Serbs, Croats, and Muslims are grudging, and there are few signs of genuine tolerance, much less reconciliation (Abadie 2004).

The situation in Kosovo is even less stable or conciliatory. After years of what amounted to repressive segregation by Serbs and exclusion from power or state-provided benefits, Albanians began a rebellion that the Serbian government could not master. Pushed into an untenable situation, the Milošević government moved to the next level, ethnic cleansing, in 1999. In response, NATO, again using mostly U.S. airpower, began a bombing campaign against Serbia that led to its withdrawal from Kosovo. This was quickly followed by the murder and forced ethnic cleansing of the Serbian minority from most of Kosovo by the Albanians (Glenny 2000, 661–62). U.S. and European troops, and a subsequent European-led United Nations occupation have failed completely to promote any kind of tolerance or even truce between Albanians and Serbians in Kosovo. Killings have continued, and the Serbians would be ethnically cleansed if they were not under armed protection. If, on the other hand, the outside world were not involved, Serbia would probably invade and reoccupy the province (*Economist* 2004a; Wood 2004). Again, outside intervention did stop the mass murder and ethnic cleansing but has not brought a self-sustaining peace.

One of the presumed triumphs of external intervention in the Yugoslav wars was the eventual overthrow of Slobodan Milošević in October 2000 by his own people, tired of their increasing poverty and isolation. Milošević was eventually turned over in June 2001 to an international tribunal to be judged for his war crimes. This, and a similar war crimes tribunal to deal with those responsible for the Rwandan genocide are now frequently cited as examples of how an international rule of law can punish leaders who have ordered genocidal acts and create an international climate that, by criminalizing such acts, will prevent them.

The legal basis for the trial is a United Nations 1993 resolution to set up an International Criminal Tribunal for the Former Yugoslavia. This resolution is based on the precedent of the Nuremburg trials of Nazis (Grosscup 2004, 355–81). The tribunal has successfully prosecuted a small number of others for the mass murders perpetrated during the Yugoslav wars, but the Milošević trial dragged on for years at great expense without ever being resolved before his death in 2006. Nor has it done much to help ameliorate the continuing ethnic hostilities in this region (Judah 2004, 23–25).

Much the same kind of argument can be made with respect to the Rwanda tribunal that is also costly and has been bogged down for years. In both the Yugoslav and Rwandan cases it should be pointed out that there would have been no end to the genocides and ethnic cleansing without military action (victory by the Tutsi rebel army in Rwanda, American-led NATO intervention in the Yugoslav wars). The same, of course, is true of the earlier trials of Nazi and Japanese leaders after World War II. Justice, whatever its merits, followed total military victory after both Germany and Japan had been flattened. In Yugoslavia and Rwanda, the trials have brought little reconciliation or toleration, and the intervention by outside powers would have been impossible had the Serbian and Hutu regimes been strong enough to resist. No one dreams of bringing Chinese leaders to justice for what they have done in Tibet or of arresting Vladimir Putin, the president of Russia, for Russian brutality in Chechnya. International action is a slender reed on which to count even when the offending state is relatively weak.

An *Economist* editorial about Darfur shows why this is so: "The great powers are not all pulling in the same direction. An arms embargo [against Sudan] would be a start, but Russia, which is selling fighter jets to Khartoum, is likely to oppose it. The threat of an oil embargo would be more potent. [Sudan depends on oil exports.] The French and Chinese governments may not like this idea, however, as their oil firms have interests in Sudan" (*Economist* 2004b).

The same piece goes on to suggest international intervention by "a coalition of the willing" on the model of Kosovo, but staffed with African soldiers. This is not very promising. After the American and British experience in Iraq in 2003–4, when their "coalition of the willing" turned out to be wildly unpopular almost everywhere in the world, and not even very well liked by the American and British publics, what big powers will do this? As for African soldiers, there are no African armies capable of handling such a giant task as bringing peace to Sudan, especially since Sudan's Muslim Arabs would call this a Christian Crusade and mobilize Islamic opinion against it (Sengupta 2004).

Another sad example of the ineffectiveness of other kinds of international intervention against oppressive governments that refuse to change is the case of Burma, or as its leaders call it, Myanmar. There the United States has been applying economic sanctions for fifteen years against a brutal, uncaring government that presses its people into forced labor, delivers few services, jails its opposition, persecutes its ethnic minorities, and engages in corrupt drug dealings. But European countries apply less stringent sanctions, while Asian countries, and especially China, apply none at all. So Burma's military rulers, their families, cronies, and allies are doing well while the vast majority suffer. As Jane Perlez of the *New York Times* points out, not only do sanctions fail to hurt the Burmese elite, but they probably make life even more difficult for its ordinary people (Perlez 2004; for more background on Burma, see Chirot 1996). Even worse is the case of Rwanda, discussed in the previous chapter, where an internationally established, United Nations–sponsored power-sharing agreement between rival Tutsi and Hutu political forces prompted the Hutu elite to engage in genocide in order to avoid its provisions (Prunier 1997, 223–29).

This does not mean that such efforts are completely without value. Any set of rules that limits conflict, even if it does not eliminate it, is worth having. Over time, if such tribunals become more routine, they will establish some sort of boundary about what is internationally acceptable or not, and the prosecution of a few cases, even if mostly symbolic, helps do that. As Guy Lesser notes in a recent article about the Milošević trial, "if such tribunals can be made to work, and succeed in earning world respect, they might help determine when peace enforcement is necessary and decisive collective international community action is imperative. Perhaps in [the] future, when policymakers begin to see a distant tragedy unfolding, the argument that they must take action because it is their legal duty to do so will start to sound like a winning one" (2004, 46). So, although international interventions are rare and do not guarantee peaceful resolutions, they do at least create the potential for applying international justice in a way that might, sometimes, deter future tragedies.

USING INTERNATIONAL PRESSURE TO BRING THE PERPETRATORS TO JUSTICE

It is this hope that animates a legal effort to create a universal system of human rights that would bring to trial those responsible for mass murder and the abuse of human rights. For example, Princeton University's Program in Law and Public Affairs has devised a set of principles on "universal jurisdiction" that brought together a group of respected jurists from many countries to draw up such a code. In her introduction to this proposed system, Mary Robinson, then the United Nations Commissioner for Human Rights, cites a number of promising precedents. Belgium was willing to prosecute officials in other countries who have violated human rights. The British House of Lords decreed in the case of Augusto Pinochet, a former dictator of Chile accused of having thousands tortured and killed when he took power in 1974, that former heads of state do not enjoy immunity under British law. When the United Nations took over the governance of Sierra Leone to end an extraordinarily bloody civil war in 2002, it specified that amnesty and pardon would not apply to international crimes of genocide as defined by the 1948 convention on that topic (and cited here at the start of chapter 1). Robinson concludes that "the exercise of universal jurisdiction holds the promise for greater justice for the victims of serious human rights violations around the world" (*Princeton Principles* 2001, 17–18).

The *Princeton Principles*, however, like all other such legal remedies, run into three problems: the issue of sovereignty, the question of definition, and the problem of enforcement. Supporters of the proposed laws answer the first by claiming that "with respect to serious crimes under international law (piracy, slavery, war crimes, crimes against peace, crimes against humanity, genocide, and torture) the official position of any accused person, whether as head of state or government or as a responsible government official, shall not relieve such person of criminal responsibility nor mitigate punishment" (29, 31).

That means that if a sovereign country designates a person, say its former president or a general, as innocent, some international authority may still prosecute, especially if the accused happens to visit the prosecuting country. In other words, the *Princeton Principles* simply deny this aspect of state sovereignty.

Granting that certain crimes may be prosecuted internationally, the question remains as to who then defines whether or not such crimes have been committed? In democratic Western countries, the issue may seem clear, but even there, it is heavily weighted by ideological and political considerations. Was dropping the atomic bomb on Hiroshima tantamount to genocide? Some would argue that it was, and others say not. The United States' war in Vietnam was undeclared. Were U.S. leaders, who rightly or wrongly believed they were serving the greater interests of freedom in the war against communist dictatorship, therefore criminals? Some would so argue; others would say not. The *Princeton Principles* raise the same question in a different way, by pointing out that "particular states [may] abuse universal jurisdiction to pursue politically motivated prosecutions. Mercenary governments and rogue prosecutors could seek to indict the heads of state or other senior public officials in countries with which they have political disagreements" (43). Unfortunately, it is not simply the worst and most obviously criminal "mercenary" governments and "rogue" prosecutors who are likely to abuse universal jurisdiction. Ingrained political problems such as the Israeli-Palestinian conflict, the Turkish-Kurdish dispute, revolutionary and counterrevolutionary warfare in Guatemala, hostilities in Algeria between its fundamentalist Muslims and its government, and dozens of other cases come to mind. There is no obvious answer to this question unless one were to suppose that everyone could agree about when self-defense of one nation's or one community's interests justify extreme measures.

Finally, the possibility of enforcement, as we have seen, supposes that the offending individuals have lost power or are not supported by a strong state. Enforcement against the officials of failed African states or of states unable to resist attacks by a great power, such as Serbia, might not be such a bad idea, since those standing accused have committed atrocities. But is a law that is enforced against the weak but not the strong a fair one?

This is not a counsel of despair, because establishing rules does contribute to limiting mayhem; but it is a reminder that international intervention is a tenuous way to solve such problems, particularly when few powers are able or willing to take military action and when powerful states are less likely to be subjected to the rules. Nevertheless, in democratic states, where public opinion counts, the existence of international laws that allow intervention and tribunals to judge those who have committed atrocities can make a limited contribution to reestablishing old-fashioned rules of war similar to those decreed long ago in the epigraph from the Quran at the start of this chapter. If we remember that limiting slaughter is often a more realistic option than establishing absolute justice or peace, then anything that reinforces rules of engagement between warring parties within particular states or between them is a positive development. Recall also that in chapter 3 we cited cases in the past where rules of conflict were gradually developed to limit the damages of warfare—rules that worked for considerable periods of time even though there was no enforcement mechanism. It is possible, therefore, to develop standards of decency even if they are not strictly policed.

It is important to emphasize, however, that rules to limit conflict do very little to establish a tolerant atmosphere or to solve competing ethnic, religious, or regional group disputes that lead to violence. To change social attitudes and create institutions able to promote tolerance requires something else. Macro-level, purely state-centered institutional reform that can be imposed from above or well-publicized efforts to bring perpetrators of mass murder to trial can make a contribution, but more modest solutions are sometimes equally or more important. We will return to the role of state-centered, macropolitical institutions and influence below, but first we need to look at lower-level ways of limiting the damage of intercommunal conflicts. These are not necessarily complete solutions, either, but without them the broad-scope remedies are almost certain to remain inadequate in the long run.

Limiting Demands for Justice and Revenge

There is an intermediate approach between large-scale institutional reforms from above and micro-level local projects—one that was pio-
neered by South Africa after its black majority gained power from the
segregationist apartheid white regime in 1994. We will discuss this strategy briefly before turning to genuinely small-scale ones.

When the white South African government negotiated the transfer
of power to Nelson Mandela's African National Congress (ANC) in
1994, this ended a decades-long struggle by majority black Africans to
obtain political equality, which meant power, from the minority whites,
who consisted mostly of Afrikaan descendants of Dutch settlers and
English-speaking white immigrants. Many of the English speakers were
descendants of or themselves immigrants from other European countries, including a sizable number of European Jews. The South African
ethnic situation was vastly more complicated than this, however, because it also included a number of major African-language groups that
regarded themselves as distinct ethnicities, as well as significant numbers of Asians, some from east Asia, but mostly descendants of Indian
immigrants who had come when South Africa had been a British colony. Mixed white-black people called *coloureds* were part of the picture,
too. Coloureds and Asians had been granted more privileges than
blacks under the old apartheid system, but not as many as whites
(A. Marx 1998, 84–119, 194–216).

Any sort of attempt to impose rule by one ethnic group over the
others would have ended in catastrophe, and Mandela understood this.
There had been what amounted to a civil war between the ANC and
the white government, with many thousands killed or imprisoned (including Mandela himself, from 1962 to 1990) and many cases of torture
by the government. Revenge against the whites who had oppressed his
people would result in white flight and the collapse of the relatively
prosperous economy. Domination by his own African ethnic group
would create a civil war with other Africans, a situation made all the
more plausible by the near civil war that was raging at that moment
between the ANC and a Zulu movement that had made a tactical alli-

ance with the white government. Furthermore, the ANC itself was potentially split between hard-line leftists who wanted to socialize the
economy by confiscating the wealthy whites' assets in mining, manufac-
turing, and farming, and accommodationists willing to settle for political power and gradual improvement of the situation for the many poor,
often unemployed, and undereducated blacks. As the apartheid system
fell apart in the early 1990s and the white government and the ANC
negotiated a transfer of power, the level of violence between black communities actually increased, such that from 1990 to 1994 nearly fifteen
thousand people were killed, a number almost three times as high as
in the preceding five years (Hamber 2001, 239–40; and more generally,
Sparks 1995).

Almost no knowledgeable observer predicted a happy ending, but
Mandela, helped by his moral authority and that of Archbishop Des-
mond Tutu, a black Anglican who had gained world fame as an advocate of peaceful change, devised a way out. What became known as the
Truth and Reconciliation Commission (TRC) was established, in
which those who had committed crimes in the pursuit of political ends
could confess and receive amnesty. This was to make everyone feel
better, to heal old wounds, and to make it clear that such crimes,
whether committed by whites or blacks, were not simply being swept
under the rug. For all but a tiny handful whose crimes were deemed
to be too extreme, there was to be no actual punishment (Hamber 2001,
246–56; Villa-Vicencio and Verwoerd 2000).

Nothing like this had ever been attempted, and it worked, at least up
to a point. South Africa turned into a working democracy, its economy
survived, and a formal reconciliation took place. The TRC is popularly
attributed a significant role in this success, although many disagree. For
many of the black victims who appeared before the TRC it was a difficult experience (Byrne 2004). They were promised economic compen-
sation, but little has been provided. They expected to see remorseful
perpetrators, but in many cases saw stony faces reciting in monotone
the horrors perpetrated. This was just sufficient to bring amnesty for
the speaker. Some had no word in their language for amnesty and believed that the government and the TRC were demanding that they

forgive their perpetrator. In short, it is not clear what victims took away from their experience at the TRC.

Perhaps more important politically is the experience of the TRC among the millions of South Africans who composed its audiences, both those who actually attended the sessions and the much larger number who saw them on television, or more numerous yet, listened to the radio. Though the usual form of audience research that would have measured intergroup attitudes and optimism for a "rainbow nation" before, during, and after the TRC broadcasts was not undertaken, a substitute of sorts is available.

Polls were conducted in 2001, after the TRC had completed its term (1995–2001), to see if people accepted its message (Gibson 2004). This message was fivefold: apartheid was a crime against humanity, the ideas behind apartheid were bad, the struggle to preserve apartheid was unjust, both those struggling for and those struggling against the apartheid system did unforgivable things to people, and the abuses under apartheid were committed by state institutions rather than by just a few evil individuals. The 2001 polling data showed that individuals who accepted this message had more positive intergroup attitudes than those who did not. So, at least among those who accepted the TRC's message, it may be that attitudes toward intergroup relations changed for the better. How many changed their minds is not known, but given the high level of hostility that had existed between groups before the TRC, that number could have been substantial.

Whether the current level of peace and democracy in South Africa will last is another question, as unemployment among blacks is still, in the early 2000s, at 40 to 50 percent; the whites who have stayed remain far richer than the overwhelming majority of blacks; crime rates are very high; and there is continuing anger among many blacks that justice has not been done. Yet, as in Malaysia, where the Malay middle and business classes share some interests with their Chinese equivalents, so is it in South Africa. There a slowly growing black middle class does not want to jeopardize its prosperity. This middle class's cross-cutting economic and ethnic interests work against each other to promote toleration of white wealth (Hamber 2001, 250–51; Murphy 2002). To be sure, there are many who see this outcome as unjust and who call for both more punishment and forced redistribution of wealth (Frost 1998; Mamdani 1996). Yet, it is this messy compromise that has made South Africa's somewhat miraculous emergence from violent conflict possible (see various positions on these issues by the authors in Rotberg and Thompson 2000). Whatever the reality, the TRC is given some of the credit for this outcome and thus has come to be seen as a solution in many other conflict situations.

There are now many "truth commissions" in conflict-ridden societies all over the world (Humphrey 2002). The problem, of course, is that in some ways the South African model is the exact opposite of what "justice" would call for, something completely missed by those who keep demanding that internal wars fought with desperate means that include murder, torture, and in some cases ethnic cleansing and genocidal acts be resolved by punishing those guilty of committing such crimes. If they were merely criminals, there would be no problem, but these political acts represent a set of interests, fears, and ideological commitments, not simple crimes. If justice means punishment, rather than a confession followed by a purely symbolic admission of guilt as in South Africa, there is no reason for those who have committed such acts to submit unless they have been totally defeated. Suspecting that punishment, confiscation of their property, imprisonment, or even death will ensue is unlikely to persuade them to accept a compromise peace. Had the South African government, its thousands of soldiers and policemen, politicians, and prominent elites felt that this would be their fate, they could have fought on for decades more, or at best, all fled, leaving the country in ruins. Is this what the calls for "justice" really mean to do?

Thoughtful people have come to contradictory conclusions on such issues. Aryeh Neier, a well-known human rights activist, takes the uncompromising position that the guilty should be punished, though it is not quite clear how far down the hierarchy of those who ordered and committed mass murder justice should go (1998). Martha Minow believes that truth commissions without retribution can help (2002, 24–29). Gary Bass has argued that the trial of a few top perpetrators on narrow legalistic grounds is a far better solution than either widespread vengeance or wholesale prosecutions. Any realistic assessment of what such justice can accomplish has to admit that its effects are limited, but such trials can at least produce good documentation of what abuses actually took place, and that is itself a useful contribution to resolution (Bass 2000, 276–310).

As long as the argument is about a fairly small number of leaders, a good case can be made that justice and revenge may serve a useful end. The situation changes whenever mass repression, especially to the point of mass murder or ethnic cleansing, has occurred. When many have committed these acts, sometimes with approval of their entire communities, even those who did not physically participate, the situation is far more delicate. Realistically, punishing a substantial portion of the guilty may be more likely to perpetuate rancors and divisions than to provide solutions.

This is what the western Europeans understood after World War II, when the countries occupied by Germany faced civil wars between those who had collaborated with the occupiers and those who had resisted. Forgetting, after some limited reprisals and trials, was the better path toward reconstructing societies. This was reinforced by creating the myth that all of the horrors of the war were perpetrated by only Germans with a small number of local collaborators, and the even more fantastic myth that majorities had participated in resistance to German occupation. The Germans themselves accepted blame for what the Nazis had done, with the understanding that relatively few would be blamed and even fewer punished, and they did not press any claims for retribution for the expulsion and murder of many Germans from eastern Europe and the Soviet Union. Yet, what was the choice? (Judt 2000, 294–303).

It is easy, a half century later, to blame European leaders of that time such as Charles de Gaulle for having placed national reconciliation above justice, which would have meant large-scale punishment and revenge. Moralizing about the need for more complete justice is a favorite attitude taken by more recent academic studies of this period, but what would it have meant in terms of continuing the hatreds and divisions of the war? Even Tony Judt, who condemns the unifying mythologizing and deliberate amnesia that occurred in the late 1940s and early 1950s, recognizes that, after all, it may have served some purpose.

He writes: "In return for the myth of an ethically respectable past and an impeccably untainted identification with a reborn Europe, we have been spared the sorts of language and attitudes that so polluted and degraded the public realm between the wars" (2000, 314). Indeed, the violence of the political debate in the 1930s, the hypernationalist xenophobia, the call to class warfare, the demeaning of minorities, and the unwillingness to compromise or tolerate opposition lay behind both the rise of fascism and the brutality unleashed throughout Europe after the start of the war in 1939. Forgetting and pretending that it had not been so, on the other hand, prepared the way for a much more benign postwar western Europe.

Ernest Renan's phrase about how nations are held together comes to mind once more: "Now, the essence of a nation is that all individuals have many things in common and also that all have forgotten many things" (cited in B. Anderson 1991, 199–translation by Chirot). Renan goes on to cite the terrible religious wars between Protestants and Catholics in France in the sixteenth century, and the other major episode of religious war in thirteenth-century France, the Albigensian Crusade. The critical notion here is that if the remembrance of these events had not been pushed aside as a basis for continuing rancor and desire for revenge, it would have been impossible to construct a French national identity able to incorporate both Protestants and Catholics, and perhaps as well, different French regions that had been characterized by different religious inclinations. This is the precise opposite of the call to memory put forth by those who engage in ethnic or religious warfare on behalf of "historical justice" and revenge. William Butler Yeats's lines about Ireland, which only in the twenty-first century is showing some signs of coming to terms with ethnic and religious divisions that go back more than three centuries, are apt:

> Out of Ireland have we come.
> Great hatred, little room,
> Maimed us at the start. (Quoted in Foster 1989, 229)

This brings us back to the central question: how is it possible to promote tolerance? Having exceptional leaders such as Nelson Mandela helps, of course, as does the realism that understands it is better to overlook past sins in order to lessen future conflict. We could ask, what would have happened if Slobodan Milošević had Nelson Mandela's personality? Would it have made a difference? Undoubtedly so, but neither psychologists nor political scientists can provide much help in trying to make leaders less vindictive and selfish. One need only contrast Mandela with his neighbor, Robert Mugabe, president of Zimbabwe. Mugabe murdered at least twenty-five thousand Ndebeles, the ethnic rivals of his Shona people, when he took power in the early 1980s, but then became more benign until his increasingly corrupt rule caused him to lose popularity and legitimacy. Furious, he turned not only on the white farmers he had tolerated until then but also against his old ethnic rivals and against the multiethnic political opposition. In the process he has ruined his country's economy, brought famine and starvation, and brutalized his population. He has gotten his revenge, but at a formidable cost. As no outside power wants to intervene, his abuses remain unchecked (Power 2003). Unfortunately, a great many African intellectuals and leaders see only the confiscation of white property and applaud the "justice" of this act, even if it has ruined Zimbabwe.

Other than hoping for good leaders or very occasional international intervention, can more be done? Samantha Power, in her award-winning book *A Problem from Hell* (2002) has argued that a great power such as the United States has a responsibility to act when it sees genocides occurring. But of course, that happens only rarely, at great cost, and as we have seen, it is very difficult to get widespread international consensus on such cases. Nor does it begin to address the issue of "little genocides," the kinds of systematic persecutions and murders that kill a hundred or a few thousand at a time without attracting significant international attention.

Some structures, some kind of genuine federalism and democracy can help reduce conflict in multiethnic or multireligious societies, but what about creating a sense of tolerance, so that whatever institutional arrangements are made, the tolerant rather than the intolerant version will be more likely? This is where we need to turn to a more microscopic, local approach, and away from grand state policies and state-sponsored commissions.

Modest Solutions and Small-Scale Changes to Promote Tolerance

Direct international interventions, particularly military ones, or political bargains by far-sighted leaders may be the only way to quickly end genocidal campaigns, but even when successful, these hardly guarantee the kinds of change that lead to more open-minded societies. What is wanted are ways to move competing ethnic, religious, regional, ideological, and class-based groups to resolve their conflicts tolerantly and peacefully, or at least learn to limit the violence that may erupt. One of the strategies that has emerged over the past twenty or so years for carrying out this kind of more basic change is the slow construction of personal contacts between individuals from communities in conflict.

Building Friendships between Communities

Perhaps the most popular approach to building peace between groups in conflict is founded on the "contact hypothesis." If individuals in the two groups get a chance to know one another personally, hostility and support for violence will decrease. This idea is usually traced to Gordon Allport's classic, *The Nature of Prejudice* (1954). Allport was well aware that contact between members of groups in conflict can often exacerbate hostility and violence, particularly contact in the context of competition. But he argued that contact would have positive impact if it occurred under four conditions: contact should be interpersonal, with potential for friendship formation; it should be between those who perceive themselves to be of equal status; it should be supported by authority; and, perhaps most important, it should involve cooperation for common goals.

An immediate limitation of this formulation is that it is very difficult to arrange this kind of contact when groups are in violent conflict. Particularly difficult is the requirement of cooperation for common goals; nontrivial goals are not easily arranged in a classroom or weekend workshop. We will see in the next section of this chapter that the missing piece in many instances is the existence of well-integrated civil society institutions. Where these exist, the possibility that different communities can work through such organizations toward important common goals may be much higher.

If the conditions of the contact hypothesis can be satisfied, and if individuals come to know and like individual members of the "enemy" group, then it is plausible that the impact on intergroup relations will be positive. How can one hate a whole group if one knows and likes individual members of the group? This idea is familiar to many who have never heard of Allport or his hypothesis, and it has been the inspiration of many different forms of contact-based peace education.

Some idea of the size of the investment in contact-based interventions is conveyed by the following observations. In the United States, about two-thirds of all colleges and universities are using some form of "diversity workshop" or "multicultural education" in which individuals from different ethnic groups are brought together to talk about their own experiences of discrimination and bias (McCauley, Wright, and Harris 2000). In addition, many U.S. corporations are using something similar to improve relations between ethnic groups in the workplace. Each year in Israel, donors (mostly American) commit about nine million U.S. dollars to contact-based Jewish-Arab coexistence projects in Israel (Maoz 2006). Each year in Northern Ireland, government spending on projects to improve relations between Protestants and Catholics, including contact-based reconciliation groups and integrated groups set up in response to some particular act of political violence, is about eight million pounds sterling (Knox and Hughes 1996).

What do we know about the success of contact-based peace programs? Research is only beginning to catch up with the popularity of such interventions. The obvious form of evaluation is to compare measures of attitude toward the out-group before and after a workshop, which may last a few hours on one day, or a weekend, or more rarely continue as a series of meetings over months. The few dozen studies that have been published tend to share several limitations. Most measure attitudes toward the out-group at the end of the workshop; unfortunately few include follow-up measures to determine whether changes found at the end of the intervention persist over time. Most use paper-and-pencil measures of beliefs about, or feelings and intentions toward, members of another group; few include any measure of actual behavior of participants. A few studies have included behavioral observations of interactions between participants from different groups *during the intervention*, on the plausible assumption that if behavior in the workshop does not show integration and respect, the chance is small that behavior after the workshop will change (Maoz 2005).

With these limitations in mind, what are results of this research? A review of Israeli studies of programs bringing Jews and Palestinians together found that most report very positive attitudes toward individuals from the "enemy" group who were met in the program (Maoz 2005). At least small changes also occur toward the out-group in general. Arabs start to view Jews somewhat more positively, and Jews also improve their general opinion of Arabs. Similarly, a review of studies of multicultural education in the United States found that the best predictor of positive impact on perceptions of the out-group was whether the program included contact with out-group members (Stephan, Renfrow, and Stephan 2004).

In short, there is developing evidence that contact-based peace education has a small but significant effect on improving intergroup attitudes. Meeting and liking individual members of a group in conflict with one's own group can make a contribution toward humanizing the enemy. Nevertheless, the limitations of contact-based interventions must also be noted. They are slow, in the sense that building one-on-one acquaintances takes time. Even in a small country like Israel, with a big investment in contact programs per capita, polling data indicate that only one in seven Israeli Jewish adults have participated in Jewish-Arab contact projects (Maoz 2006). Contact-based interventions are also limited in their focus on the interpersonal, whereas the origins of intergroup conflict and violence are at the level of intergroup relations. The fact that your group has some nice individuals in it is not directly an answer to my perception that your group is humiliating, threatening, or victimizing my group. Indeed, it is possible for contact-based education to move participants toward more positive attitudes—seeing racial stereotypes as hurtful, feeling more comfortable about approaching a stranger from another race—even as essentializing of racial differences is increasing (McCool, DuToit, Petty, and McCauley 2006).

If building peace through personal acquaintance is slow, and building peace through state institutions and state leadership is difficult, there is yet another alternative between these two extremes of large-scale and very small-scale intervention. In the space between family and state are "civil society" institutions that can play a role in limiting violence between groups in conflict. It is these, we will suggest, that can link the interpersonal and intergroup levels to provide stable support and a more peaceful way to handle competition and conflict between communities.

Building Civil Society from the Ground Up

In his pathbreaking work, Ashutosh Varshney has found evidence to suggest that the single most critical variable in determining which cities in India have or have not experienced intercommunal violence between Muslims and Hindus is the strength of their civil society institutions. In cities where community leaders were in regular contact through integrated civic organizations and could reassure each other at times of heightened political tension that they would keep their communities quiet, and when they could use their organizational authority to tell their own people to remain peaceful, there was little violence, even when other nearby places were erupting in deadly ethnic riots. This outcome reflects more than a routine interaction of Muslims and Hindus with each other during their normal lives. Simply knowing people of other communities and interacting with them on a daily basis—in line with the contact hypothesis—is a less sturdy protection against attempts by politicians to polarize ethnic communities than formal associations led by local elites who interact with and have some trust in each other (Varshney 2002, 3–15; review by McCauley 2005).

This is a crucial point, as some psychological work has focused on bringing together elites from conflicting factions in unofficial groups to learn tolerance in discussing common problems. Herbert Kelman's work (1997) in assembling influential Israeli Jews and Palestinians, usually in some neutral setting outside of Israel/Palestine, is frequently cited as a good example. Kelman provides evidence that participants in his groups, which sometimes continue over periods of years, do develop substantially increased abilities to plan together for a future in which both Jewish and Palestinian needs can be accommodated. The difficulty, however, is in the situation that participants return to after group meetings. They have trouble getting support for their new ideas from members of organizations back home that have not, as organizations, been involved in Kelman's program.

The quick collapse of intercommunal cooperation between Jews and Arabs after 2000, and the almost complete failure to ever establish trust between their leaders, suggests the limitations of even elite contacts as long as these are unofficial and not connected to existing institutions and organizations. In the Israeli-Palestinian case, integration at the level of elite participation in formal civil society institutions has probably been impossible since the 1930s, if not earlier (Segev 2001). Any settlement of this particular situation will require an internationally imposed, pragmatic separation of the two societies into two states and a deliberate abandonment of anything that might be called historical justice.

There is some disagreement among psychologists who specialize in contact-based peace building as to whether association between communities—even if it satisfies the four conditions of the contact hypothesis—necessarily promotes tolerance. One of us (McCauley 2001, 359) is skeptical (see also Forbes 1997), but most psychologists think that it does (Pettigrew and Tropp 2000). Varshney's work can clarify the issue by pointing out that ordinary association probably helps somewhat, but without institutional support buttressed by civil society institutions and active interaction among community leaders, such connections are unlikely to resist polarization in politically tense situations.

This confirms much of the political science literature about ethnic and religious violence, including, in particular, the work already cited by Donald Horowitz. Such violence is rarely "spontaneous." It is directed and encouraged by leaders. The leadership may come from the very top, as it did when German Nazi or Rwandan Hutu leaders organized systematic genocides, or when Serbian leaders encouraged genocidal ethnic cleansing in parts of Yugoslavia. It may be local, or pushed by a particular political party acting at the local level, as has typically been the case in India (Brass 1997). What Varshney's work shows is that if local leaders want to maintain peace, if they trust each other, and if they communicate effectively with their communities, it is far more difficult for political opportunists to mobilize these communities for violent action (Bock and McCauley 2003). It may be impossible to stop heavily armed outsiders from entering a region and committing outrages, but strong community civil society institutions can at least keep locals from joining in and worsening the damage. And after violent conflicts, reconciliation is also far easier if neighbors know that they have not been responsible for the atrocities committed by outsiders.

We have seen that one way to limit mass political murder is to have tolerant leaders at the top of the political structure, though it is difficult to devise either domestic or international institutions to guarantee this. Approaching the problem through local community leadership, however, is equally important, and more amenable to specific programmatic action.

It is possible to construct community-based institutions that can serve to calm passions in times of political crisis and intercommunal conflict. That is what "civil society" means—organized groups at a level above that of the family but below that of the state that bring together people for any number of social, political, religious, or economic activities. Where these exist, they can be reinforced; where they are absent, they can be initiated. Not all such institutions have as their explicit purpose to promote intercommunal tolerance and cooperation, but they can be encouraged to do so, whatever their original purpose may have been. If, on top of that, they bring together leading members of diverse communities, by the very act of existing and functioning, they provide mechanisms that can mitigate hostility and conflict.

The procedures for creating and strengthening such institutions have been tried by various organizations, particularly some NGOs in recent years. Such an attempt by CARE in Ivory Coast, where one of us (Chirot) participated in 2003–4, can serve as an example. Ivory Coast was one of the rare economic success stories in sub-Saharan Africa after independence. Until the 1980s, its economy grew quickly, based largely on tropical export crops. Immigrants were welcomed in the country to provide needed labor, new lands were cleared for coffee and cocoa production, and its sixty or so different linguistic groups, along with its Muslims, Christians, and Animists, intermixed with only occasional, and fairly limited, conflicts. All was not peace and harmony, but disputes were contained by handing out benefits very widely and by President Houphouët-Boigny's ability to co-opt regional leaders through material and honorific distributions. One of the main problems, however, was that all of these distributions came from the top, with very little development of independent civil society organizations to bring together leaders of various communities. Their point of contact was at the national political level, where they competed for power and rewards (Berthélemy and Bourguignon 1996; Rothchild 1997, 14–15; Zolberg 1969).

The system began to break down in the 1980s because the economy ceased to grow while population continued increasing rapidly. After Houphouët's death in 1993, the prospect of elections in 1995 unbalanced the entire situation. Northerners, mostly but not entirely Muslim, had grown to be more numerous than southerners, who were largely but far from entirely Christian. The old political elites were heavily southern Christian, and to keep control they changed citizenship laws to effectively disenfranchise most northerners. Such action also threatened the property rights of northerners and of immigrants from neighboring northern countries, mostly Burkina Faso and Mali, who had been cultivating coffee and cocoa lands in the south that they had cleared decades earlier. There followed a series of tainted elections, increasing harassment of northerners by southern gendarmes and officials, land seizures in the south of property long owned by northerners, and then a series of coups and countercoups.

The upshot was another attempted coup in September 2002 that split the country in two, north and south. Both sides had their armies and retain them as of mid-2006. There were massacres of northerners in the south, especially in the main city of Abidjan, which is ethnically and religiously very mixed, and of southerners in the north. Up to ten thousand people died, and more than a million fled from one part of the country to another or to neighboring states. Local disputes over land and other resources such as fishing rights merged with national politics and the struggle for control of state resources to produce a situation that could have led to hundreds of thousands more deaths and massive ethnic cleansing in each region. France, the former colonial power, intervened by placing an army of four thousand to five thousand between the contending north and south, and this has been reinforced by six thousand more UN troops (Berthélemy and Bourguignon 1996; Chirot 2005; Human Rights Watch 2001; S. Smith 2003, 2004b, as well as many other articles by Smith in *Le Monde*).

CARE, the World Bank, and other international organizations understood perfectly well that there was little to be done to control the behavior of the political authorities in the rebel north or the government-held south. That is something the French government, the United Nations, and the major African states who are afraid that this civil war could spill over and destroy the entire region have worked on with mixed results. But underneath the turbulent, contentious, and now deadly political conflict for control of the state, a host of local problems emerged to contribute to distrust, fear, and the separation of ethnic and religious groups in affected regions. Most of the country, and particularly its middle zone on the borders between north and south were quite ethnically and religiously mixed, but the war separated communities, reinforced suspicions, and broke apart prior ordinary links (Chirot 2003).

With very modest World Bank funding, CARE encouraged notables in the area of Bouaké, the rebel capital in the very center of the country, to form a steering committee. This committee included representatives of the key communities—Muslims, Catholics, Protestants, a number of major ethnolinguistic groups, and the main immigrant groups. The steering committee was to send out the word to rural villages and to urban districts that similar local committees should be formed to ask for reconstruction funding to repair the damages of the civil war. This could include activities ranging from repairing schools, dispensaries, and wells to providing small amounts of capital to get markets and small businesses functioning again. The only requirement was that, as much as possible, local committees running these projects also had to include representatives of as many ethnic and religious communities as possible, so that the act of working together could establish regular communications and a basis for trust. Local groups were then to produce plans for reconstruction projects to be judged by the central regional steering committee, and the winning proposals were financed, typically with grants of two thousand to four thousand dollars (Chirot 2004).

Though these were only short-term pilot projects, in just a few months they produced something unusual. In the past, before the civil war, villages or urban groups could send requests into the central government, but this actually promoted conflictual relations, as grants were handed out on the basis of political favoritism. Such procedures increased the stakes in disputes over control of the state, worsened suspicion among those who did not receive benefits, and did nothing at all to get different ethnicities cooperating in joint projects. By providing very small amounts of funding controlled by local multiethnic and multireligious committees, however, incentives were put into place to reward cooperation, toleration, and discussion of major issues between groups.

Catherine Boone's research in Ivory Coast has found that there are, first of all, large local variations in the kinds of rural institutions that exist throughout that country. Looking particularly at the southwest, where some of the worst episodes of killing took place in connection with land disputes between different communities, she noted an absence of local integrating institutions. Thus, when the civil war broke out, neither the central government nor local institutions were able to cope with the tensions that long predated the war itself. She writes: "Possibilities for local institution building may be the most open-ended in these settings . . . [and] one can envision a wide variety of workable forms" (Boone 2003, 326). Clearly, whatever solution might be found at the level of national politics for their problems, without building local institutions as well, new violence will arise sooner or later.

A somewhat older example is another CARE project, but in Niger. There, in the Department of Maradi, sedentary farmers and herders have been brought together in joint commissions to delineate boundaries through which cattle may be walked in search of pasture without damaging fields. This has been particularly important with increasing population densities that have strained resources all through the African savannah and Sahel (the mixed agro-herding dry zone, from the Atlantic to the Red Sea south of the Sahara desert). In the past three decades, traditional tensions between herders and sedentary farmers have vastly increased as a result of desiccation and population growth, so that what used to be fairly minor local disputes have become major ethnic battles.

Similar commissions set up in eastern Niger have been established to resolve water rights disputes between ethnically different groups of herders vying for the same scarce pasturage and water. Given the nearly complete failure of the state to resolve these problems, and their explosive potential for creating deadly ethnic wars, as in Sudan, such local efforts are probably the only way to prevent catastrophes. They cannot eliminate the problems of population growth and resource shortage, but they can limit the damages of conflict by promoting mediating institutions for joint discussion and exchange of views (CARE 2004; Thébaud 1998, 2002).

This is exactly what the Sudanese region of Darfur needs to lessen conflict, not just an international military force to impose peace, and not just, or perhaps not even mainly, an international court of justice to condemn those responsible for genocidal ethnic cleansing. Mechanisms for resolving local disputes and containing competition between ethnic groups within acceptable boundaries are also necessary.

Projects like these CARE endeavors in western Africa have been tried in many places. In some cases they can succeed as long as no one expects rapid and miraculous resolutions of conflicts from such modest projects. They effectively build or rebuild civil society institutions that can, on lines similar to those witnessed by Varshney in India, promote greater local calm in very tense political situations. In the long run, it is even possible to envision such local institutions creating national councils of local NGO leaders who could act as a moderating counterweight to warring political forces and who could create a general atmosphere of greater tolerance and understanding. Even without such a grand plan, very local successes do some good. In a sense, what they can accomplish is to eliminate some of the flammable tinder that turns national political struggles into vicious local fires whose lasting effects are to make reconciliation and ethnic or religious tolerance almost impossible. (Some examples of such projects can be found in Archibald and Richards 2002; Biabo 2003; Brusset, Hasabamagara, and Ngendakuriyo 2002; Millie and Paiwastoon 2003; Ndayizeye 2002; UNDP 2001; Young 2002.)

Ivory Coast is not the only place where the failure of local institutions to resist political pressures from the center turned struggles over control of the state into vicious civil wars with catastrophic local consequences. Even where, before open warfare, people had mixed together fairly peacefully, such national breakdowns can quickly create deadly local fighting between previously nonviolent communities. That is exactly what happened in Yugoslavia, too, though in that case, where multiethnic local institutions did try to resist, they were destroyed by outside military intervention (Oberschall 2001, 123–24, 144–48). Yet, in Yugoslavia, the prior tradition of excessive socialist centralization meant that there were few multiethnic, local, nongovernmental civil society institutions to resist these pressures.

No one would claim that even the strongest local organizations can successfully resist a large influx of well-armed strangers. When soldiers, mercenaries, militants, or gangs can undermine the state's monopoly on violence to attack some groups and claim to "represent" other local communities, civic integration can offer only limited resistance. But even that helps slow the destructive effects of civil conflict and to provide the basis for social reconstruction and reconciliation after order is reestablished. Civil society institutions are not by any means a perfect protection against violent intercommunal conflict, but there is probably no other intervention with more potential for mitigating conflict at the local level.

THE ROLE OF DECENTRALIZATION AND DEMOCRACY

As we saw above, one of the macropolitical solutions to limiting conflict is federalism or some sort of devolution of power to local regions and communities. This is also not a comprehensive solution, but in many cases it has succeeded in limiting the damages of competition for resources between different communities. As we noted, such solutions work best in a democratic environment where political competition can be resolved by elections rather than violence. That was exactly what James Madison prescribed for the United States when he observed that decentralization would insure a society ". . . broken into so many parts, interests, and classes of citizens, that the rights of individuals, or of the minority, will be in little danger from interested combinations of the majority" (Madison [1788] 1941).

A study of democracy and decentralization in southern Asia and western Africa concluded that decentralization does contribute to democratic practices and social peace, but that it works best when strong local civil society organizations are already in place. Thus, decentralization worked to enhance democracy and the responsiveness of government in the Indian province of Karnataka, and to promote peaceful rather than conflictual competition for resources. It worked much less well in Bangladesh and Ivory Coast, particularly the latter. The main reason was that in India, and specifically in Karnataka, civil society institutions were much stronger to begin with, there was greater trust in local elites, and there were means for maintaining communications between various communities and the government. The authors of the study found that this was not the case in Ivory Coast. Their information predates the civil war by a decade, but given what we now know, the study seems prophetic. In Bangladesh, and in a part of Ghana that was studied as well, the results were also less impressive than in India, though somewhat better than in Ivory Coast (Crook and Manor 1998). The point is that when local groups effectively control more resources, and the way in which these are distributed is both transparent and reasonably fair, political struggle for control of the central government then becomes less critical, and local communities can work out their conflicts without appealing to it. That, in turn, makes state politics less dangerous.

It might seem somewhat circular to say that strong civil society institutions promote democracy, better governance, and ultimately greater tolerance so that decentralization is more effective, and then to promote decentralization as a strategy for reducing the potential damages of political competition. It is more than a tautology, however, because it brings out, once more, the fact that fiddling with macropolitical structures is insufficient if the social base remains prone to intolerance and has no practice in local conflict resolution. The lesson we can draw from this is that it is well worth supporting and slowly building local organizations that bring together different, competing communities so that they acquire the means of settling some of their disputes.

The contemporary enthusiasm for the promotion of civil society structures among international NGOs and development agencies, and among those who wish to encourage tolerant democracy, should not, however, obscure some reservations long held by classical political philosophers. Alexis de Tocqueville admired early-nineteenth-century American civil society institutions because they strengthened local power and kept the potential tyranny of the majority at bay. No central power, however popular and strongly backed by the majority, could impose this tyranny of the majority on the entire land. Yet, it was precisely this decentralization that also allowed the nineteenth century's worst abuses of human freedom and tolerance in the United States—slavery in the south and the expulsion and genocide of Indians on the western frontier (Wolin 2001, 262–68).

This is why it would be foolish to think that civil society institutions and local-level projects are sufficient to control intergroup violent competition, or that democracy and decentralization are the solution to everything, particularly in highly divided societies. In a number of African cases, as well as in Yugoslavia, the sudden move to democracy only provoked greater intolerance because it intensified competition without reassuring losers that they could survive; and it became an incentive to extremist politicians to play up ethnic, religious, and ethnic tensions (Hayden 1992; Sandbrook 2000). That is exactly what happened in the case of Ivory Coast when the "winner take all" mentality of the major political parties pushed those in power to initiate intolerant repression in order to prevent northerners from winning elections. A strong civil society helps, as do decentralization and democracy, but there are no panaceas for the problem of destructively violent intercommunal competition. It takes a combination of many mechanisms that limit violence to develop the habits of tolerance able to resist the occasional crisis. In the package of solutions, we ought not to forget the role of the modern central state and the macropolitical changes discussed earlier in this chapter.

The Crucial Role of States in Promoting Peaceful Exchanges

In chapter 3 we presented evidence that exchange between groups mitigates conflict by setting boundaries on its expression. Like other conflict limitation strategies, it is hardly perfect and can break down, but in general, the more exchange there is between ethnic groups, religious communities, regions, elites—or for that matter, states—the less likely it is that they will engage in competition to the death. Similarly, exchanges of marriage partners, or of goods between different ethnic, religious, or nationally defined groups lessens the chances of uncontrolled conflict between them.

How, then, can greater exchange between groups be promoted? It is not feasible to force people to intermarry, though it is possible to remove rules that prohibit intermarriage, such as the ones that used to outlaw black-white marriage in the United States and South Africa. On the other hand, there are all kinds of commercial possibilities for increasing exchanges between groups. The great danger is that increasing commercial exchange is often accompanied by ethnic specialization such that one particular group, say, Jews in Poland up to the early twentieth century, or Chinese in Indonesia and Malaysia to this day, predominates as owners of shops and controllers of capital. Greater exchange can then lead to perceived greater inequality, and majority ethnic or religious populations might then become increasingly intolerant instead of more accommodating (Chirot and Reid 1997). Economic growth in the modern world greatly expands the rate of exchange, but again, if it results in some groups gaining greater wealth than others, it also exacerbates conflict. A minority doing better than the majority may be a particularly inflammable situation (Chua 2003).

The point is that almost any structure that brings different communities together helps create rules between them that limit the intensity of conflict, but it simultaneously opens up new areas of competition. This means that open trading systems within and between states, open marriage arrangements that give individuals freer choice of partners and allow intermarriage, schools that mix various groups together within a society, and institutions such as armies that enroll soldiers from all classes, regions, and ethnic groups promote greater tolerance but also a greater potential for conflict if particular communities feel they are falling behind.

Here is where strong and impartial modern states can play a vital role and where institutions at levels below the state are much less effective. If states can guarantee that individuals will be protected and treated equally, then ethnic or religious particularism will seem less appealing, as individuals will need their community less. Thus, strong states that build a sense of common nationhood are double-edged swords. By creating "super tribes" they increase the danger of wars between nations, and by excluding or failing to assimilate some groups within their national boundaries they promote intolerance that in times of crisis may lead to mass murder and ethnic cleansing. But without the existence of strong national states, competing communities have an incentive to close ranks to protect themselves in troubled times. It was because the Yugoslav central state's authority collapsed, and the various regions in the country lost faith in the state's ability to protect them, that federalism failed and ethnic war broke out.

This is the dilemma of trying to promote strong local civil society institutions, federalism, consociationalism, or other kinds of decentralization that may reduce local conflict but also weaken modern states. A balance needs to be reached between local and central power, between nongovernmental civil society and the state, between regionalism and nationalism. Finding the right balance is an unending challenge that must repeatedly deal with new crises and threats to tolerance.

The European Union that emerged after World War II is an outstanding recent example of the construction of a large political institution that is often cited as having superseded the state. It did this by creating a new kind of weak state that has some real powers but remains a confederal structure in which the original states retain more power than the center. As it unites states that were frequently at war with each other until the end of World War II, the European Union has effectively curbed violent competition between them and allowed the old regions within each to become more autonomous. The existing states, France, Germany, Spain, and so on, no longer need to worry that if they have less control over their provinces or people they will be weakened in military competition with other states. Their inhabitants no longer need the protection of their state as much, because they are also protected by Europe's strong norms of tolerance. Therefore, in the new balance being worked out there is greater unity as well as a greater acceptance of diversity, and all this is bound together by a vast increase in trade within the Union and movement across boundaries by its people, who now mix so thoroughly that war between them seems unthinkable. There remain many problems, but on the whole this is an experiment that has worked. Even if full political integration never occurs, and each nation-state retains its identity, as seems most likely, the peace achieved by Europe after so many centuries of terrible warfare is a significant accomplishment (Caporaso 2000; McKay 2001).

Alan Milward's economic history of postwar Europe, however, shows that the effect of greater unity was to rescue the European nation-state from the discredit into which it had fallen as a result of the horrendous war that had just been fought in the name of nationalism, and to allow the reconstruction of both economies and societies that had been terribly damaged (Milward 1992). It is doubtful that an effective European Union would have been possible had its constituent members not been both strongly nationalistic and united. Democracy and surrendering limited powers to the Union itself, as well as gradually allowing regions within the state to obtain more autonomy, were dependent on having self-confident and united states as building blocks. Moreover, the western Europeans who created the Union were wedded to a particular Enlightenment ideology of respect for individual rights. Nazism and communism had taught them that the consequences of abandoning the Enlightenment were catastrophic, and the entire premise of the Union is that democracy and tolerance are its essential founding ideology, along with free trade and the free movement of people.

This brings us to a final, crucial point. Without leaders and elites who accept some of the right values, tolerance will ultimately fail. Adjusting institutions at both the national and the local level is important but not sufficient. The promotion of civil society institutions can create a lasting basis for more harmonious relations between groups. Increasing opportunities for exchange and state protection of rights also contribute to the reduction of violent tension. But the vital step without which, ultimately, most attempts to limit violence will fail, is the promotion of a particular view of social relations. This was something broached at the end of chapter 3, but not yet discussed in our inventory of ways to mitigate conflict between communities—the realm of social values and political philosophies.

Individual Rights and Pluralist Histories

In April 2003 one of us (Chirot) was interviewing people in Bouaké, the rebel capital of the northern Ivory Coast to get their views about the causes of the civil war that had split the country in two. Roadblocks manned by armed rebels—men and boys who were rowdy and often drunk—held sway over the streets of the city. Rebels were careening around in stolen cars. There had been massacres of southern policemen and civil servants in the city a few months before. Most stores had been looted, and gas stations were stripped of their pumps. Burnt-out cars littered the streets from the fighting that had taken place. The rebel "chief of security," one "Chef" Daouda Konaté was using his men to extract as much cash as possible from the intimidated population. (He subsequently participated in a major bank heist and vanished with a small fortune.) Most of the civil servants, doctors, and teachers who were southerners had fled, but many people from ethnicities associated with the south remained, and had been subjected to murder, looting, and rape, and they were still being threatened.

One of the interviews was with the local leaders of an ethnic community from the north. It took place in a courtyard under a large shade tree. After the usual exchange of greetings and drinks of cold juice, the senior elder of the group took out a thick sheaf of papers and began reading in French. He read for almost two hours a history of ethnic relations in Ivory Coast from before colonial times, through the entire colonial era, and since independence in 1960. The message was simple. Southerners were lazy and uncivilized. They had relied on northerners for all the work that had once made Ivory Coast prosperous. While northerners had built impressive chiefdoms and states and understood what it was to respect authority and tradition, southerners were savages who had lived in anarchy in their southern forests until the colonial period. The French had given the southerners too much power and could not be trusted either. Peace could only be reestablished if southerners shared power with northerners and recognized their contributions, but given the natural inclinations of southerners, this was unlikely.

Aside from the details, this story is all too common and could have been repeated in one form or another throughout the world. It combines a mythologized history of the past full of resentment about various injustices with a demeaning, essentializing description of whole ethnic, religious, and regional groups who are deemed to be enemies. Needless to say, the southern view is the exact mirror image of the northern one. Southerners, according to their own explanation offered in great detail, especially by educated professionals, is that they were kind enough to allow the impoverished northerners to come and work on southern lands and share in the wealth of the land, but now these ungrateful and backward people from the north want to take over and run a country that is not theirs. In its most extreme form, this southern, increasingly racist ideology is expressed by the so-called Young Patriots, Ivory Coast President Gbagbo's Brown Shirts, who are sent out to kill and terrorize northerners and the president's political foes in the main southern city, Abidjan (based on Chirot's interviews in Abidjan in April 2003). Much can be done to mitigate conflict at the local level. If, however, such stereotypical group images and historical rancors become widely accepted, the chances of having tolerant political leaders who can rise above such simplifications are not high.

In all the many twentieth-century and contemporary situations that have led to large-scale genocidal killings and ethnic cleansing, the causes are subject to debate. Did the catastrophe occur because of economic and political pressures, because of a pervasive culture of prejudice, or because of acts by ideological or perhaps merely opportunistic leaders? Such questions are what underlie the perpetual controversy about Nazi motivations, particularly the debates stirred up by Daniel Goldhagen's book (1996). Goldhagen believes that a pervasive, centuries-old culture of German anti-Semitism was behind the Holocaust. His critics point out that this is a simplistic exaggeration that overlooks the presence of anti-Semitism elsewhere in Europe while essentializing German sentiments that were much more divided than Goldhagen suggests. Even though there was widespread anti-Semitism, most of it was fairly mild and not genocidal until the Nazi period, when Hitler used his popularity and the most drastic theories about the dangers of race mixing and of Jews as a polluting race to legitimize his own extreme views (Bauer 2002, 93–118). An even more contrary view has been presented by Benjamin Valentino, who claims that genocides in general, and the Nazi one in particular, did not need widespread popular support or deep structural causes but were primarily the work of a small group of ideologues who happened to seize power (2004, 30–65).

The genocide of Jews is the most studied of all cases, but similar controversies exist about all major cases of modern episodes of mass killing for political ends. Our argument in this last chapter is that all of these approaches have considerable merit. There is no single explanation, neither in the rhetoric of those who commit genocide (see chapter 1) nor in the analysis of the psychological foundations of genocide (see chapter 2). Long-held views about other ethnic, religious, class, or regional groups matter, as do extremist leaders, both local and at the level of the central state. Crises that exacerbate competition and intensify fears also make a difference, as do international maneuvers. Those who seek simple explanations believe there are simple solutions, but they are wrong. In the case of Germany, had there been no widespread anti-Semitism, it is unlikely that a party whose central platforms included vicious and well-publicized anti-Semitism would have been able to garner substantial popular support. Had there been no humiliating defeat in World War I and a series of subsequent economic crises, the Nazis would have remained marginal. Had Hitler and a small cadre of his closest followers not been obsessed with matters of race, there would have been no genocide.

We ought not forget, however, that the intellectual climate among many leading German thinkers and elites led them to believe that Germany's redemption from its failures and corruption had to begin with the purification of the race and the elimination of the Jews. Jews were said to have abused and taken advantage of the commercialization of modern life and therefore been responsible for the alienation and miseries wrought by modernity (Herf 1984). The Nazi propaganda machine would have been unable to produce an accepting consensus among Germans had the stage not been set by this elite ideological bias. Having this base with which to work, Nazi propaganda after they came to power made extermination policies more acceptable to the general population. During the mass killings, many Germans may not

206 Chapter Four

have known all the gory details, but awareness that something like this was happening was certainly widespread, and protests were rare; the Nazi government and Hitler in particular retained the loyalty of most of the population (Craig 1982, 207–10; Friedländer 1997; Weiss 1996).

We could look at the Armenian genocide, the Rwandan one, and at lesser cases, and find a similarly complex combination of causes behind them, but also historical mythologies of ethnicity and nation that created an atmosphere conducive to the triumph of extremism. The same could be said of Ivory Coast in 2003 and 2004, where a genocide has not taken place, but where there have been mass murders and where the potential for a much larger and deadlier civil war exists. Ivory Coast is only one of almost countless other cases spread through history and around the world. Beyond the structural causes, the economic difficulties, and the political bungling that began the civil war, there is also a climate of opinion in which stories like the ones told above by northern elders or southern extremists can thrive. People do not need to read sophisticated German philosophers like Nietzsche or Heidegger or even *Mein Kampf* to create a climate in which extremist leaders full of righteous anger come to the fore.

Two elements of such stories are of particular importance. One is the obvious essentializing that says that "they" are all alike and must be treated as a single entity. We have discussed this at some length in chapter 2. To combat this requires a special ideology that has become widespread only in political cultures suffused with Enlightenment values. That ideology recognizes that individuals are in a real sense more important than communities. Not only do individuals have rights, but they are to be judged as individuals responsible for their actions, not as members of any group. As human beings find it easy to essentialize groups, to lump individuals into communities, and to judge the group as a whole, making individual distinctions in difficult times of intercommunal competition is a rare accomplishment.

Isaiah Berlin points out that the doctrine of individual liberty was almost entirely absent in the legal conceptions of the ancient Greeks and Romans, in Jewish, Chinese, and in fact all other ancient laws (1998, 201). A sense of the individual certainly existed, but legal traditions were based on community, not individual obligations and privileges. The individual operated within a community, not as an autonomous entity with distinct rights above those of the community. Yet, that notion of inviolable individual as opposed to community rights is at the very heart of the Enlightenment's preoccupation with law. The central theme in John Locke's *Second Treatise* is his concern with how the individual can best preserve his or her independence within a community or commonwealth, and what must be done to make sure that governments do not impinge on that essential individual freedom ([1689] 1955, 144–45). Immanuel Kant's prescription for enlightenment was that every (adult) individual be free from the tutelage of others, that is, from the received opinion of the community, the powers that be, or anything other than one's own reason ([1784] 1959, 85–92).

Of course these philosophical positions are idealizations, but if the notion of individual rights is inculcated and widely accepted in a society, it can play a role in limiting the power of essentializing. Doing this is not easy because it runs against some of our deepest impulses, against both traditional thinking and even contemporary communitarianism. Isaiah Berlin wrestled with the need to balance community solidarity with individual rights and concluded that we must continue to believe that we are more than mere members of any community, that we "have plural allegiances, belong to diverse communities, and know the experience of conflicting roles. Plurality and conflict are integral to our identities" (quoted in Gray 1996, 103).

Teaching this in Western liberal societies is hard enough, and doing so in societies without much of a tradition of Enlightenment philosophy is even harder, but it is an important part of trying to lessen the probability of murderous ethnic, religious, or other intercommunal deadly conflicts. Both Nazism and communism were explicit rejections of individualism in favor of community solidarity, and it is the error of much milder forms of communitarianism to forget that rejecting individual rights and autonomy in favor of what is often called more organic solidarity creates the potential for dangerous abuse (Chirot 1995).

The second important aspect of the Ivorian account of how their history explained the civil war and justified their own side's position is that all communities, but especially self-conscious ethnic, religious, and national groups, have such stories based on remembered experiences. These remembrances, however, are not only frequently false, but insofar as they recall memories of injustice committed by others, they perpetuate hostilities and make tolerance and compromise more difficult.

Human societies understand themselves as historical processes. That is why the first five books of the Hebrew Bible are a compendium of laws, along with stories of struggles and killing meant to explain why God's favorite people could triumph when they obeyed God but were bound to fail if they did not. These books also contain long genealogies. It is these stories accompanied by genealogies that situate and define the Jewish people and religion, and such historical explanations are almost universal in one form or another. Furthermore, in every historical tradition recent events are incorporated and history changed to accommodate them, so that, for example, Ivorian, or German, or Rwandan, or Cambodian histories were reshaped to make the past fit the conflicts and ideologies uppermost in the minds of those who led the massacres in order to justify themselves and energize their followers. That reshaping sometimes involved outright fabrication, but it also harped on past injustices, failures, and tragedies to focus the desire for revenge and to stoke fears that if mass murders were not carried out, more disasters would occur.

Ernest Renan is right to claim that forgetting is crucial if there is to be social peace, and the South African truth and reconciliation commissions were right to try to paper over recent injustices. Can such forgetting be taught? Should it be? Memory cannot be eradicated, nor should it be. Any group's identity is partly based on and legitimized by its members' sense of their history. Forgetting too much in order to ensure social peace and political stability can be undesirable, as it may lead to a denial of past wrongs. Ian Buruma, for example, correctly praised Germany for teaching its people to evaluate its murderous past, whereas Japan's failure to do so leads many to question how sincere a transformation has occurred there (1994). The issue is not what needs to be forgotten or remembered, but *how* history is to be interpreted.

What should be opposed is the use of history to perpetuate a sense of community grievance by turning contemporary groups into proxies for the essentialized past perpetrators of injustices. To recognize that the Germans conducted the Holocaust is important; to go from there to saying that all Germans, or any of their institutions that exist today and worked with the Nazis generations ago are still responsible, and will be forever, is to go too far. To admit that terrible massacres and ethnic cleansing continue to take place in some parts of the world is critical; but to blame whole communities and their descendants for generations to come is only to guarantee future catastrophes.

Achieving the right balance is neither easy nor obvious, but the effort needs to be made wherever conflict exists. Because reality is always complex, the more we know about the past, and the more simplifying mythologies we can expose to demystification, the more difficult it is to use history as the basis for claims against past opponents, the harder it is to reshape the past to fit contemporary political competition, and the easier it is to effect reconciliation. The argument about whether or not there is such a thing as objective history is not one we should try to resolve. Hardly any historian would accept today the seemingly naive statement by J. B. Bury that history is a science (quoted in Berlin 1998, x). We are convinced, however, that in the long run a more tolerant atmosphere is created if history ceases to be taught as a set of received truths, as a set of simplified morality tales, but comes to be transmitted to the young as a subject to be approached the way the Enlightenment came to view science. As outlined by Ernest Gellner (with some of our own additions in brackets to summarize related statements in his book), this means:

> There are no privileged a priori substantive truths. This . . . eliminates the sacred from the world [of history and science, at least]. All facts and all observers are equal [in that what is claimed to be fact should be tested to see if it can be supported]. There are no privileged Sources or Affirmations, and all of them can be queried. In inquiry, all facts and features are separable: it is always proper to inquire whether combinations could not be other than what has previously been supposed. In other words, the world does not arrive as a package deal—which is the customary manner in which it appears in traditional cultures [and in both strong political ideologies and religions]—but piecemeal. (Gellner 1992, 80)

This is not the way history is taught to schoolchildren in most of the world, or perhaps anywhere. It is not the way the young are taught their communities' histories by their elders. It is, on the other hand, largely the way history is now discussed in good universities, particularly in the liberal democracies with a strong Enlightenment tradition.

If even some of that skepticism and willingness to question and test received facts were to become more widespread, there would be fewer intellectual and political leaders wedded to communal myths about "our" purity and perfectly just cause. Some leaders who can balance the need to mobilize support for just causes while avoiding deadly essentializing of enemies occasionally do emerge, and we tend to remember the most famous ones as exceptional heroes. The Abraham Lincolns, Jawaharlal Nehrus, and Nelson Mandelas of this world are rare. But educating substantial numbers of young potential elites about history in this manner would certainly increase the likelihood that there will be more, and at many different levels of leadership. It may seem utopian to even mention such a long-term project, but that, after all, is one of the functions of higher education. In a world that seems to be going in the opposite direction, that is something worth considering. It is the final suggestion we want to make, one that is as important as all the others and that must be part of any durable approach to minimizing the risks of mass political murder.

Our Question Answered

"The best thing for being sad," replied Merlyn, beginning to
puff and blow, "is to learn something. That is the only
thing that never fails. You may grow old and trembling in
your anatomies, you may lie awake at night listening to the
disorder in your veins, you may miss your only love, you may
see the world about you devastated by evil lunatics, or
know your honour trampled in the sewers of baser minds.
There is only one thing for it then—to learn. Learn why the
world wags and what wags it."
—*Terence H. White, The Once and Future King*, 1958

There is no sign that the occasions of intergroup violence are de-
creasing. Conflicts based on economic, ethnic, religious, and
ideological divides are now considerably more likely within states than
between states, but that does not mean that international wars are a
thing of the past or irrelevant to understanding genocide and ethnic
cleansing. The genocide in Cambodia was the outcome of a process
begun by the international Vietnam War; the Rwandan genocide led
to the Zaire/Congo war that involved several African countries and resulted in more than three million deaths; and the potential for international wars that could lead to genocidal massacres, even nuclear war,
remains significant in the Middle East, between India and Pakistan,
and in Korea. Some of these conflicts could easily unleash massacres
on a scale as large as anything we have seen.

Amitai Etzioni has argued that international rivalries should give way
to a kind of global communitarianism (2004), but it takes a kind of
utopian blindness to believe that anything like that is about to happen.
Ethnic identities and nationalist passions are not disappearing, even

though many learned observers think they should be considered dangerously obsolete (Hobsbawm 1992). Scholars point to the fuzzy and uncertain boundaries of ethnicity, to the change in these boundaries over a few generations, and conclude that ethnicity is imagined, constructed, and therefore somehow an irrational superficiality or a matter of what Marxists long called "false consciousness" (B. Anderson 1991). Whatever its intellectual merits, this kind of argument is lost on most people and has not erased the widespread, very strong sense of ethnicity among them, including Americans and western Europeans.

Psychologist-anthropologist Francisco Gil-White offers strong evidence that however much good scholars may believe that ethnicity is constructed, imagined, and flexible, that is not how real people see it. Based primarily on evidence from Mongolia, but with many comparative examples, Gil-White suggests that human beings have a strong tendency to identify with particular ethnic groups and to think of these groups in primordialist terms, that is, as basic, biological, and unchanging (1999). Most humans think that their ethnic group is a kind of large, extended family and that, therefore, they owe it some kind of loyalty and can look to it for protection (Pinker 2002, 323).

A recent study by Monica Toft (2003) of ethnic disputes that emerged from the breakup of the Soviet Union and a comparison with other ethnoterritorial quarrels in the contemporary world comes to the conclusion that when there are concentrated ethnic minorities within a state who are actually majorities within their own region, and where they have some serious grievances against the dominant state, violent civil war is likely as soon as state control weakens. This is particularly the case if the ethnic group in question has a strong allegiance to its own way of life and sees that as being tied to its territory.

A very obvious contemporary case is Chechnya, where Russia is conducting a brutal war against the Chechens, filled with massacres and countermassacres. Russia has little prospect of winning without resorting to near genocidal ethnic cleansing, which is the direction in which it is heading (Lieven 1998; Toft 2003). In her study, Toft contrasts Chechnya with Tatarstan, where Muslim Tatars in Russia were too dispersed and not a clear majority on any piece of territory significant enough to organize a revolt or aspire to independence, and so their ethnoreligious consciousness did not lead to war. In Czechoslovakia, a case we discussed in chapter 4, Czechs and Slovaks never contested each other's territories, and their populations were not highly mixed except in a few urban centers, so the two split apart amicably. In Yugoslavia, on the other hand, particularly in Bosnia and Kosovo, overlapping claims to territory by pockets of concentrated groups of various ethnicities interspersed among each other led to very bloody wars.

Following this logic, it becomes clear why a situation like the one in Israel/Palestine, with two different ethnicities reinforced by different religions and claiming the same territory, cannot be resolved either by power sharing or by a compromise that will be fully accepted as legitimate by both sides (Toft 2003). This does not mean that compromise is impossible—only that any compromise has to involve one or both sides giving up something it deeply believes to be just, and this means that any arrangement will leave many on one or both sides discontented. Toft's point is that contemporary Western scholars have forgotten the importance of ethnicity and territory in producing major conflicts, and that until we all learn to take these into account once more, we will fail to understand much of the violence that occurs in the world. As scholars, we may know that primordial sentiments are not, strictly speaking, true. We have abundant evidence that ethnic boundaries do change, and that genealogies and histories trying to demonstrate purity of descent are often fabrications; but that hardly negates the perception of ethnic groups themselves. It is, after all, what they believe that determines their behavior toward other groups, not some scholar's reconstruction of historical facts.

Similarly, wars of religious ideology that might have seemed relics of a distant past now once again seem to be on the agenda. That is most evident in the case of Islam, where recent studies have emphasized both the vehemence and modernity of the kind of fundamentalism at war with the West, with India, with Russia, and with Israel (Kepel 2004; Roy 2004). But fundamentalism is far from being a purely Islamic phenomenon, and in fact extends across the world with ramifications among Christians, Jews, Hindus, and in many other groups (Juergensmeyer 2000). In China, however much we may condemn the government's persecution of Falun Gong, its rise is symptomatic of a return to the tradition of religiously inspired, revolutionary secret societies with a messianic vision about the coming end of the world (M. H. Chang 2004). Remembering that the Taiping Rebellion, motivated by its own messianic vision, and enlisting the discontented in a rapidly changing society, was the bloodiest war in Chinese history until the twentieth century, it is no wonder that the Chinese government is worried.

Just as much as scholars underplayed the role of ethnicity and territory until the wars and massacres of the 1990s and early 2000s brought these issues back, so have reports about the end of ideology been premature (Bell 1965; Fukuyama 1992). The ideological disputes of one age may well start to seem irrelevant when the world changes. Communism and fascism, the major enemies of liberal capitalist democracies, have been defeated, but other ideologies remain to rally people, to offer means for coping with the problems of social life, and to provide strong identities to groups and societies in conflict with each other. Not only that, but identities and ideologies that once seemed to be fading may easily reappear with renewed vigor. That is what has happened in many parts of the former communist world, from the Balkans to the Caucasus to central Asia. In a modern world that was supposed to become ever more secular, extremist religious ideologies have clearly become far stronger than they were a few decades ago. Many Western scholars have been surprised that this has happened, though perhaps it was as naive to think that religion no longer matters as to believe that ethnic particularism and hypernationalism are relics of a less rational past.

Martin Jaffee has written a provocative analysis of the major monotheistic religions that developed out of the "Abrahamic" tradition: Judaism, Christianity, and Islam. He notes that many would like to say that these variants are all compatible with each other, believe in the same God, and emerged from the same region and cultural tradition. There is indeed a common philosophical tradition shared by all three, but Jaffee points to the powerful forces for intergroup violence that can emerge from a monotheism "framed as a moral imperative to transform a historical community in a project of divine service" (Jaffee 2001, 757–58). This imperative, which emerges from the Hebrew prophetic tradition, is one in which God calls the elect to form a community to transform the human order to bring it into line with God's will. A group that resists God's will can easily be seen as the kind of threat and pollution we have found associated with mass killing. This is the fundamentalism that may be growing even in developed countries with an Enlightenment tradition and a strong culture of human rights.

Martin Marty and Scott Appleby, who led a massive effort to study the growing trend toward fundamentalism throughout the world, concluded that it is particularly well suited to monotheistic "People of the Book," that is Jews, Christians, and Muslims, though they note that in some of the cases in eastern Asia newer texts have been written that make some of the same claims as the monotheistic, ancient texts of the Abrahamic religions. They ascribe the rise of fundamentalism in various parts of the world to the unsettling effects of rapid social change and the resulting demand for more secure, unquestioned communal identities (Marty and Appleby 1994, 817–33). Even in the United States, the more widespread the perception of political, economic, or social threat becomes, the more fundamentalist Protestant churches gain members at the expense of mainline Episcopalians and Presbyterians (McCann 1999).

Though the most virulent forms of religious fundamentalism today are modern, fundamentalists usually claim historical legitimacy on the basis of older texts. They reject secular-scientific notions of progress and clearly define those who are not with them as enemies to be converted, dominated, or eventually eliminated. This means that they combine a high level of ideological certitude with a sense of hostility and fear against outsiders who are viewed as threatening their existence (Marty and Appleby 1994, 817–33). This is exactly the kind of ideology that easily leads to genocidal violence when there are conflicts between competing communities and states, even when these conflicts originate less in ideological differences than in economic and political rivalries.

Ideologies, whether secular, ethnic, nationalist, or religious, are not the only sources of conflict. Throughout much of the world there are failed or failing states, particularly in Africa but also in parts of the Middle East, in central Asia, in the Caucasus, and in Latin America and the Caribbean, and these are sources of both international and domestic unrest (Fukuyama 2004). It is in failed states that people are most likely to fall back on closed ethnic or religious groups for protection and to turn to extreme ideologies that promise salvation. And it is in such situations that competition for scarce resources is most apt to produce violent conflicts.

We have in this volume emphasized the normality of genocidal mass murder, even if it rarely reaches the level of the most notorious cases. It will not help to minimize the problem by pretending that things like that will not happen again or that they are anomalies produced by sick minds. In the midst of war, in the face of threats to ourselves and those we care about, it is all too easy to reach the conclusion that we should kill them all. Steven Pinker, discussing human violence, has emphasized that "if anything, it is the belief that violence is an aberration that is dangerous, because it lulls us into forgetting how easily violence may erupt in quiescent places" (2002, 314). So it is with mass political murder.

Just how easy it is to slip into massacres becomes evident by considering one of the charts in a chapter titled "Ground Troop Combat Motivations" in one of the pioneering studies of war, *The American Soldier* (Stouffer et al. 1949, 158). In March—April 1944, researchers administered a survey to 4,064 enlisted infantrymen with combat experience fighting the Japanese in the Pacific. The survey asked: "What would you like to see happen to the Japanese after the war?" Responses were as follows: "Punish leaders but not ordinary Japanese" (43 percent), "Make Japanese people suffer plenty" (9 percent), "Wipe out whole Japanese nation" (42 percent). The rest had no opinion.

One might be tempted to attribute the popularity of wiping out the Japanese people to the personal suffering and loss of those engaged in combat against Japanese soldiers. But the same survey administered in November 1943 and April 1944 to 1,022 veteran enlisted infantrymen fighting in Europe showed that 61 percent favored wiping out the whole Japanese nation. And an identical survey given in February 1944 to 472 infantrymen in training in the United States showed 67 percent in favor of wiping out the whole Japanese nation. In other words, American soldiers fighting the Germans and even American soldiers who had not yet seen combat were more in favor of getting rid of all Japanese than the soldiers actually fighting the Japanese!

Identification with a group, particularly when other group members are suffering more from the enemy than oneself, is evidently more powerful than personal suffering in producing hatred of the enemy. A survey of veteran enlisted infantrymen in the Pacific in March—April 1944 asked: "When the going was tough, how much were you helped by thoughts of hatred for the enemy?" Of the 4,734 soldiers responding, 46 percent said thoughts of hatred for the enemy "Helped a lot" (Stouffer et al. 1949, 174). Although the survey respondents were not the same for the two kinds of question, probably many of the soldiers who favored wiping out the Japanese nation (42 percent) were also likely to feel that hatred of the enemy helped when the going was tough (46 percent).

The point here is not that Americans are particularly bloodthirsty and hate-filled. On the contrary, the point is how easy it is to link hatred of the enemy with an impulse to kill them all — easy even for individuals raised in a developed country with a culture of individual and civil rights. Had America's leaders decided that the Japanese should be subject to wholesale massacres after the war to punish them for their behavior in World War II, there is little doubt that a large percentage of the American military would have been all too happy to follow these orders.

Human rights advocates see the extension of humanitarian principles as a way in which to regulate conflicts in the world and bring about a more kindly approach to governance and conflict resolution everywhere. They are right, but as Timothy McDaniel has pointed out, this is a peculiarly Western notion that has been attacked elsewhere as ethnocentric and hypocritical. He cites Morocco's Council of Religious Scholars that answered the demand for human rights by claiming: "We in Islam have had it [human rights] since the beginning. We have no differences between whites, blacks, Jews, Muslims—everyone is free. We never persecuted the Jews here the way they did in France and England" (quoted in McDaniel 2000, 212–13).

Some of the historical precedent cited in this statement is of dubious accuracy, but the statement reflects a common view throughout the non-Western world, including China and most of Asia, that it is no one's business but their own how they regulate their internal conflicts, and that extreme threats to their states and societies justify extreme, large-scale violence. There is no reason to believe that Western democracies would act all that differently if they felt seriously threatened. Not only World War II, but also the wars fought by the major Western powers in the third world since then have had more than their share of human rights abuses.

The problem of intolerance and conflicting identities is far deeper than any merely structural issue—unequal prosperity, competition for resources, fixing broken states, and so on. Our social lives are fundamentally centered on group identities that are defined by difference, that is, by boundaries that divide us from other groups, especially competing groups. The nature and boundaries of these groups may change, but their importance remains. Small clans can be grouped into tribes. Tribes can become large nations. National boundaries can change. Religions can go from being purely local to encompassing vast areas with worldviews transcending ethnicity and nation. But group identities remain a vital part of all our lives, and they all have insiders and outsiders. Such boundaries may remain semidormant for long periods of time, but when conflict intensifies, they are quickly reinforced and become highly contentious as groups try to protect themselves from outsiders viewed as dangerous. They become what Ken Jowitt has called "barricaded" entities "whose primary imperative is 'absolute' separation from what are seen as contaminating others. . . . Social, religious, ideological, cultural and political connections among members who share a barricaded identity are dogmatically and hysterically defined and defended, as are disconnections from nonmembers. . . . Violence between barricaded entities tends to be recurrent. The threshold for violence is very low" (2001, 28–29).

Everything we have said points to the conclusion that we need to do our utmost to avoid barricading ourselves. The first step in that direction is to learn. If we understand "why the world wags and what wags it," as Merlyn says in the epigraph to this chapter, we necessarily become more tolerant. The more we know about each other and the more we exchange with others, the less likely we are to fall into the essentializing trap and the more likely we are to learn to negotiate and compromise, and to better control our emotions. The more we can do that, the more we will see the answer to our original question.

Why not kill them all? Because they are like us.

References

Abadie, Laurent. 2004. "À Mostar, la symbolique du vieux pont reste assez éloignée du réel." *Le Monde*, July 27. Electronic edition at http://www.lemonde.fr/.

Adanır, Fikret. 2001. "Armenian Deportations and Massacres in 1915." In Chirot and Seligman, eds., *Ethnopolitical Warfare*, 71–81.

Allport, Gordon. 1954. *The Nature of Prejudice*. Cambridge, Mass.: Addison-Wesley.

Anderson, Benedict. 1991. *Imagined Communities*. Rev. and expanded ed. London: Verso.

———. 1998. *The Spectre of Comparisons: Nationalism, Southeast Asia, and the World*. London: Verso.

Anderson, David L. 1998. *Facing My Lai: Moving beyond the Massacre*. Lawrence: University of Kansas Press.

Anderson, William L., ed. 1991. *Cherokee Removal: Before and After*. Athens: University of Georgia Press.

Archibald, Steve, and Paul Richards. 2002. "Seeds and Rights: New Approaches to Postwar Rehabilitation in Sierra Leone." Atlanta: CARE.

Arendt, Hannah. 1951. *The Origins of Totalitarianism*. New York: Harcourt, Brace.

———. 1963. *Eichmann in Jerusalem: A Report on the Banality of Evil*. New York: Viking.

Aron, Raymond. 1951. "Du Marxisme au Stalinisme." In Aron, *Les guerres en chaîne*, 159–77. Paris: Gallimard.

Axelrod, Robert. 1984. *The Evolution of Cooperation*. New York: Basic Books.

Banac, Ivo. 1984. *The National Question in Yugoslavia: Origins, History, Politics*. Ithaca, N.Y.: Cornell University Press.

Barany, Zoltan. 2002. *The East European Gypsies: Regime Change, Marginality, and Ethnopolitics*. Cambridge: Cambridge University Press.

Barany, Zoltan, and Robert G. Moser, eds. *Ethnic Politics after Communism*. Ithaca, N.Y.: Cornell University Press.

Barkey, Karen. 1994. *Bandits and Bureaucrats: The Ottoman Route to State Centralization*. Ithaca, N.Y.: Cornell University Press.

Barkey, Karen, and Mark von Hagen, eds. 1997. *After Empire: Multiethnic Societies and Nation-Building*. Boulder, Colo.: Westview.

Barth, Fredrik. 1973. "Descent and Marriage Reconsidered." In Goody, ed., *The Character of Kinship*, 3–19.

Bass, Gary Jonathan. 2000. *Stay the Hand of Vengeance: The Politics of War Crimes Tribunals*. Princeton, N.J.: Princeton University Press.

Bauer, Yehouda. 2002. *Rethinking the Holocaust*. New Haven, Conn.: Yale University Press.

Bauman, Zygmunt. 1989. *Modernity and the Holocaust*. Ithaca, N.Y.: Cornell University Press.

Baumeister, Roy, Ellen Bratslavsky, Catrin Finkenauer, and Kathleen D. Vohs. 2001. "Bad Is Stronger Than Good." *Review of General Psychology* 5 (4): 323–70.

Beal, Merrill D. 1966. *I Will Fight No More Forever: Chief Joseph and the Nez Perce War*. Seattle: University of Washington Press.

Bell, Daniel. 1965. *The End of Ideology: On the Exhaustion of Political Ideas in the Fifties*. Glencoe, Ill.: Free Press.

Beller, Steven. 1989. *Vienna and the Jews 1867–1938: A Cultural History*. Cambridge: Cambridge University Press.

Bergsma, Wiebe. 1995. "Britain and the Dutch Republic." In Davids and Lucassen, eds., *A Miracle Mirrored*, 196–228.

Berkowitz, Leonard. 1989. "Frustration-Aggression Hypothesis: Examination and Reformulation." *Psychological Bulletin* 106:59–73.

Berlin, Isaiah. 1998. *The Proper Study of Mankind*. New York: Farrar, Straus and Giroux.

Berndt, Ronald M. 1964. "Warfare in the New Guinea Highlands." *American Anthropologist* 66 (4): 183–203.

Berthélemy, Jean-Claude, and François Bourguignon. 1996. *Growth and Crisis in Côte d'Ivoire*. Washington, D.C.: World Bank.

Biabo, Prosper. 2003. "Community Action for Reintegration and Recovery for Youth and Women Project, Republic of Congo." Brazzaville: United Nations Development Programme Mission in Congo.

Blackburn, Robin. 2000. "Kosovo: The War of NATO Expansion." In Wasserstrom, Hunt, and Young, eds., *Human Rights and Revolutions*, 191–210.

Blass, Thomas. 1999. "The Milgram Paradigm after 35 Years: Some Things We Now Know about Obedience to Authority." *Journal of Applied Social Psychology* 29: 955–78.

Blick, Jeffrey P. 1988. "Genocidal Warfare in Tribal Societies as a Result of European-induced Culture Conflict." *MAN* 28 (4) (December): 654–70.

Bock, Joseph G., and Clark McCauley. 2003. "A Call to Lateral Mission: Mobilizing Religious Authority against Ethnic Violence." *Mission Studies* 20 (Spring): 9–34.

Bonte, Pierre, ed., 1994. *Épouser au plus proche.* Paris: École des Hautes Études en Sciences Sociales.

Boone, Catherine. 2003. *Political Topographies of the African State: Territorial Authority and Institutional Choice.* Cambridge: Cambridge University Press.

Botev, Nikolai. 1994. "Where East Meets West: Ethnic Intermarriage in the Former Yugoslavia, 1962–1989." *American Sociological Review* 59 (3): 461–80.

Bothwell, Robert. 1995. *Canada and Quebec: One Country, Two Histories.* Vancouver: University of British Columbia Press.

Boxer, Charles R. 1965. *The Dutch Seaborne Empire 1600–1800.* New York: Knopf.

Bozdoğan, Sibel, and Reşat Kasaba, eds. 1997. *Rethinking Modernity and National Identity in Turkey.* Seattle: University of Washington Press.

Brass, Paul. 1997. *Theft of an Idol: Text and Context in the Representation of Collective Violence.* Princeton, N.J.: Princeton University Press.

———. 2003. "The Partition of India and Retributive Genocide in the Punjab, 1946–47: Means, Methods, and Purposes." *Journal of Genocide Research* 5 (1): 71–101.

Bratton, Michael, and Nicolas van de Walle. 1997. *Democratic Experiments in Africa: Regime Transitions in Comparative Perspective.* Cambridge: Cambridge University Press.

Braudel, Fernand. 1973. *The Mediterranean and the Mediterranean World in the Age of Phillip II.* Vol. 2. New York: Harper and Row.

Brook, Timothy, ed. 1999. *Documents on the Rape of Nanking.* Ann Arbor: University of Michigan Press.

Browning, Christopher R. 1992a. *The Path to Genocide.* Cambridge: Cambridge University Press.

———. 1992b. *Ordinary Men: Reserve Police Battalion 101 and the Final Solution in Poland.* New York: HarperCollins.

Brubaker, Rogers. 1992. *Citizenship and Nationhood in France and Germany.* Cambridge, Mass.: Harvard University Press.

Brubaker, Rogers. 1996. *Nationalism Reframed: Nationhood and the National Question in the New Europe*. Cambridge: Cambridge University Press.

Brusset, Emery, Joseph Hasabamagara, and Augustin Ngendakuriyo. 2002. "Evaluation of the Burundi Community Rehabilitation Project 1999–2002." Washington, D.C.: World Bank and United Nations High Commission for Refugees.

Burke, Peter, ed. 1980. *The New Cambridge Modern History*. Vol. 13, *Companion Volume*. Cambridge: Cambridge University Press.

Burleigh, Michael, and Wolfgang Wippermann. 1991. *The Racial State: Germany 1933–1945*. Cambridge: Cambridge University Press.

Buruma, Ian. 1994. *The Wages of Guilt: Memories of War in Germany and Japan*. New York: Farrar, Straus and Giroux.

Byrne, Catherine. 2004. "Benefit or Burden: Victims' Reflections on TRC Participation." *Peace and Conflict: Journal of Peace Psychology* 10 (3): 237–56.

Caesar, Julius, and Aulus Hirtius. [51–50 B.C.] 1980. *The Battle for Gaul*. Translated by Ann Wiseman and Peter Wiseman. Boston: David R. Godine.

Canny, Nicholas. 1989. "Early Modern Ireland, c. 1500–1700." In Foster, ed., *The Oxford History of Ireland*, 88–133.

Caporaso, James A. 2000. *The European Union: Dilemmas of Regional Integration*. Boulder, Colo.: Westview.

CARE. 2004. "Niger Projects NER 048, 053, 067." http://www.careusa.org. (Click "CARE's Work," country of Niger, and, respectively, "Dakoro Household Livelihood," "DANIDA-Diffa Pastoral HLS," and "Capacity and Good Governance in Southern Maradi.")

Carneiro, Robert. 1990. "Chiefdom-level Warfare as Exemplified in Fiji and the Cauca Valley." In Haas, ed., *The Anthropology of War*, 190–211.

Chagnon, Napoleon A. 1988. "Life Histories, Blood Revenge, and Warfare in a Tribal Population (Yanomamo Indians of Amazonas)." *Science* 239 (February 26): 985–92.

———. 1990. "Reproductive and Somatic Conflicts of Interest in the Genesis of Violence and Warfare among Tribesmen." In Haas, ed., *The Anthropology of War*, 77–104.

Chalk, Frank, and Kurt Jonassohn. 1990. *The History and Sociology of Genocide: Analyses and Case Studies*. New Haven, Conn.: Yale University Press.

Chan, Hok-lam. 1988. "The Chien-wen, Yung-lo, Hung-his, and Hsüan-te Reigns." In Mote and Twitchett, eds., *The Cambridge History of China*, 7:182–304.

Chang, Iris. 1998. *The Rape of Nanking: The Forgotten Holocaust of World War II.* New York: Penguin.

Chang, Maria Hsia. 2004. *Falun Gong: The End of Days.* New Haven, Conn.: Yale University Press.

Chazan, Robert. 2000. *God, Humanity, and History: The Hebrew First Crusade Narratives.* Berkeley: University of California Press.

Chirot, Daniel. 1995. "Modernism without Liberalism: The Ideological Roots of Modern Tyranny." *Contention* 5 (1): 141–66.

———. 1996. *Modern Tyrants: The Power and Prevalence of Evil in Our Age.* Princeton, N.J.: Princeton University Press.

———. 2003. "Proposals for Future CARE Programs in Côte d'Ivoire: Understanding the Political Crisis, Dealing with Its Consequences, and Mitigating Ethnic Conflict." Unpublished report. Atlanta: CARE USA.

———. 2004. "Suggestions for Reconstruction, Reinsertion, and Rehabilitation (RRR) Projects to Be Financed by the Government of Côte d'Ivoire with World Bank Funding and a Preliminary Evaluation of RRR Pilot Projects in the Region of Bouaké." Unpublished report. Atlanta: CARE USA.

———. 2005. "What Provokes Violent Ethnic Conflict? Political Choice in One African and Two Balkan Cases." In Barany and Moser, eds., *Ethnic Politics after Communism*, 140–65.

Chirot, Daniel, and Anthony Reid, eds. 1997. *Essential Outsiders: Chinese and Jews in the Modern Transformation of Southeast Asia and Central Europe* Seattle: University of Washington Press.

Chirot, Daniel, and Martin E. P. Seligman, eds. 2001. *Ethnopolitical Warfare: Causes, Consequences, and Possible Solutions.* Washington, D.C.: American Psychological Association Press.

Chua, Amy. 2003. *World on Fire: How Exporting Free Market Democracy Breeds Ethnic Hatred and Global Instability.* New York: Doubleday.

Cialdini, Robert. 2001. *Influence: Science and Practice.* Boston: Allyn and Bacon.

Clifton, Robin, 1999. "An Indiscriminate Blackness? Massacre, Countermassacre, and Ethnic Cleansing in Ireland, 1640–1660." In Levene and Roberts, eds., *The Massacre in History*, 107–26.

Codere, Helen. 1967. "Fighting with Property." In McFeat, ed., *Indians of the North Pacific Coast*, 92–101.

Cohen, Mark R. 1994. *Under Crescent and Cross: The Jews in the Middle Ages.* Princeton, N.J.: Princeton University Press.

Collier, Paul, and Anke Hoeffler. 1998. "On Economic Causes of Civil War." *Oxford Economic Papers* 50 (4) (October): 563–673.

Courtois, Stéphane et al. 1999. *The Black Book of Communism: Crimes, Terror, Repression*. Cambridge, Mass.: Harvard University Press.

Craig, Gordon A. 1982. *The Germans*. New York: G. P. Putnam's Sons.

Crook, Richard C., and James Manor. 1998. *Democracy and Decentralization in South Asia and West Africa*. Cambridge: Cambridge University Press.

Crouch, Harold. 1978. *The Army and Politics in Indonesia*. Ithaca, N.Y.: Cornell University Press.

Crouzet, Denis. 1990. *Les guerriers de Dieu: La violence au temps des troubles de religion (vers 1525–vers 1610)*. Seyssel, France: Champ Vallon.

Dardess, John W. 1983. *Confucianism and Autocracy: Professional Elites in the Founding of the Ming Dynasty*. Berkeley: University of California Press.

Davids, Karel, and Jan Lucassen, eds. 1995. *A Miracle Mirrored: The Dutch Republic in European Perspective*. Cambridge: Cambridge University Press.

Davis, Natalie Z. 1975. "The Rites of Violence." In Natalie Z. Davis, *Society and Culture in Early Modern France*, 152–87. Stanford, Calif.: Stanford University Press.

Davis, Robert Penn. 1979. "Chaos in Indian Country." In King, ed., *The Cherokee Indian Nation*, 129–47.

Deák, István. 1997. "Holocaust Views: The Goldhagen Controversy in Retrospect." *Central European History* 34 (2): 295–307.

Deák, István, Jan T. Gross, and Tony Judt, eds. 2000. *The Politics of Retribution in Europe: World War II and Its Aftermath*. Princeton, N.J.: Princeton University Press.

Dedering, Tilman. 1999. " 'A Certain Rigorous Treatment of All Parts of the Nation': The Annihilation of the Herero in German South West Africa, 1904." In Levene and Roberts, eds., *The Massacre in History*, 205–22.

Degler, Carl N. 1991. *In Search of Human Nature: The Decline and Revival of Darwinism in American Social Thought*. New York: Oxford University Press.

Deng, Francis M. 1995. *War of Visions: Conflict of Identities in the Sudan*. Washington, D.C.: Brookings Institution Press.

de Vries, Jan, and Ad van der Woude. 1997. *The First Modern Economy: Success, Failure, and Perseverance in the Dutch Economy, 1500–1815*. Cambridge: Cambridge University Press.

Díez Medrano, Juan. 1995. *Divided Nations: Class, Politics, and Nationalism in the Basque Country and Catalonia.* Ithaca, N.Y.: Cornell University Press.

Dittmer, Lowell. 1987. *China's Continuous Revolution: The Post-liberation Epoch 1949–1981.* Berkeley: University of California Press.

Djilas, Aleksa. 1991. *The Contested Country: Yugoslav Unity and Communist Revolution 1919–1953.* Cambridge, Mass.: Harvard University Press.

Dollard, John, Leonard W. Doob, Neal E. Miller, O. H. Mower, and Robert R. Sears. 1939. *Frustration and Aggression.* New Haven, Conn.: Yale University Press.

Donald, Lelan. 1997. *Aboriginal Slavery on the Northwest Coast of North America.* Berkeley: University of California Press.

Doran, Michael S. 2004. "The Saudi Paradox." *Foreign Affairs* 83 (1): 35–49.

Douglas, Mary. 1984. *Purity and Danger: An Analysis of the Concepts of Pollution and Taboo.* London: Routledge.

Dower, John W. 1986. *War without Mercy: Race and Power in the Pacific War.* New York: Pantheon Books.

———. 1999. *Embracing Defeat: Japan in the Wake of World War II.* New York: W. W. Norton.

Drechsler, Horst. 1980. *"Let Us Die Fighting": The Struggle of the Herero and Nama against German Imperialism (1884–1915).* London: Zed Books.

Duby, Georges. 1977. *The Chivalrous Society.* Berkeley: University of California Press.

Dumont, Jean-Paul. 1987. "Quels Tasadays? De la découverte et de l'invention d'autrui." *Homme* 27 (103): 27–42.

Dumont, Louis. 1980. *Homo Hierarchicus: The Caste System and Its Implications.* Chicago: University of Chicago Press.

Dwyer, Leslie, and Degung Santikarma. 2003. "When the World Turned to Chaos: 1965 and Its Aftermath in Bali, Indonesia." In Gellately and Kiernan, eds., *The Specter of Genocide,* 189–214.

Early, John D., and John F. Peters. 2000. *The Xilixana Yanomami of the Amazon: History, Social Structure, and Population Dynamics.* Gainesville: University Press of Florida.

Economist. 2004a. "Thick Skin Required: Kosovo's Future; A Power Vacuum in the UN's Balkan Mission." May 22.

———. 2004b. "The World Notices Darfur: Sudan" and "The World Can't Wait: Genocide in Darfur." July 31.

El-Khazen, Farid. 2000. *The Breakdown of the State in Lebanon, 1967–1976.* Cambridge, Mass.: Harvard University Press.

Ellingson, Ter. 2001. *The Myth of the Noble Savage.* Berkeley: University of California Press.

Elster, Jon. 1999. *Alchemies of the Mind: Rationality and the Emotions.* Cambridge: Cambridge University Press.

Etzioni, Amitai. 2004. *From Empire to Community: A New Approach to International Relations.* New York: Palgrave Macmillan.

Evans-Pritchard, Edward E. 1940. *The Nuer.* Oxford: Oxford University Press.

Farb, Peter. 1968. *Man's Rise to Civilization as Shown by the Indians of North America from Primeval Times to the Coming of the Industrial State.* New York: E. P. Dutton.

Farmer, Sarah B. 1999. *Martyred Village: Commemorating the 1944 Massacre at Oradour-sur-Glane.* Berkeley: University of California Press.

Fearon, James D., and David D. Laitin. 1996. "Explaining Interethnic Cooperation." *American Political Science Review* 90 (4) (December): 715–35.

Fein, Helen. 1990. "Genocide: A Sociological Perspective." *Current Sociology* 38 (1) (Spring): 1–126.

Fenton, Steve. 2003. *Ethnicity.* Cambridge: Polity Press.

Ferguson, Brian R. 1984. "A Reexamination of the Causes of Northwest Coast Warfare," 267–328. In Brian R. Ferguson, ed., *Warfare, Culture, and Environment.* Orlando, Fla.: Academic Press.

———. 1995. *Yanomami Warfare: A Political History.* Santa Fe, N.M.: School of American Research Press.

Fest, Joachim C. 1970. *The Face of the Third Reich.* New York: Pantheon.

———. 1975. *Hitler.* New York: Vintage.

Fine, John V. A., Jr. 1994. *The Late Medieval Balkans: A Critical Survey from the Late Twelfth Century to the Ottoman Conquest.* Ann Arbor: University of Michigan Press.

Finkelstein, Israel, and Neil Asher Silberman. 2001. *The Bible Unearthed.* New York: Free Press.

Fitness, Julie, and Garth J. O. Fletcher. 1993. "Love, Hate, Anger, and Jealousy in Close Relationships." *Journal of Personality and Social Psychology* 65:942–58.

Fitzpatrick, David. 1989. "Ireland since 1870." In Foster, ed., *The Oxford History of Ireland,* 174–229.

Fogel, Joshua A., ed. 2000. *The Nanjing Massacre in History and Historiography*. Berkeley: University of California Press.

Forbes, Hugh Donald. 1997. *Ethnic Conflict: Commerce, Culture, and the Contact Hypothesis*. New Haven, Conn.: Yale University Press.

Fortes, Meyer. 1969. *Kinship and the Social Order*. Chicago: Aldine.

Fossier, Robert. 1986. "The Great Trial." In Robert Fossier, ed., *The Middle Ages: Volume III (1250–1520)*, 52–118. Cambridge: Cambridge University Press.

Foster, Robert F., ed. 1989. *The Oxford History of Ireland*. Oxford: Oxford University Press.

Frank, Richard B. 1999. *Downfall: The End of the Imperial Japanese Empire*. New York: Random House.

Fraser, Angus. 1995. *The Gypsies*. Oxford: Blackwell.

Freeman, Michael. 1995. "Genocide, Civilization and Modernity." *British Journal of Sociology* 46 (2) (June): 207–23.

Fried, Morton, Marvin Harris, and Robert Murphy, eds. 1986. *War: The Anthropology of Armed Conflict and Aggression*. Garden City, N.J.: American Museum of Natural History Press.

Friedländer, Saul. 1997. *Nazi Germany and the Jews*. New York: Harper Collins.

Frijda, Nico H. 2000. "The Psychologist's Point of View." In Lewis and Haviland-Jones, eds., *Handbook of Emotions*, 59–74.

Frost, Brian. 1998. *Struggling to Forgive: Nelson Mandela and South Africa's Search for Reconciliation*. London: HarperCollins.

Fukuyama, Francis. 1992. *The End of History and the Last Man*. New York: Free Press.

———. 2004. *State Building: Governance and World Order in the 21st Century*. Ithaca, N.Y.: Cornell University Press.

Gallagher, Tony. 2001. "The Northern Ireland Conflict: Prospects and Possibilities." In Chirot and Seligman, eds., *Ethnopolitical Warfare*, 205–14.

Garrett, Stephen A. 1993. *Ethics and Airpower in World War II: The British Bombing of German Cities*. New York: St. Martin's Press.

Gaylin, Willard. 2003. *Hatred: The Psychological Descent into Violence*. New York: Public Affairs.

Geary, Patrick J. 2002. *The Myth of Nations: The Medieval Origins of Europe*. Princeton, N.J.: Princeton University Press.

Gellately, Robert, and Ben Kiernan, eds. 2003. *The Specter of Genocide: Mass Murder in Historical Perspective*. Cambridge: Cambridge University Press.

Gellner, Ernest. 1983. *Nations and Nationalism*. Ithaca, N.Y.: Cornell University Press.

———. 1992. *Postmodernism, Reason and Religion*. London: Routledge.

Gibson, James L. 2004. "Does Truth Lead to Reconciliation? Testing the Causal Assumptions of the South African Truth and Reconciliation Process." *American Journal of Political Science* 48 (2): 201–17.

Gil-White, Francisco. 1999. "How Thick Is Blood?" *Ethnic and Racial Studies* 22 (5): 789–820.

Glenny, Misha. 1993. *The Fall of Yugoslavia: The Third Balkan War*. London: Penguin.

———. 2000. *The Balkans: Nationalism, War and the Great Powers, 1804–1999*. New York: Viking.

Glover, Jonathan. 2000. *Humanity: A Moral History of the Twentieth Century*. New Haven, Conn.: Yale University Press.

Goldhagen, Daniel J. 1996. *Hitler's Willing Executioners: Ordinary Germans and the Holocaust*. New York: Knopf.

Goodson, Larry P. 2001. *Afghanistan's Endless War: State Failure, Regional Politics, and the Rise of the Taliban*. Seattle: University of Washington Press.

Goody, Jack, ed. 1973. *The Character of Kinship*. Cambridge: Cambridge University Press.

Gottesman, Evan. 2003. *Cambodia after the Khmer Rouge*. New Haven, Conn.: Yale University Press.

Gould, Roger. 1999. "Collective Violence and Group Solidarity: Evidence from a Feuding Society." *American Sociological Review* 64 (3) (June): 357–81.

Grant, Michael. 1984. *The Ancient History of Israel*. New York: Charles Scribner's Sons.

Gray, John. 1996. *Isaiah Berlin*. Princeton, N.J.: Princeton University Press.

Greenfeld, Liah. 1992. *Nationalism: Five Roads to Modernity*. Cambridge, Mass.: Harvard University Press.

Greengrass, Mark. 1999. "Hidden Transcripts: Secret Histories and Personal Testimonies of Religious Violence in the French Wars of Religion." In Levene and Roberts, eds., *The Massacre in History*, 70–87.

Gregor, Thomas. 1990. "Uneasy Peace: Intertribal Relations in Brazil's Upper Xingu." In Haas, ed., *The Anthropology of War*, 15–124.

Gross, Jan T. 1979. *Polish Society under German Occupation: The General-gouvernement, 1939–1944*. Princeton, N.J.: Princeton University Press.

————. 1988. *Revolution from Abroad: The Soviet Conquest of Poland's Western Ukraine and Western Belorussia.* Princeton, N.J.: Princeton University Press.

————. 2001. *Neighbors: The Destruction of the Jewish Community in Jedwabne, Poland.* Princeton, N.J.: Princeton University Press.

Grosscup, Scott. 2004. "The Trial of Slobodan Milošević: The Demise of Head of State Immunity and the Specter of Victor's Justice." *Denver Journal of International Law and Policy* 32 (Spring): 355–81.

Guilmartin, John F., Jr. 1989. "Ideology and Conflict: The Wars of the Ottoman Empire, 1453–1606." In Rotberg and Rabb, eds., *The Origins and Prevention of Major Wars*, 149–75.

Gurr, Ted Robert. 1993. *Minorities at Risk: A Global View of Ethnopolitical Conflict.* Washington, D.C.: United States Institute of Peace.

Gurr, Ted Robert, and Barbara Harff. 1994. *Ethnic Conflict in World Politics.* Boulder, Colo.: Westview.

Haas, Jonathan, ed. 1990. *The Anthropology of War.* Cambridge: Cambridge University Press.

Hall, John A., and Charles Lindholm. 1999. *Is America Breaking Apart?* Princeton, N.J.: Princeton University Press.

Hamber, Brandon. 2001. "Who Pays for Peace? Implications of the Negotiated Settlement in Post-apartheid South Africa." In Chirot and Seligman, eds., *Ethnopolitical Warfare*, 235–58.

Hamilton, Alastair. 2000. "Introduction," 1–9. In Alastair Hamilton, Alexander H. deGroot, and Maurits H. van den Boogert, eds., *Friends and Rivals in the East.* Leiden: Brill.

Handlin, Oscar. 1973. *The Uprooted.* 2nd ed. Boston: Little, Brown.

Hardin, Russell. 1995. *One for All: The Logic of Group Conflict.* Princeton, N.J.: Princeton University Press.

Harmand, Jacques. 1984. *Vercingétorix.* Paris: Fayard.

Harris, Marvin. 1996. "Yanomami Warfare: A Political History." *Human Ecology* 24 (3): 413–16.

Hart, Marjolein't. 1995. "The Dutch Republic: The Urban Impact upon Politics." In Davids and Lucassen, eds., *A Miracle Mirrored*, 57–98.

Hartz, Louis. 1955. *The Liberal Tradition in America.* New York: Harcourt, Brace and World.

Haslam, Nick O., Louis Rothschild, and Donald Ernst. 2000. "Essentialist Beliefs about Social Categories." *British Journal of Social Psychology* 39:13–127.

Hay, Denys, ed. 1975. *The New Cambridge Modern History*. Vol. 1, *The Renaissance 1493–1520*. Cambridge: Cambridge University Press.

Hayden, Robert M. 1992. "Constitutional Nationalism in the Formerly Yugoslav Republics." *Slavic Review* 51 (4): 654–73.

Hechter, Michael. 2000. *Containing Nationalism*. Oxford: Oxford University Press.

Hefner, Robert W. 1990. *The Political Economy of Mountain Java: An Interpretive History*. Berkeley: University of California Press.

———, ed. 1998. *Democratic Civility: The History and Cross-cultural Possibility of a Modern Political Ideal*. New Brunswick, N.J.: Transaction Publishers.

Heider, Karl G. 1970. *The Dugum Dani: A Papuan Culture in the Highlands of West New Guinea*. Chicago: Aldine.

Hemley, Robin. 2003. *Invented Eden: The Elusive, Disputed History of the Tasaday*. New York: Farrar, Straus and Giroux.

Herbst, Jeffrey. 2000. *States and Power in Africa: Comparative Lessons in Authority and Control*. Princeton, N.J.: Princeton University Press.

Herf, Jeffrey. 1984. *Reactionary Modernism: Technology, Culture, and Politics in Weimar and the Third Reich*. Cambridge: Cambridge University Press.

Heuveline, Patrick. 2001. "Approaches to Measuring Genocide: Excess Mortality during the Khmer Rouge Period." In Chirot and Seligman, eds., *Ethnopolitical Warfare*, 93–108.

Hilberg, Raul. 1992. *Perpetrators, Victims, Bystanders: The Jewish Catastrophe 1933–1945*. New York: HarperCollins.

Hilsman, Roger. 1996. *The Cuban Missile Crisis: The Struggle over Policy*. Westport, Conn.: Praeger.

Hinton, Alexander L., ed. 2002. *Annihilating Difference: The Anthropology of Genocide*. Berkeley: University of California Press.

Hironaka, Ann. 2005. *Neverending Wars: The International Community, Weak States, and the Perpetuation of Civil War*. Cambridge, Mass.: Harvard University Press.

Hirschfeld, Lawrence A. 1996. *Race in the Making: Cognition, Culture, and the Child's Construction of Human Kinds*. Cambridge, Mass.: MIT Press.

Hirschman, Albert O. 1977. *The Passions and the Interests*. Princeton, N.J.: Princeton University Press.

Hirschman, Charles. 1987. "The Meaning and Measurement of Ethnicity in Malaysia: An Analysis of Census Classifications." *Journal of Asian Studies* 46 (3): 555–82.

Hitler, Adolf. [1925–26] 1971. *Mein Kampf*. Translated by Ralph Manheim. Boston: Houghton Mifflin.

———. [1941–43] 1973. *Hitler's Table Talk 1941–1943*. Introduced by Hugh R. Trevor-Roper. London: Weidenfeld and Nicolson.

Hobsbawm, Eric J. 1987. *The Age of Empire 1875–1914*. New York: Pantheon.

———. 1992. *Nations and Nationalism since 1780: Programme, Myth, Reality*. Cambridge: Cambridge University Press.

Hochschild, Adam. 1999. *King Leopold's Ghost*. Boston: Houghton Mifflin.

Hodson, Randy, Dusko Sekulic, and Garth Massey. 1994. "National Tolerance in the Former Yugoslavia." *American Journal of Sociology* 99 (6): 1,534–58.

Hoig, Stanley W. 1998. *The Cherokees and Their Chiefs*. Fayetteville: University of Arkansas Press.

Holt, Mack P. 1995. *The French Wars of Religion 1562–1629*. Cambridge: Cambridge University Press.

Homans, George C. 1974. *Social Behavior: Its Elementary Forms*. New York: Harcourt Brace Jovanovich.

Horowitz, Donald L. 2001. *The Deadly Ethnic Riot*. Berkeley: University of California Press.

Hughes, Robert. 1988. *The Fatal Shore*. New York: Vintage.

Human Rights Watch. 2001. *The New Racism: The Political Manipulation of Ethnicity in Côte d'Ivoire*. New York: Human Rights Watch.

Humphrey, Michael. 2002. *The Politics of Atrocity and Reconciliation: From Terror to Trauma*. London: Routledge.

Hunt, Lynn. 2000. "The Paradoxical Origin of Human Rights." In Wasserstrom, Hunt, and Young, eds., *Human Rights and Revolutions*, 3–17.

Huntington, Samuel P. 2004. *Who Are We? The Challenges to America's National Identity*. New York: Simon and Schuster.

Ignatieff, Michael. 1997. *The Warrior's Honor: Ethnic War and the Modern Conscience*. New York: Henry Holt.

International Crisis Group. 2004. "Sudan: Now or Never in Darfur." Africa Report no. 80. http://www.crisisweb.org/home/index.cfm?id=2765&1=1 (accessed May 23).

IRIN News.org. 2004. "Chad-Sudan: Janjawid Militia in Darfur Appears to Be out of Control." U.N. Office for the Coordination of Humanitarian Affairs. http://www.irinnews.org/repor.asp?ReportID=41067 (accessed July 18).

Isiguro, Yoshiaki. 1998. "The Japanese National Crime: The Korean Massacre after the Great Kanto Earthquake of 1923." *Korea Journal* (Winter): 331–32.

Jaffee, Martin S. 2001. "One God, One Revelation, One People: On the Symbolic Structure of Elective Monotheism." *Journal of the American Academy of Religion* 69 (4) (December): 753–75.

Janos, Andrew C. 1997. *Czechoslovakia and Yugoslavia: Ethnic Conflict and the Dissolution of Multinational States*. Berkeley: International and Area Studies of the University of California.

Japanese Ministry of Education. 1937. "Kokutai no Hongi" ("The Unique National Policy"). In Morris, ed. *Japan 1931–1945: Militarism, Fascism, Japanism?*, 46–52.

Jelavich, Barbara. 1983. *History of the Balkans*. Vol. 2, *Twentieth Century*. Cambridge: Cambridge University Press.

Johnson, James T. 1999. *Morality and Contemporary Warfare*. New Haven, Conn.: Yale University Press.

Jomo, K. S. 1997. "A Specific Idiom of Chinese Capitalism in Southeast Asia: Sino-Malaysian Capital Accumulation in the Face of State Hostility." In Chirot and Reid, eds. *Essential Outsiders*, 237–57.

Jones, James R. 1996. *The Anglo-Dutch Wars of the Seventeenth Century*. London: Longman.

Jordan, William C. 1996. *The Great Famine: Northern Europe in the Early Fourteenth Century*. Princeton, N.J.: Princeton University Press.

Jowitt, Ken. 1992. *New World Disorder: The Leninist Extinction*. Berkeley: University of California Press.

———. 2001. "Ethnicity: Nice, Nasty, and Nihilistic." In Chirot and Seligman, eds., *Ethnopolitical Warfare*, 27–36.

Judah, Tim. 1997. *The Serbs: History, Myth and the Destruction of Yugoslavia*. New Haven, Conn.: Yale University Press.

———. 2004. "The Fog of Justice." *New York Review of Books* (January 15): 23–25.

Judt, Tony. 2000. "The Past Is Another Country: Myth and Memory in Postwar Europe." In Deák, Gross, and Judt, eds., *The Politics of Retribution in Europe*, 293–323.

Juergensmeyer, Mark. 1993. *The New Cold War: Religious Nationalism Confronts the Secular State*. Berkeley: University of California Press.

———. 2000. *Terror in the Mind of God: The Global Rise of Religious Violence*. Berkeley: University of California Press.

Kaiser, David. 2000. *Politics and War: European Conflict from Philip II to Hitler*. Cambridge, Mass.: Harvard University Press.

Kamen, Henry. 1998. *The Spanish Inquisition: A Historical Revision*. New Haven, Conn.: Yale University Press.

Kant, Immanuel. [1784] 1959. *"Foundations of the Metaphysics of Morals" and "What Is Enlightenment?"* Indianapolis: Liberal Arts Press of Bobbs Merrill.

Kapelle, William E. 1979. *The Norman Conquest of the North: The Region and Its Transformation, 1000–1135*. Chapel Hill: University of North Carolina Press.

Karpat, Kemal H. 1973. *An Inquiry into the Social Foundation of Nationalism in the Ottoman State*. Princeton, N.J.: Center for International Studies, Princeton University.

Kasaba, Reşat. 1997. "Kemalist Certainties and Modern Ambiguities." In Bozdoğan and Kasaba, eds., *Rethinking Modernity and National Identity in Turkey*, 15–36.

Kaufman, Stuart J. 2001. *Modern Hatreds: The Symbolic Politics of Ethnic War*. Ithaca, N.Y.: Cornell University Press.

Kedourie, Elie. 1960. *Nationalism*. London: Hutchinson.

Keegan, John. 1978. *The Face of Battle: A Study of Agincourt, Waterloo and the Somme*. London: Penguin Books.

———. 1994. *A History of Warfare*. New York: Knopf.

Keil, Frank C. 1989. *Concepts, Kinds, and Cognitive Development*. Cambridge, Mass.: MIT Press.

Keller, Edmond J. 1998. "Transnational Ethnic Conflict in Africa." In Lake and Rothchild, eds., *The International Spread of Ethnic Conflict*, 275–92.

Kelman, Herbert C. 1997. "Group Processes in the Resolution of International Conflicts: Experiences from the Israeli-Palestinian Case." *American Psychologist* 52:212–20.

Kepel, Gilles. 2004. *The War for Muslim Minds: Islam and the West*. Cambridge, Mass.: Harvard University Press.

Kershaw, Ian, and Moshe Lewin. 1997. "Introduction. The Regimes and Their Dictators: Perspectives and Comparisons." In Ian Kershaw and Moshe Lewin, eds., *Stalinism and Nazism: Dictatorship and Comparison*. Cambridge: Cambridge University Press.

Khalidi, Rashid. 1986. *Under Siege: P.L.O. Decisionmaking during the 1982 War*. New York: Columbia University Press.

Kiernan, Ben. 1985. *How Pol Pot Came to Power*. London: Verso.

Kiernan, Ben. 1996. *The Pol Pot Regime: Race, Power and Genocide in Cambodia under the Khmer Rouge, 1975–1979.* New Haven, Conn.: Yale University Press.

———. 2001. "Myth, Nationalism, and Genocide." *Journal of Genocide Studies* 3 (2): 187–206.

Kieval, Hillel. 1997. "Middleman Minorities and Blood: Is There a Natural Economy of the Ritual Murder Accusation in Europe?" In Chirot and Reid, eds., *Essential Outsiders*, 208–33.

Kinealy, Christine. 1997. *A Death-Dealing Famine: The Great Hunger in Ireland.* London: Pluto Press.

King, Duane H., ed. 1979. *The Cherokee Indian Nation: A Troubled History.* Knoxville: University of Tennessee Press.

Knox, Colin, and Joanne Hughes. 1996. "Crossing the Divide: Community Relations in Northern Ireland." *Journal of Peace Research* 33 (1): 83–98.

Konner, Melvin. 1990. *Why the Reckless Survive—And Other Secrets of Human Nature.* New York: Viking.

Kressel, Neil J. 1996. *Mass Hate: The Global Rise of Genocide and Terror.* New York: Plenum Press.

Kugel, James L. 1997. *The Bible as It Was.* Cambridge, Mass.: Harvard University Press.

Kuper, Adam. 1994. *The Chosen Primate: Human Nature and Cultural Diversity.* Cambridge, Mass.: Harvard University Press.

Kuper, Leo. 1981. *Genocide.* New Haven, Conn.: Yale University Press.

Lacey, Marc. 2004. "Despite Appeals, Chaos Still Stalks the Sudanese" and "Amnesty Says Sudan Militias Use Rape as Weapon." *New York Times,* July 18 and 19, respectively.

Lake, David A., and Donald Rothchild, eds. 1998. *The International Spread of Ethnic Conflict: Fear Diffusion, and Escalation.* Princeton, N.J.: Princeton University Press.

Lamaison, Pierre. 1994. "Tous cousin? De l'héritage et des stratégies matrimoniales dans les monarchies européennes à l'âge classique." In Bonte, ed., *Épouser au plus proche*, 341–67.

Lamin, Abdul Rahman. 2003. "Building Peace through Accountability in Sierra Leone: The Truth and Reconciliation Commission and the Special Court." *Journal of Asian and African Studies* 38 (August): 295–321.

Lane Fox, Robin. 1992. *The Unauthorized Version: Truth and Fiction in the Bible.* New York: Knopf.

Langer, Walter C. 1972. *The Mind of Adolf Hitler.* New York: Basic Books.

Lape, Peter V. 2000. "Political Dynamics and Religious Change in the Late Pre-colonial Settlement in the Bunda Islands, Eastern Indonesia." *World Archeology* 32 (1): 138–55.

Laqueur, Walter. 1990. *Stalin: The Glasnost Revelations.* New York: Scribner's.

Lardy, Nicholas. 1983. *Agriculture in China's Modern Economic Development.* New York: Cambridge University Press.

Larson, Deborah W. 1997. *Anatomy of Mistrust: U.S.-Soviet Relations during the Cold War.* Ithaca, N.Y.: Cornell University Press.

Lee Hock Guan. 2000. "Ethnic Relations in Peninsular Malaysia: The Cultural and Economic Dimensions." *Social and Cultural Issues* (Singapore: Institute of Southeast Asian Studies) 1 (August).

Lemarchand, René. 1996. *Burundi: Ethnic Conflict and Genocide.* Cambridge: Cambridge University Press.

Lemkin, Raphael. 1944. *Axis Rule in Occupied Europe.* Washington, D.C.: Carnegie Endowment for International Peace.

Lesser, Guy. 2004. "War Crime and Punishment: What the United States Could Learn from the Milošević Trial." *Harper's Magazine* (January): 37–52.

Lester, Robert E. 1996. *The Peers Inquiry of the Massacre at My Lai.* Microfilmed from the Judge Advocate General's School, U.S. Army, Charlottesville, Va. Bethesda, Md.: University Publications of America.

Levene, Mark, and Penny Roberts, eds. 1999. *The Massacre in History.* New York: Berghahn Books.

Lévi-Strauss, Claude. 1969. *The Elementary Structures of Kinship.* Boston: Beacon Press.

Lewis, Bernard. 1984. *The Jews of Islam.* Princeton, N.J.: Princeton University Press.

Lewis, Michael, and Jeanette M. Haviland-Jones, eds. 2000. *Handbook of Emotions.* New York: Guilford Press.

Lieven, Anatol. 1998. *Chechnya: Tombstone of Russian Power.* New Haven, Conn.: Yale University Press.

Lih, Lars T. 1995. "Introduction," 1–63. In Lars T. Lih, Oleg V. Naumov, and Oleg V. Khlevnik, eds., *Stalin's Letters to Molotov.* New Haven, Conn.: Yale University Press.

Lijphart, Arend. 1977. *Democracy in Plural Societies: A Comparative Exploration.* New Haven, Conn.: Yale University Press.

Lim, Linda Y. C., and L. A. Peter Gosling. 1997. "Strengths and Weaknesses of Minority Status for Southeast Asian Chinese at a Time of Economic Growth and Liberalization." In Chirot and Reid, eds., *Essential Outsiders*, 285–317.

Lipstadt, Deborah E. 1986. *Beyond Belief: The American Press and the Coming of the Holocaust, 1933–1945*. New York: Free Press.

Locke, John. [1689] 1955. *Of Civil Government: Second Treatise*. Chicago: Henry Regnery.

Lumpkin, Wilson. 1969. *The Removal of the Cherokee Indians from Georgia*. 2 vols. in 1. New York: Arno Press.

MacFarquhar, Roderick. 1983. *The Origins of the Cultural Revolution*. Vol. 2, *The Great Leap Forward 1958–1960*. New York: Columbia University Press.

Madigan, Tim. 2001. *The Burning: Massacre, Destruction, and the Tulsa Race Riot of 1921*. New York: Thomas Dunne Books/St. Martin's Press.

Madison, James. [1788] 1941. "The Federalist Number 51." In Alexander Hamilton, John Jay, and James Madison, *The Federalist*, 335–41. New York: Modern Library. (Some scholars believe Alexander Hamilton may have written no. 51.)

Maier, Charles S. 1989. "Wargames: 1914–1919." In Rotberg and Rabb, eds., *The Origin and Prevention of Wars*, 249–79.

Mamdani, Mahmood. 1996. "Reconciliation without Justice." *Southern African Review of Books* 46:3–5.

———. 2001. *When Victims Become Killers: Colonialism, Nativism, and Genocide in Rwanda*. Princeton, N.J.: Princeton University Press.

Manent, Pierre. 1995. *An Intellectual History of Liberalism*. Princeton, N.J.: Princeton University Press.

Manz, Beatrice F. 1989. *The Rise and Rule of Tamerlane*. Cambridge: Cambridge University Press.

Maoz, Ifat. 2005. "Evaluating the Quality of Communication between Groups in Dispute: Equality in Contact Interventions between Jews and Arabs in Israel." *Negotiations Journal* 31:131–46.

———. 2006. "Moving between Coexistence and Conflict: Planned Encounters between Jews and Arabs in Israel." In Podeh and Kaufman, eds., *Arab-Jewish Relations*, forthcoming.

Maoz, Ifat, and Clark McCauley. 2005. "Psychological Correlates of Support for Compromise: A Polling Study of Jewish-Israeli Attitudes toward Solutions to the Israeli-Palestinian Conflict," *Political Psychology* 26: 791–807.

Marty, Martin E., and R. Scott Appleby. 1994. "Conclusion: An Interim Report on a Hypothetical Family," 814–42. In Marty and Appleby, eds., *Fundamentalism Observed*. Vol. 1. Chicago: University of Chicago Press.

Marx, Anthony W. 1998. *Making Race and Nation: A Comparison of the United States, South Africa, and Brazil*. Cambridge: Cambridge University Press.

Marx, Karl. [1848] 1977. "The Communist Manifesto," 221–47. In *Karl Marx: Selected Writings*, edited by David McLellan. Oxford: Oxford University Press.

Massey, Garth, Randy Hodson, and Dusko Sekulic. 1999. "Ethnic Enclaves and Intolerance: The Case of Yugoslavia." *Social Forces* 78 (2): 669–93.

Mattern, Susan P. 1999. *Rome and the Enemy: Imperial Strategy in the Principate*. Berkeley: University of California Press.

Maybury-Lewis, David. 2002. "Genocide against Indigenous Peoples." In Hinton, ed., *Annihilating Difference*, 43–53.

McCann, Stewart J. H. 1999. "Threatening Times and Fluctuations in American Church Membership." *Personality and Social Psychology Bulletin* 25 (3): 325–36.

McCauley, Clark. 2000–2001. "How President Bush Moved the U.S. into the Gulf War: Three Theories of Group Conflict and the Construction of Moral Violation." *Journal for the Study of Peace and Conflict* (annual edition): 32–42.

———. 2001. "The Psychology of Group Identification and the Power of Ethnic Nationalism." In Chirot and Seligman, eds., *Ethnopolitical Warfare*, 343–62.

———. 2005. "Review of A. Varshney's *Ethic Conflict and Civic Life: Hindus and Muslims in India*." *Terrorism and Political Violence* 17 (4): 646–53.

McCauley, Clark, Mary Wright, and Mary Harris. 2000. "Diversity Workshops on Campus: A Survey of Current Practice at U.S. Colleges and Universities." *College Student Journal* 34:100–114.

McCool, Alan, Fanie DuToit, Christopher Petty, and Clark McCauley. 2006. "The Impact of a Program of Stereotype Reduction Seminars in South Africa." *Journal of Applied Social Psychology* 36 (3): 586–613.

McDaniel, Timothy. 2000. "The Strange Career of Radical Islam." In Wasserstrom, Hunt, and Young, eds., *Human Rights and Revolutions*, 211–29.

McDowall, David. 1997. *A Modern History of the Kurds*. London: I. B. Taurus.

McFeat, Tom, ed. 1967. *Indians of the North Pacific Coast*. Seattle: University of Washington Press.

McGarry, John, and Brendan O'Leary. 1995. *Explaining Northern Ireland: Broken Images*. Oxford: Blackwell.

McKay, David H. 2001. *Designing Europe: Comparative Lessons from the Federal Experience*. Oxford: Oxford University Press.

McLoughlin, William G. 1986. *Cherokee Renascence in the New Republic*. Princeton, N.J.: Princeton University Press.

McNeill, William H. 1979. *The Human Condition: An Ecological and Historical View*. Princeton, N.J.: Princeton University Press.

Melson, Robert. 1992. *Revolution and Genocide: On the Origins of the Armenian Genocide and the Holocaust*. Chicago: University of Chicago Press.

Mendes-Flohr, Paul R., and Jehuda Reinharz, eds. 1980. *The Jew in the Modern World: A Documentary History*. New York: Oxford University Press.

Milgram, Stanley. 1974. *Obedience to Authority*. New York: Harper and Row.

Miller, Donald E., and Lorna Touryan Miller. 1993. *Survivors: An Oral History of the Armenian Genocide*. Berkeley: University of California Press.

Millie, Hambastigee, and Millie Paiwastoon. 2003. *National Solidarity Program: Draft Operation Manual*. Kabul: Afghan Ministry of Rural Rehabilitation and Development.

Milward, Alan. 1979. *War, Economy and Society 1939–1945*. Berkeley: University of California Press.

———. 1992. *The European Rescue of the Nation-State*. Berkeley: University of California Press.

Minow, Martha. 2002. "Breaking the Cycles of Hatred," 14–76. In Martha Minow, ed., *Breaking the Cycles of Hatred: Memory, Law, and Repair*. Princeton, N.J.: Princeton University Press.

Morgan, David. 1986. *The Mongols*. Oxford: Basil Blackwell.

Morren, George E. 1984. "Warfare on the Highland Fringe of New Guinea: The Case of the Mountain Ok." In Ferguson, ed., *Warfare, Culture, and Environment*, 169–207.

Morris, Ivan, ed. 1963. *Japan 1931–1945: Militarism, Fascism, Japanism?* Boston: Heath.

Moss, Michael. 2000. "The Story behind a Soldier's Story." *New York Times*, May 31.

Mosse, George L. 1964. *The Crisis of German Ideology*. New York: Grosset and Dunlap.

Mote, Frederick W., and Denis Twitchett, eds. 1988. *The Cambridge History of China*. Vol. 7, *The Ming Dynasty, 1368–1644*, pt. 1. Cambridge: Cambridge University Press.

Mukherjee, Kudrangshu. 1990. " 'Satan Let Loose upon Earth': The Kanpur Massacre in India in the Revolt of 1857." *Past and Present* 128 (August): 92–116.

Murphy, Sean. 2002. "The Strange Bedfellows of Justice Politics in South Africa." B.A. honors thesis, University of Washington.

Murray, Williamson A. 1995. "The West at War 1914–18." In Parker, ed., *Cambridge Illustrated History of Warfare*, 266–97.

Naimark, Norman M. 2001. *Fires of Hatred: Ethnic Cleansing in Twentieth-Century Europe*. Cambridge, Mass.: Harvard University Press.

Nance, John. 1975. *The Gentle Tasaday: A Stone Age People in the Philippine Rain Forest*. New York: Harcourt Brace Jovanovich.

Naphy, William G., and Penny Roberts, eds. 1997. *Fear in Early Modern Society*. Manchester: Manchester University Press.

Ndayizeye, Judith. 2002. "Prévention des conflicts au Burundi." Washington, D.C.: World Bank (Postconflict Unit).

Neier, Aryeh. 1998. *War Crimes*. New York: Random House.

Neillands, Robin. 2001. *The Bomber War: Arthur Harris and the Allied Bomber Offensive, 1939–1945*. London: John Murray.

Netanyahu, Benzion. 1995. *The Origins of the Inquisition in Fifteenth-Century Spain*. New York: Random House.

Nicolson, Harold. 1962. *Kings, Courts and Monarchy*. New York: Simon and Schuster.

Nierop, Henk van. 1995. "Similar Problems, Different Outcomes: The Revolt of the Netherlands and the Wars of Religion in France." In Davids and Lucassen, eds., *A Miracle Mirrored*, 26–56.

Nirenberg, David. 1996. *Communities of Violence: Persecution of Minorities in the Middle Ages*. Princeton, N.J.: Princeton University Press.

Nisbett, Richard E., and Dov Cohen. 1996. *Culture of Honor: The Psychology of Violence in the South*. Boulder, Colo.: Westview.

Oberschall, Anthony. 2001. "From Ethnic Cooperation to Violence and War in Yugoslavia." In Chirot and Seligman, eds., *Ethnopolitical Warfare*, 119–50.

Ó Gráda, Cormac. 1999. *Black '47 and Beyond: The Great Irish Famine in History, Economy, and Memory*. Princeton, N.J.: Princeton University Press.

Öhman, Arne. 2000. "Fear and Anxiety: Evolutionary, Cognitive, and Clinical Perspectives." In Lewis and Haviland-Jones, eds., *Handbook of Emotions*, 573–93.

O'Leary, Brendan. 2001. "Nationalism and Ethnicity: Research Agendas on Theories of Their Sources and Their Regulation." In Chirot and Seligman, eds., *Ethnopolitical Warfare*, 37–48.

Olson, Mancur. 2000. *Power and Prosperity*. New York: Basic Books.

Orogun, Paul S. 2002. "Crisis of Government, Ethnic Schism, Civil War, and Regional Destabilization of the Democratic Republic of the Congo." *World Affairs* 165:25–42.

Oskamp, Stuart, ed. 2000. *Reducing Prejudice and Discrimination*. Mahwah, N.J.: Lawrence Erlbaum Associates.

Padfield, Peter. 1990. *Himmler*. New York: Henry Holt.

Pakenham, Thomas. 1979. *The Boer War*. London: Weidenfeld and Nicolson.

Pape, Robert A. 1995. *Bombing to Win: Air Power and Coercion in War*. Ithaca, N.Y.: Cornell University Press.

Parker, Geoffrey. 1980. "Warfare." In Burke, ed., *The New Cambridge Modern History*, 201–19.

———, ed. 1995. *Cambridge Illustrated History of Warfare*. Cambridge: Cambridge University Press.

Parry, J. H. 1975. "The Ottoman Empire (1481–1520)." In Hay, ed., *The New Cambridge Modern History*, 395–419.

Patterson, Orlando. 1998. *The Ordeal of Integration: Progress and Resentment in America's "Racial" Crisis*. Washington, D.C.: Civita/ Counterpoint.

Perdue, Theda. 1979. "Cherokee Planters: The Development of Plantation Slavery before Removal." In King, ed., *The Cherokee Indian Nation*, 110–28.

Perlez, Jane. 2004. "Despite U.S. Penalties, Burmese Junta Refuses to Budge." *New York Times*, August 1.

Persico, Richard V. 1979. "Early Nineteenth-Century Cherokee Political Organization." In King, ed., *The Cherokee Indian Nation*, 92–109.

Pettigrew, Thomas F., and Linda R. Tropp. 2000. "Does Intergroup Contact Reduce Prejudice? Recent Meta-analytic Findings." In Oskamp, ed., *Reducing Prejudice and Discrimination*, 93–114.

Pinker, Steven. 2002. *The Blank Slate: The Modern Denial of Human Nature*. New York: Viking.

Podeh, Elie, and Asher Kaufman, eds. 2006. *Arab-Jewish Relations*. Sussex, Eng.: Sussex Academic Press.

Power, Samantha. 2002. *A Problem from Hell: America and the Age of Genocide*. New York: Perseus Publishing.

———. 2003. "How to Kill a Country: Turning a Breadbasket into a Basket Case in Ten Easy Steps the Robert Mugabe Way." *The Atlantic* (December): 86–94.

———. 2004. "Dying in Darfur: Can Ethnic Cleansing in Sudan Be Stopped?" *New Yorker* (August 30): 56–73.

Prawdin, Michael. 1967. *The Mongol Empire: Its Rise and Legacy*. New York: Free Press.

The Princeton Principles on Universal Jurisdiction. 2001. Compiled by the Princeton Project on Universal Jurisdiction. Princeton, N.J.: Princeton University Program in Law and Public Affairs.

Prunier, Gérard. 1997. *The Rwanda Crisis: History of a Genocide*. New York: Columbia University Press.

———. 2005. *Darfur: The Ambiguous Genocide*. Ithaca, N.Y.: Cornell University Press.

Reed, John S. 1993. *Surveying the South: Studies in Regional Sociology*. Columbia: University of Missouri Press.

———. 2001. "Why Has There Been No Race War in the American South?" In Chirot and Seligman, eds., *Ethnopolitical Warfare*, 275–86.

Reed, John S., and Dale V. Reed. 1996. *1001 Things Everyone Should Know about the South*. New York: Doubleday.

Remini, Robert V. 1977. *Andrew Jackson and the Course of American Empire*. Vol. 2. New York: Harper and Row.

———. 2001. *Andrew Jackson and His Indian Wars*. New York: Viking.

Rieff, David. 2000. "A New Age of Liberal Imperialism?" In Wasserstrom, Hunt, and Young, eds., *Human Rights and Revolutions*, 177–90.

———. 2002. *A Bed for the Night: Humanitarianism in Crisis*. New York: Simon and Schuster.

Riley-Smith, Jonathan. 1987. *The Crusades: A Short History*. New Haven, Conn.: Yale University Press.

Robinson, Geoffrey. 1995. *The Dark Side of Paradise: Political Violence in Bali*. Ithaca, N.Y.: Cornell University Press.

Rodrik, Dani. 1997. *Has Globalization Gone Too Far?* Washington, D.C.: Institute for International Economics.

Rossabi, Morris. 1988. *Khubilai Khan: His Life and Times*. Berkeley: University of California Press.

Rotberg, Robert I., and Theodore K. Rabb, eds. 1989. *The Origin and Prevention of Major Wars*. Cambridge: Cambridge University Press.

Rotberg, Robert I., and Dennis Thompson, eds. 2000. *Truth v. Justice: The Morality of Truth Commissions*. Princeton, N.J.: Princeton University Press.

Rothchild, Donald. 1997. *Managing Ethnic Conflict in Africa: Pressures and Incentives for Cooperation*. Washington, D.C.: Brookings Institution Press.

Roy, Olivier. 2004. *Globalized Islam: The Search for a New Ummah*. New York: Columbia University Press.

Royzman, Edward B., Clark McCauley, and Paul Rozin. 2006. "Four Ways to Think about Hate." In Sternberg, ed., *The Psychology of Hate*, forthcoming.

Rozin, Paul, Jonathan Haidt, and Clark McCauley. 2000. "Disgust." In Lewis and Haviland-Jones, eds., *Handbook of Emotions*, 637–53.

Rozin, Paul, and Edward B. Royzman. 2001. "Negativity Bias, Negativity Dominance and Contagion." *Personality and Social Psychology Review* 5 (4): 296–320.

Ruane, Joseph, and Jennifer Todd. 1996. *The Dynamics of Conflict in Northern Ireland: Power, Conflict, and Emancipation*. Cambridge: Cambridge University Press.

Rummel, Rudolph J. 1994. *Death by Government*. New Brunswick, N.J.: Transaction Publishers.

Sabini, John. 1995. *Social Psychology*. New York: W. W. Norton.

Salisbury, Harrison E. 1992. *The New Emperors: China in the Era of Mao and Deng*. Boston: Little, Brown.

Samson, Ross. 1991. "Economic Anthropology and the Vikings," 87–96. In Ross Samson, ed., *Social Approaches to Viking Studies*. Glasgow: Cruithne Press.

Sandbrook, Richard. 2000. *Closing the Circle: Democratization and Development in Africa*. London: Zed Books.

Satz, Ronald N. 1991. "Rhetoric versus Reality: The Indian Policy of Andrew Jackson." In W. Anderson, ed., *Cherokee Removal*, 29–54.

Schapiro, Leonard. 1987. *Russian Studies*. New York: Viking.

Scheff, Thomas J. 1994. *Bloody Revenge: Emotions, Nationalism and War*. Boulder, Colo.: Westview.

Schelling, Thomas C. 1966. *Arms and Influence*. New Haven, Conn.: Yale University Press.

Schorske, Carl E. 1981. *Fin-de-siècle Vienna: Politics and Culture*. New York: Vintage Books.

Schumpeter, Joseph. [1919] 1955. *Social Classes and Imperialism: Two Essays*. Cleveland, Ohio: Meridian Books.

Segev, Tom. 2001. *One Palestine Complete: Jews and Arabs under the British Mandate*. New York: Henry Holt.

Sengupta, Somini. 2003. "Congo War Toll Soars as U.N. Pleads for Aid." *New York Times*, May 27.

———. 2004. "Crisis in Sudan: Thorny Issues Underlying Carnage in Darfur Complicate World's Response." *New York Times*, August 16.

Seton-Watson, Hugh. 1977. *Nations and States: An Enquiry into the Origins of Nations and the Politics of Nationalism*. Boulder, Colo.: Westview Press.

Shand, Alexander F. 1920. *The Foundations of Character*. London: Macmillan.

Shankman, Paul. 1991. "Culture Contact, Cultural Ecology, and Dani Warfare." *MAN* 26 (2) (June): 299–321.

Shepher, Joseph. 1983. *Incest: A Biosocial View*. New York: Academic Press.

Shenfield, Stephen D. 1999. "The Circassians: A Forgotten Genocide?" In Levene and Roberts, eds., *The Massacre in History*, 149–62.

Singer, Peter. 1981. *The Expanding Circle: Ethics and Sociobiology*. New York: Farrar, Straus and Giroux.

Sivan, Emmanuel. 1985. *Radical Islam: Medieval Theology and Modern Politics*. New Haven, Conn.: Yale University Press.

Skerry, Peter. 1993. *Mexican Americans: The Ambivalent Minority*. New York: Free Press.

Slezkine, Yuri. 2004. *The Jewish Century*. Princeton, N.J.: Princeton University Press.

Smith, Anthony D. 1986. *The Ethnic Origins of Nations*. Oxford: Blackwell.

———. 2001. *Nationalism*. Cambridge: Polity Press.

Smith, Stephen. 2003. "La crise ivoirienne: Un condensé des caractéristiques de tout un continent." *Le Monde*, February 20. Electronic edition at http://www.lemonde.fr.

———. 2004a. "Côte d'Ivoire: Le processus de paix menacé par le limogeage de trois ministres de l'opposition." *Le Monde*, May 25. Electronic edition at http://www.lemonde.fr.

Smith, Stephen. 2004b. "La France et l'ONU impuissants face à la crise en Côte d'Ivoire." *Le Monde*, June 4. Electronic edition at http://www.lemonde.fr.

Sorel, Georges. 1941. *Reflections on Violence*. New York: Peter Smith.

Sparks, Allister H. 1995. *Tomorrow Is Another Country: The Inside Story of South Africa's Road to Change*. New York: Hill and Wang.

Spence, Jonathan D. 1990. *The Search for Modern China*. New York: W. W. Norton.

———. 1997. *God's Chinese Son: The Taiping Heavenly Kingdom of Hong Xiuquan*. New York: W. W. Norton.

Spencer, Herbert. 1897. *The Principles of Sociology*. New York: D. Appleton.

Staples, Brent. 1999. "Unearthing a Riot." *New York Times Magazine*, December 19.

Staub, Ervin. 1989. *The Roots of Evil: The Origins of Genocide and Other Group Violence*. Cambridge: Cambridge University Press.

———. 2001. "Ethno-Political and Other Group Violence: Origins and Prevention." In Chirot and Seligman, eds., *Ethnopolitical Warfare*, 289–304.

Steinberg, Jonathan. 1996. *Why Switzerland?* Cambridge: Cambridge University Press.

Stephan, Cookie White, Lausanne Renfro, and Walter G. Stephan. 2004. "The Evaluation of Multicultural Educational Programs: Techniques and a Meta-analysis," 266–79. In Walter G. Stephan and W. Paul Vogt, eds., *Education Programs for Improving Intergroup Relations: Theory, Research, and Practice*. New York: Teachers College Press.

Stern, Fritz. 1974. *The Politics of Cultural Despair*. Berkeley: University of California Press.

Sternberg, Robert J. 2003. "A Duplex Theory of Hate: Development and Applications to Terrorism, Massacres, and Genocide." *Review of General Psychology* 7 (3): 299–328.

———, ed. 2006. *The Psychology of Hate*. Washington, D.C.: American Psychological Press.

Sternhell, Zeev. 1994. *The Birth of Fascist Ideology*. Princeton, N.J.: Princeton University Press.

———. 1996. *Neither Right nor Left: Fascist Ideology in France*. Princeton, N.J.: Princeton University Press.

Stouffer, Samuel A., et al. 1949. *The American Soldier*. Vol. 2, *Combat and Its Aftermath*. Princeton, N.J.: Princeton University Press.

Suny, Ronald G. 1993. "Rethinking the Unthinkable: Toward an Understanding of the Armenian Genocide," 94–115. In Ronald G. Suny, *Looking toward Ararat: Armenia in Modern History*. Bloomington: Indiana
University Press.

Taban, Alfred. 2004. "Sudan's Shadowy Militia." BBC News, April 10.
http://News.bbc.co.uk/1hi/world/Africa/361953.stm.

Tacitus, Cornelius. [A.D. 98] 1964. *The Agricola of Tacitus*. Translated by
Alfred J. Church and W. J. Brodribb. London: Macmillan.

Tangney, June P., and Ronda L. Dearing. 2002. *Shame and Guilt*. New
York: Guilford.

Taylor, Bruce. 1997. "The Enemy within and Without: An Anatomy of
Fear on the Spanish Mediterranean Littoral." In Naphy and Roberts,
eds., *Fear in Early Modern Society*, 78–99.

Taylor, Christopher C. 2002. "The Cultural Face of Terror in the Rwandan
Genocide of 1994." In Hinton, ed., *Annihilating Difference*, 137–78.

Taylor, Frederick. 2004. *Dresden: Tuesday, February 13, 1945*. New York:
HarperCollins.

Tefft, Stanton K., and Douglas Reinhart. 1974. "Warfare Regulation: A
Cross-cultural Test of Hypotheses among Tribal Peoples." *Behavior Science Research; Human Relations Area Files Journal of Comparative Research* 9:151–72.

Teitel, Ruti. 1996. "Judgment at The Hague." *East European Constitutional Review* 5 (4) (Fall): 80–85.

Thayer, Nate. 1997. "Day of Reckoning: Pol Pot Breaks an 18-Year Silence
to Confront His Past." *Far Eastern Economic Review* (October 30): 14–18.

Thébaud, Brigitte. 1998. *Élevage et développement au Niger: Quel avenir
pour les éleveurs du Sahel?* Geneva: Bureau International du Travail.

———. 2002. *Foncier pastoral et gestion de l'espace au Sahel: Peuls du
Niger oriental et du Yagha burkinabé*. Paris: Karthala.

Thornton, Russell. 1990. *The Cherokee: A Population History*. Lincoln:
University of Nebraska Press.

Tibi, Bassam. 1998. *The Challenge of Fundamentalism: Political Islam and
the New World Disorder*. Berkeley: University of California Press.

Tocqueville, Alexis de. [1835–40] 1954. *Democracy in America*. New York:
Vintage.

Toft, Monica Duffy. 2003. *The Geography of Ethnic Violence: Identity, Interests, and the Indivisibility of Territory*. Princeton, N.J: Princeton University Press.

Trotsky, Leon. 1937. *The Revolution Betrayed: What Is the Soviet Union and Where Is It Going?* New York: Doubleday.

Tuchman, Barbara. 1962. *The Guns of August.* New York: Bantam Books.

Tucker, Robert C. 1990. *Stalin in Power 1928–1941.* New York: W. W. Norton.

Ulam, Adam B. 1977. *Stalin: The Man and His Era.* New York: Viking.

UNDP (United Nations Development Programme). 2001. *Peace-building from the Ground Up: A Case Study of UNDP's CARERE Program in Cambodia 1991–2000.* Phnom Penh: UNDP/Cambodia.

Vaksberg, Arkady. 1994. *Stalin against the Jews.* New York: Knopf.

Valentino, Benjamin A. 2004. *Final Solutions: Mass Killing and Genocide in the 20th Century.* Ithaca, N.Y.: Cornell University Press.

Varshney, Ashutosh. 2002. *Ethnic Conflict and Civic Life: Hindus and Muslims in India.* New Haven, Conn.: Yale University Press.

Vayda, Andrew P. 1971. "Phases in the Process of War and Peace among the Maring of New Guinea." *Oceania* 42:1–24.

Villa-Vicencio, Charles, and Wilhelm Verwoerd, eds. 2000. *Looking Back, Reaching Forward: Reflections on the Truth and Reconciliation Commission of South Africa.* London: Zed Books.

Wakeman, Frederic, Jr. 1975. *The Fall of Imperial China.* New York: Free Press.

Walker, Anthony R. 1995. "The Tasaday Controversy: Assessing the Evidence," *Journal of Southeast Asian Studies* 26 (2): 458–61.

Waller, James. 2002. *Becoming Evil: How Ordinary People Can Commit Genocide and Mass Killing.* New York: Oxford University Press.

Walzer, Michael. 1977. *Just and Unjust Wars: A Moral Argument with Historical Illustrations.* New York: Basic Books.

Warwick, Peter. 1980. "Introduction to Part Two: War," 58–64. In Peter Warwick, ed., *The South African War: The Anglo-Boer War 1899–1902.* Burnt Mill, Eng.: Longman.

Wasserstrom, Jeffrey N., Lynn Hunt, and Marilyn B. Young, eds. 2000. *Human Rights and Revolutions.* Lanham, Md.: Rowan and Littlefield.

Waters, Mary C. 1990. *Ethnic Options: Choosing Identities in America.* Berkeley: University of California Press.

Wax, Emily. 2005. "Sudan's Unbowed, Unbroken Inner Circle." *Washington Post*, May 3.

Weber, Eugen. 1976. *Peasants into Frenchmen: The Modernization of Rural France, 1870–1914.* Stanford, Calif.: Stanford University Press.

Weber, Max. [1922] 1968. *Economy and Society*. New York: Bedminster Press.

Weinberg, Gerhard L. 1994. *A World at Arms: A Global History of World War II*. Cambridge: Cambridge University Press.

Weiner, Amir. 2001. *Making Sense of War: The Second World War and the Fate of the Bolshevik Revolution*. Princeton, N.J.: Princeton University Press.

Weiss, John. 1996. *Ideology of Death: Why the Holocaust Happened in Germany*. Chicago: I. R. Dee.

Weitz, Eric D. 2003. *A Century of Genocide: Utopias of Race and Nation*. Princeton, N.J.: Princeton University Press.

Welch, David A. 1995. *Justice and the Genesis of War*. Cambridge: Cambridge University Press.

Werth, Nicolas. 2003. "The Mechanism of Mass Crime: The Great Terror in the Soviet Union, 1937–1938." In Gellately and Kiernan, eds., *The Specter of Genocide*, 215–39.

White, Terence H. 1958. *The Once and Future King*. New York: Putnam.

Williamson, Jeffrey. 1996. "Globalization and Inequality Then and Now: The Late 19th and Late 20th Centuries Compared." NBER working paper no. 5491. Cambridge, Mass.: National Bureau of Economic Research.

Williamson, Samuel R., Jr. 1989. "The Origins of World War I." In Rotberg and Rabb, eds., *The Origins and Prevention of Major Wars*, 225–48.

Wilson, A. Jeyaratnam. 2000. *Sri Lankan Tamil Nationalism: Its Origins and Development in the 19th and 20th Centuries*. Vancouver: University of British Columbia Press.

Wilson, Charles. 1977. *The Dutch Republic*. New York: McGraw-Hill.

Winter, Jay M. 1985. *The Great War and the British People*. London: Macmillan.

Wolin, Sheldon S. 2001. *Tocqueville between Two Worlds: The Making of a Political and Theoretical Life*. Princeton, N.J.: Princeton University Press.

Wood, Nicholas. 2004. "Kosovo Report Criticizes Rights Progress by U.N. and Local Leaders." *New York Times*, July 14.

Young, Anna. 2002. "Integrating Relief, Recovery, and Civil Society Principles in a Conflict-affected Environment. Maluku Case Study: Mercy Corps Indonesia." Portland, Maine: Mercy Corps.

Zakaria, Fareed. 1998. *From Wealth to Power: The Unusual Origins of America's World Role*. Princeton, N.J.: Princeton University Press.

Zarinebaf-Sahr, Fariba. 1997. "Qizilbash 'Heresy' and Rebellion in Ottoman Anatolia during the Sixteenth Century." *Anatolia Moderna* 7:1–15.

Zijderveld, Anton C. 1998. "Civil Society, Pillarization, and the Welfare State." In Hefner, ed., *Democratic Civility*, 153–71.

Zolberg, Aristide R. 1969. *One-party Government in the Ivory Coast.* Princeton, N.J.: Princeton University Press.

Index